JEWS, MUSLIMS
AND JERUSALEM
Disputes and Dialogues

D1592866

"The book is concise, comprehensive, instructive and enlightening. I would turn it into mandatory reading at the cadets' course in the Ministry of Foreign Affairs and in the army."
RACHEL ELIOR, Professor of Jewish Thought, The Hebrew University of Jerusalem

"This study refashions ingrained stereotypes and scholarly precepts of a monolithic divide of the Muslim-Jewish encounter in modern times, nurtured by polemic traditions and anti-Semitism. The book presents a more complex and diffuse reality of intertwined worlds, denoting intolerance, militancy and conflicts side-by-side with reconciliation and co-existence. It will be of great interest to historians and social scientists working on interfaith relations and conflict resolution."
MEIR HATINA, Professor of Islamic and Middle Eastern Studies, The Hebrew University of Jerusalem

"Moshe Maoz's book presents an in-depth, comprehensive and thorough historical reading that examines Muslims' relations with Jews and Judaism, and attempts to view these relations in terms of contemporary reality. The book carefully analyzes the trends of religionization that flood the area and warns of its implications. Anyone who is anxious about a religious war and strives to achieve coexistence in the region must read this book."
DR. YUSRI KHAIZRAN, Shalem College, Jerusalem

"The book is rich in detail and information about every country and every period where Muslim–Jewish relations have had political and other consequences. The author sets out both the positive and negative attitudes of the dominant Muslim majority towards the Jewish minority in a balanced way. It is based on first-hand sources and on the author's many years of research experience and participation in Jewish–Muslim dialogue."
PROFESSOR MENACHEM KLEIN, Political Science, Bar-Ilan University

"The great importance of the book is its comprehensive historical account . . . the relations between Jews and Muslims, and the place of Jerusalem in these relations . . . a unique contribution is the analysis of the Shi'a and Sunni attitudes to Jews and Israel."
ITZHAK REITER, Professor and Chair of Israel Studies, Ashkelon Academic College

"Herewith a comprehensive and pioneering study on Muslims, Jews and Jerusalem that is based on substantive sources and research. It impartially examines the ambivalence in Muslim–Jewish relations throughout history and in many regions, with an emphasis on the Middle East, and the Holy City of Jerusalem and its Temple Mount and Wailing Wall. Ma'oz is sure-footed as he proposes political and cultural dialogue to solve the Palestinian problem in a spirit of peace and conciliation."
PROFESSOR EMERITUS JACOB LANDAU, Political Science, The Hebrew University of Jerusalem

"The explosive issues of the Temple Mount and East Jerusalem are at the core of the discussion. Prof. Ma'oz examines the range of ideological, political, cultural and religious perceptions regarding the Jewish-Israeli and Arab-Muslim conflict."
PROFESSOR YEHUDIT RONEN, Department of Political Studies, Academic Chair of The Special External Program, Bar-Ilan University

"Moshe Ma'oz surprises us again with another excellent book. An heir to Albert Hourani's tradition of meticulous research and analysis, Ma'oz paints a picture of a possible peace between Israelis and Palestinians – a peace that recognizes and respects the other's history and narrative. Further, against the prevalent Islamophobic narrative of Jerusalem, Ma'oz sheds light on the intertwined Muslim–Jewish history of the city. History has lessons for us about who we are, but above all, how we get out of this conflict: as the Biblical and Quranic image of Gog and Magog, or with an image of Muslim–Jewish understanding?"
PROFESSOR CAMELIA SULEIMAN, Michigan State University

"Briefly, yet clearly explaining the religious, political and geographical aspects, this book opens an encyclopedic perspective on the ambivalent relationship between Muslims and Jews throughout history. The question of Jerusalem, the symbolic and earthly center of the actual conflict, seems unsurmountable, but beside the dangers embedded in lack of solution, the book opens a vista to a possible dialogue and agreement."
PROFESSOR EMERITA RACHEL MILSTEIN, Department of Islamic and Middle Eastern Studies, The Hebrew University, Jerusalem

JEWS, MUSLIMS AND JERUSALEM
Disputes and Dialogues

Moshe Ma'oz

sussex
ACADEMIC
PRESS
Brighton • Chicago • Toronto

2 4 6 8 10 9 7 5 3 1

First published in Hebrew by Hakibbutz Hameuhad, Tel Aviv, 2019.
This English-language edition published 2021 in Great Britain by
SUSSEX ACADEMIC PRESS
PO Box 139
Eastbourne BN24 9BP

Distributed in North America by
SUSSEX ACADEMIC PRESS
Independent Publishers Group
814 N. Franklin Street
Chicago, IL 60610

The Author and Publisher acknowledge the financial support received from the Harry S.
Truman Research Institute for the Advancement of Peace at
The Hebrew University of Jerusalem.

This book was published with the support of the Israel Science Foundation.

British Library Cataloguing in Publication Data
A CIP catalogue record for this book is available from the British Library.

Library of Congress Cataloging-in-Publication Data
To be applied for.

Hardcover ISBN 978-1-78976-081-1
Paperback ISBN 978-1-78976-082-8

Typeset and designed by Sussex Academic Press, Brighton & Eastbourne.
Printed by TJ International, Padstow, Cornwall.

Contents

Contents

Preface

Since 1967, and especially in the past few years, Jerusalem and the Temple Mount have become the epicenter of the Muslim–Jewish conflict in Israel and throughout the Arab and Muslim world. The worst-case scenario is an apocalypse, the Armageddon that will erupt between Muslims, led by Shi'ite Iran and Hizbullah and supported by many Sunni Muslims as well, and Israel and Jewish communities throughout the world. Significant indications of such a potential catastrophe appeared for example with the riots that broke out with the excavation of the Western Wall tunnels in 1996; the al-Aqsa Intifada in 2000; the al-Quds ("the knives") Intifada in 2015; and numerous violent confrontations and killings on the Temple Mount and in related incidents. These events claimed the lives of hundreds of Muslims and Jews. A recent outbreak of riots on the Temple Mount occurred on *Tisha B'Av*, a Jewish fast day (August 11, 2019), in protest against the hundreds of Jews who entered the Temple Mount while tens of thousands of Muslim worshippers were praying at the Al-Aqsa Mosque on the Islamic holiday of Id al-Adha (Festival of the Sacrifice). These and other harsh events led to raging demonstrations in Arab states (including Egypt and Jordan that have signed peace treaties with Israel) and Muslim countries, mainly in Shi'ite Iran and Sunni Turkey, that promoted severe protests and threats against the Jewish state. Similar reactions from Arab and Muslim countries were forthcoming when American president Donald Trump moved the U.S. Embassy to Jerusalem on May 14, 2018, and after Israel's parliament, the Knesset, ratified the Nationality Law on July 19, 2018, which states, inter alia, that "a whole and united Jerusalem is the capital of Israel".

Trump's "Deal of the Century" (January 28, 2020) endorses Israel's stand on a united Jerusalem, thus provoking stern protests by the Palestinians and most Arab and Muslim states.

Moreover, at various times Muslim extremists reacted violently against the plans and attempts of extremist Jews to attack the

Al-Aqsa Mosque and the Dome of the Rock and build the third Holy Temple upon their ruins. As mentioned, an attack of such a severe nature can lead to an all-out apocalyptic war between Muslims and Jews, as reckoned by high-ranking officials in Israel's security forces as well as clergy from both sides, rabbis and imams.

It was Hussein Fadlalla, a senior Lebanese Shi'ite cleric, who claimed that the Qur'an calls for a dialogue (*hiwar*) with the Jews, but it is the Jews, supported by Fundamentalist Christians, who are seeking to destroy the Al-Aqsa Mosque and initiate the "Armageddon". Israel's former Chief Rabbi. Shlomo Goren, also wrote some years ago that such a war will indeed erupt, as part of the process of redemption and the rebuilding of the Holy Temple. American Christian Evangelists, supporters of Israel, hold a similar premise.

The deep concern in the Muslim Arab world, especially among the Palestinians, as to the fate of the Al-Aqsa Mosque and the Dome of the Rock, and also of Israel's continued occupation of the West Bank and especially of East Jerusalem, has reinforced since 1967 the anti-Jewish (Judeophobia) and anti-Israel movements. The most prominent among these are the Hamas, the "Liberation" Party (*tahrir*), the Islamic Jihad, the northern faction of the Islamic Movement in Israel, Hizbullah, and of course the Islamic rule in Iran, and recently Turkey as well. Turkey's President, Erdoğan in response to the Nationality Law passed by the Knesset, once again stated that Israel is a terrorist, fascist, racist state, similar to Nazism (*Haaretz* newspaper, 25 July, 2018).

Conversely, amongst Jews in Israel and the Diaspora (and amongst many Christians) the last several decades have witnessed a rise in extreme Islamophobia in reaction to dreadful terrorist attacks by Muslims, and also out of a religious-cultural patronization of and prejudice against Muslims (similar to the Muslims' attitude towards Jews). Spearheading these trends are members of the Jewish underground, *Gush Emunim*, Loyalists of the Temple Mount, Holy Temple organizations (about twenty in number), rabbis and leaders of the religious Zionist movement, the *Bayit Yehudi* Party and *Likud* Party members. On the other hand, it is noteworthy that there are numerous proactive movements for coexistence and peace amongst Jews and Muslims in Israel and throughout the world, and in that prevailing spirit dozens of ongoing religious and cultural dialogues are maintained between leaders from both sides, alongside political and economic dialogues between Israel and a line of Arab and Muslim countries, thanks to mutually shared interests, political considerations, etc. However, in order to achieve an historic reconciliation and coexistence between the nations, it is mandatory that both sides reach a consensus regarding the Palestinian problem, and especially the question of East Jerusalem (*al-Quds al-Sharif*) and the Temple Mount (al-Ḥaram al-Šharīf). Such a solution may also lead to expanding the relationships between Israel and Arab Muslim countries, and may thus neutralize a critical ideological motive for the violent hostility of both Sunni and Shi'ite Muslims, including Iran, Turkey, Hizbullah and Hamas.

Without question, when discussing the reciprocal relationships between Muslims and Jews in the past few generations, these relationships should be examined alongside the changes that took place throughout history and their ramifications on the present, and conclusions should be drawn – be they stringent or lenient. As we shall see in greater detail later in the book, the relationships between Muslims and Jews in Islamic lands up to the early 20th century were highly complex: ambivalent (dualistic) with similarities and differences during different periods and in different countries. On the one hand, governments and Muslim populations displayed tolerance towards the Jews via dialogue, and through cultural, economic and at times social and political cooperation. On the other hand, there were times of persecution and massacres, and even forced conversion to Islam in certain places (especially among the Shi'ites), even though the Qur'an forbids this. However, these persecutions were rare and short-lived compared to the horrific persecution of the Jews in Christian countries (from Byzantium, through the Spanish Inquisition, the Crusades, the pogroms in Russia and the Ukraine, and up to the Holocaust in Europe). Muslim tolerance towards the Jews and their preference over the Christians stemmed from theological reasons (pure monotheism vs. the Holy Trinity in Christianity), as well as considerations of politics and security: The Jews, who were relatively small in number, did not pose a security threat in Islamic countries, as did the Christians whose numbers were far greater and who were perceived as a Fifth Column of the European powers that fought against the Muslim states. At times there was also cooperation between Muslims and Jews against the Christians. Nonetheless, as previously stated, there were also times of abuse and humiliation by the Muslims towards the Jews in various Muslim countries that resulted from a religious-theological and political stance of arrogance towards Jewish (and Christian) protectorates; violent reactions towards Jews' deviation from this status or (rare) provocations by Jews; the Muslim rabble's envy of wealthy Jews (not many) and Muslim rampaging in times of a weak central government; and fanatical Muslim policies led by political rulers and religious leaders (due to which Maimonides was outwardly forced to convert to Islam), especially during a certain time period in the 12th century.

In contrast, the majority of the Jews living in Islamic countries generally accepted Islamic rule passively and submissively, and remained loyal and supportive subjects at times of war, and their leaders even praised the sovereign rule of Ishmael as a "moderate/benevolent kingdom". For centuries, Jews in these countries prayed facing Jerusalem for the rebuilding of the Holy Temple. But in fact only very few Jews lived in Jerusalem or made a pilgrimage to Jerusalem, and were grateful to the Muslim rulers who allowed them to pray at the Western Wall (but not to ascend to the Temple Mount). As we shall see further on, the collapse of the Muslim-Ottoman Empire during World War I, and the establishment of nationalist Jewish-Zionist and Arab movements (with Islamic foundations), had a crucial and even critical impact on Muslim–Jewish relationships in the Holy Land and environs. To this religious nucleus were added nationalist political, psychological and territorial elements in these relationships in the Holy Land/Palestine, with harsh consequences to the Jewish congregations in the Arab and Muslim world. Many Muslims in the Holy Land and outside it perceived the nationalist-Jewish-Zionist movement as a branch of European imperialism that was gaining control over Muslim land and damaging its cultural-traditional character. In contrast, many Jews, supported by Britain, believed that they were returning to their historic homeland in order to re-establish a national entity. A great number of them displayed political hostility and cultural arrogance towards the local Muslim Arabs; while others tried to maintain cultural, social and political dialogues with them and reach agreements with their Muslim neighbors, but with little positive results. The majority of the Zionist Jews were secular and showed no interest in Jerusalem and the Temple Mount, though they did see in the Western Wall a cultural-national-historical symbol. Alongside them, however, were small nationalist-secular organizations, such as *Beitar* [a Revisionist youth movement], *Etzel/Irgun* [the National Military Organization] and *Lechi* [Fighters for the Freedom of Israel], who aspired and worked towards rebuilding the Holy Temple upon the ruins of the Dome of the Rock and the Al-Aqsa Mosque. For many years, the religious Zionist movement was not a partner to these nationalist aspirations, but waited and prayed for the coming of the Messiah, at which time the Holy Temple will be rebuilt and the people of Israel will be redeemed.

However, following the occupation of East Jerusalem and the Temple Mount in June 1967, a critical change commenced along with great radicalization of the religious Zionists' viewpoint, which gradually spread among the Jewish population, regarding the issues of East Jerusalem, the Temple Mount, the Palestinians and Muslims. Conversely, there increasingly grew among the Muslims in Israel and throughout the world radical anti-Jewish/anti-Israeli movements, which included calls for Jihad [a Holy war] against Israel. These mutually extreme movements nurture one another and in the worst-case scenario, may lead to a Muslim–Jewish Armageddon.

This book, which is based on many years of research, as well as a variety of sources and studies, examines these extremist movements, alongside dialogues and the cooperation between Muslims and Jews. This cooperation aspires to educate towards peace and reconciliation between the nations on the basis of shared historical-cultural traditions and correlating strategic interests. Prior to that, the fundamental changes in Muslim–Jewish relationships will be discussed, from the appearance of Islam in the 7th century in the Middle East, including in Turkey and Iran and in extensive parts of Asia and Africa, whilst noting the lack of symmetry in these relationships – rulers vs. inferior subjects – and the duality in the Muslims' position towards Jews – dialogues and cooperation on the one hand, and oppression, humiliations and violence, on the other hand. Further on, a broader examination will be made of the critical changes that took place in these relationships from the start of the 20th century and till today, with emphasis on the issues of Jerusalem and the Temple Mount.

Countless research studies, books and articles have been published in European languages, in English, Arabic and Hebrew, on the different aspects and eras in Jewish–Muslim relationships, and several books have discussed the entirety of these relationships, but not in an encompassing and updated manner, without examining the reciprocal influences between Muslims and Jews, mainly in modern times. Quite a number of publications are tendentious or one-sided and are not based on academic research.

This book aims to examine these relationships in different time periods and regions, while relying on objective academic research as much as possible. The research, which forms the basis of this book, includes reading and analyzing materials from Arabic, Hebrew and other language sources; academic research studies alongside newspaper and archival segments, interviews and discussions with people whom I met throughout my journeys in the past few years to Arab countries and Muslim communities throughout the world. The research also draws upon my involvement of many years with this subject: In research, teaching, observation and active participation in conferences, seminars and dialogues. Additionally, I have included in this book a number of previous research studies of mine that were done on a variety of issues regarding the relationships of Israel and the Jews to Muslims and Arabs (most Arabs are Muslim).

I wish to thank the Truman Institute of the Hebrew University of Jersualem for the research grants that allowed me to work with research assistants, and especially Yael Gadenian, in collecting material from various sources. Special thanks to Yael Kuperman, a student in the Department of Islamic and Middle Eastern Studies, who helped to locate materials from Hebrew-Jewish sources. My deep gratitude goes to Anthony Grahame, Editorial Director at Sussex Academic, for his outstanding work in bringing this English-language edition to publication; and to Miriam Frank,for her help and support.

I hope this book will serve as a significant contribution towards increased awareness and understanding of Muslim–Jewish relationships, as they actually are, and will contest the inaccurate generalizations and stereotypes widely held by the general public worldwide.

"God has ordained for you the same religion which He enjoined . . . upon Abraham, Moses and Jesus, so that you should remain steadfast in religion and not become divided in it."
Qur'an Sura 42, verse 13

"The Kingdom of Ishmael is moderate; a benevolent Kingdom."
From the Jewish Midrash

"Islam is a much greater reality than we wish to admit . . . hence we [Jews] have been remiss in not acquainting ourselves with Islam."
Jewish Philosopher Martin Buber, Jerusalem, 1929

"In our current peace treaty with Israel we are optimistic that we will regain our land and our honor, and that (East) Jerusalem will return – sacred and dear – to the sphere of Islam, and in the shade of peace."
Jad al-Haqq, Chief Mufti of Egypt, 1979

Introduction
Judeophobia and Islamophobia

The past few decades have witnessed a rise in anti-Semitism or Muslim Judeophobia as expressed in speech, in writing and extensive terrorism; on the other hand, mainly in reaction to this, a new Jewish (and Christian) Islamophobia is developing and finds expression in acts of violence, or inciting and harmful language. These trends are especially prominent among religious and extreme nationalist factions on both sides, guided by fanatic religious leaders (and radical politicians) who selectively exploit verses from the sacred scriptures – the Qur'an and the Hadith, the Bible and the Talmud. For example, Muhammad Mursi, President of Egypt (2012–2013) and one of the leaders of the "Muslim Brotherhood" movement, used an anti-Semitic phrase several years ago, claiming that the Jews are "the descendants of apes and pigs" (based on a verse in the Qur'an)[1]. Muslim clerics again accused the Jews of using the blood of children to bake the *matzot* of Passover, and once more acclaimed the anti-Semitic *The Protocols of the Elders of Zion*. These Judeophobic trends focus mainly on Israel – the Jewish State that has "conquered" Jerusalem. Thus, for instance, the renowned Egyptian Muslim preacher, shaykh Yusuf Qardawi, recently called for "the liberation of Jerusalem" from the Israeli occupation through Jihad (also in Palestinian textbooks as well). Similar calls by Muslim religious leaders were publicized since the end of 2017.[2]

At the same time, in 2011 and 2012, mass violent demonstrations were held in front of Israel's embassies in Cairo and Amman (in 2017 as well), and also in Morocco (May 2018), Tunisia and Iran by Sunni and Shi'ite Muslims who called for "Death to the Jews, Death to Israel".[3] Similar demonstrations were held in Muslim Arab countries and in European countries in July 2014 in reaction to the IDF military operation in the Gaza Strip, known as Operation Protective Edge (in Hebrew: *Mivtza Tzuk Eitan*), while at the same

1

time Turkish President Erdoğan repeatedly compared Israel to Nazi Germany. Moreover, fanatic Muslims – both Sunni and Shi'ites – implemented hundreds of murderous terrorist attacks on Israeli and Jewish targets in Israel and in other countries, such as the terrorist attack on the Jewish school in Toulouse, France in March 2012; the deadly attacks of the Jewish deli in Paris in January 2015; and prior to that, the Jewish community center and the Israeli Embassy in Buenos Aires, 1992 and 1994.

According to a survey of the Anti-Defamation League from 2014, 93% of Palestinians and 74% of Arabs and other Muslims harbor anti-Semitic feelings; on the other hand, many Jews (and Christians), amongst them religious leaders, politicians, researchers and commentators, define Islam – and not only radical Islam – as anti-Semitic, anti-Israel and anti-Western, as violent and terroristic. For instance, they point out that most terrorist activities in the world are instigated or committed by Muslims, and that Muslims are commanded to spread the religion of Muhammad by the sword (*"din Muhammad b'sayif"*) from the Islamic domain (*dar al-Islam*) to the domain of war (*dar al-Harb*), or in other words: All of Islam is the enemy of Israel, of the Jews and of the Judeo-Christian civilization (see further on as well).

In response to that, a substantial number of Jews developed anti-Muslim and anti-Arab positions. For example, in Israel and the Palestinian territories, the number of anti-Muslim/anti-Arab expressions and incidents has increased from year to year, especially amongst the Jewish settlers in the territories. The first quarterly report of 2013 on racism in Israel (also in 2018) noted 180 racist incidents mainly against Arab citizens, which included violence, incitement, insulting "religious sentiments", coming also from Israel's security forces, public figures, rabbis and journalists. The leader of the Orthodox religious political party *Shas*, the late Rabbi Ovadia Yosef, also former Sephardi chief rabbi of Israel, ruled in his weekly sermon (in January 2012) that Islam is "an ugly religion", and "we should pray for the death of the Palestinian Ishmaelites [Arabs, Muslims]". Other rabbis, leaning on the Holy Scriptures, labeled the Arabs 'Amalekites' that must be destroyed. The rabbi of Safed, Shmuel Eliyahu, along with the support of other rabbis, publicly called to ban renting or selling apartments to Arabs ("non-Jews"). Rabbi Itzhak Shapira, backed by dozens of other rabbis, instructed in his book, *The King's Torah*, "to kill the children of non-

Jews" (Arabs) in times of war; and in many synagogues anti Arab-Muslim pamphlets are distributed from time to time. Moreover, during soccer games (especially when the Jerusalem Beitar team plays) and generally in mass demonstrations, radical Jews shout "Death to the Arabs", "Muhammad is a pig", "Muhammad is a son-of-a-bitch", "Muhammad is dead", "Baruch Goldstein is blessed", "The Holy Temple will be built, the mosque will be burnt". Other fanatical Jews desecrated and set fire to mosques and to books of the Qur'an, burnt cars and uprooted olive trees in various locations in Israel and the West Bank.[4] Senior journalists in the media, on television and radio, called Islam a "virus" and the Arabs "animals". Even worse – in March 1994 a fanatical Jewish settler from Kiryat Arba, Dr. Baruch Goldstein, murdered 29 Muslims at prayer in Hebron, at the great mosque in the Cave of the Patriarchs (and was then murdered by other worshipers); rabbis and Jewish youth continue till today to praise Goldstein's deeds in writing and orally and to immortalize him. Similarly, earlier (in 1982), Jewish extremists tried to blow up a Muslim school for girls in Jerusalem and even the mosques on the Temple Mount (1984), with the objective of rebuilding the Holy Temple. This dangerous idea continues to be acceptable to a significant number of Israelis – 30%–40% of the Israeli Jews identified with the religious Zionist population support the re-building of the Holy Temple (upon the ruins of the mosques). There is no doubt that these events, and especially hostilities aimed at the mosques on the Temple Mount, may lead to an all-out Muslim war against Israel and Jewish congregations throughout the world (this possible scenario was also supported by testimonies brought by the former heads of Israel's Security Services in the documentary film, "The Gatekeepers").

On the other hand, it should be emphasized that many of these anti-Muslim/Arab statements and actions generated severe reactions from many Israeli Jews, including political leaders (such as Netanyahu) and religious leaders (senior rabbis), and led to the long-term imprisonment of the Jewish extremists. For example, the settler Jack Teitel, who killed Palestinians in cold blood, and is now serving two life sentences and another thirty years. A further example is the harsh public denunciation against the Jerusalem Beitar team's fans who refused to allow Muslim soccer players from Chechnya to join the team, in early 2013 ("Beitar remains forever pure").[5] Recently, Israeli leaders, including Netanyahu, have condemned the hateful actions of Jewish extremists who set fire to and killed a Palestinian youth in Jerusalem (2014) and a Palestinian infant in the village Duma (2015) (the burning of the Palestinian youth was in reaction to the kidnapping and murder of three Jewish youngsters near Hebron before the *Tsuk Eitan* military operation), whereas after the murder in Duma the Israeli government decided to define the crimes of Jewish extremists as "terrorism" and to implement against them administrative detentions.

Alongside the denunciation of Islamophobic actions, there are certain Jewish notables who claim that these actions do not represent the true Jewish religion nor the vast majority of Jews in Israel and throughout the world. Thus, for instance, wrote Rabbi Dov Halbertal, an ultra-Orthodox intellectual and lecturer on Hebrew Law:

> . . . I blame the settlers, and the religious nationalists who have allowed the nationalist ethos to gain control over the national religious sector. I blame both them and ourselves for having appropriated the authentic Judaism . . . and transforming it in one fell swoop into a violent method . . . which confers upon the value of the land priority over the value of Man . . . Many of us are silent partners to this terrifying vision . . . between Joseph's tomb and Goldstein's tomb . . . to the religious ideology that has found expression in the ultimate xenophobic creation, the book, *The King's Torah*.

Similarly, Muslim religious and political leaders have expressed themselves against extremist Muslim terrorism and anti-Semitism, which they feel does not represent the authentic values of Islam, " . . . and presents a false, distorted view of Islam". Thus, for instance, the liberal Iraqi journalist, Aziz Al-Haj, complained bitterly of "the expropriation by radical Islam and the erasure of all signs of moderation and openness that found expression for generations". According to him, Islam today is a "jihad of sickening religious rulings and numerous prohibitions that lead to dark fanaticism . . . to terrible crimes the Muslims carry out in the name of the religion of Muhammad and the holy Qur'an". Leading Muslim religious leaders also condemned from time to time anti-Semitic actions.[6] It is noteworthy that Muslim and Jewish religious leaders meet occasionally in Israel and other countries, to maintain an

4

inter-religious dialogue to promote peaceful coexistence and cooperation, on the one hand, and to combat the extremist groups in both religions, on the other hand. Thus, for example, in February 2011, Muslim religious leaders together with Jewish leaders visited the death camp Auschwitz, and released a joint media statement against Holocaust deniers; at the end of November 2011, rabbis and imams from 26 different countries gathered in Jerusalem for reciprocal lectures on the Bible and the Qur'an, on Judaism and Islam, in order to promote mutual recognition and understanding between the religions. In September 2012, 40 Muslim religious leaders met with a similar number of rabbis to maintain a dialogue "between cousins in religion". When the dialogue ended, a joint decision was taken to battle all revelations of "anti-Semitism and Islamophobia . . . that may bring about the destruction of all mankind". Hassan II, king of Morocco, declared in 1985: "The crisis in the Middle East creates a divide between the sons of Abraham . . . the future can exist only through dialogue."[7]

It is doubtful whether such dialogues, and lectures by senior Muslim religious leaders and Jewish rabbis, will be able to bring a stop to these critical phenomena. For both Muslim anti-Semitism and Jewish Islamophobia are based to a great extent on mutual ignorance of anything related to the culture and history of the other party, and on religious-theological beliefs that are drawn from the selective texts and distorted interpretations of the holy scriptures and the indoctrination of radical religious leaders from both sides. Nonetheless, Muslim anti-Semitism is far more dangerous, as it is widespread amongst extensive Muslim groups some of whom have used – and plan to use – lethal weapons, and even commit suicide, in order to harm Jews. Jewish extremists as well are ready to give their lives towards the rebuilding of the Holy Temple.[8]

Misleading Generalizations and Dangerous Stereotypes

A great danger that lies in these ugly phenomena is linked to the widespread reciprocal supplementation that generates on both sides negative generalizations and stereotypes against one another, with no distinction between extreme and moderate movements among both the Muslims and the Jews. Many Muslims do not differentiate between Israelis and Jews, and Jews do not differentiate between Muslims and Arabs. Thus, for instance, violent actions and defamatory words of fanatic Jews against Muslims, mosques and the Qur'an (as well as the Israeli government's policies against Palestinian Muslims), are perceived by many Muslims throughout the world as representative of the Jews and the Jewish State. Similarly, many terrorist actions, anti-Jewish (and anti-Christian) statements and publications of fanatic Muslims are interpreted by many Jews (and Christians) as representing Islam and Muslims throughout the world. For instance, according to surveys carried out by American research institutes in 2010, many of the Muslim Arabs in the Middle East hold the view that "Israel's goal is to take control of the Middle East, or destroy Islam and do away with the Arabs", whereas many others believe that the Jews in fact control the world and are harming Muslims.

On the other hand, many Jews (and Christians) hold similar views about Islam, which construe nearly all of Islam as violent, evil, anti-Western and anti-Semitic; whose objective is to fight the Judeo-Christian civilization, to re-establish the Muslim Khalifates and impose the *Shari'a* – Islamic law – throughout widespread areas of the world (this indeed is the aspiration of extremist Muslim movements such as Al-Qaida and the Islamic State ISIS). These viewpoints possess academic and theological backing as well. Thus, for example, Prof. Samuel Huntington, a renowned Harvard University intellectual, determined in his book, *The Clash of Civilizations* (1996), that "the borders of Islam are bloody, as are its innards"; Pope Benedict XVI (who resigned from office in March 2013), in a lecture he delivered in 2006, attributed to Muhammad, founder of Islam, "evil, inhuman" ideas. Jewish Intellectuals, rabbis and politicians in Israel and abroad, compared Islam to Nazism, to terrorism and suicide bombings. During the Arab Spring uprisings, Prof. Benny Morris, a renowned Israeli historian, claimed that, but for very short time periods, Jews in Muslim countries were persecuted for centuries and suffered many massacres, and that Islam is imposing a threatening siege on Israel in particular, and on civilization in general; according to this version, Israel will survive until it is destroyed by Islam (recently Morris has stated that it is unfortunate that Israel did not expel all the Arabs in 1948).[9]

Much to one's amazement and disappointment, these prominent personages, including Jewish Israeli academicians, make generalizations that are inaccurate, unbalanced and misleading, and hence support the increasing and dangerous phenomenon of Jewish (and Christian) Islamophobia. They do not know or are unaware of the great complexity and ambivalence of the Muslim standpoints towards Jews and the Jewish State throughout its long history, including modern-day and contemporary history that is discussed in research studies of most experts on Islam, and first and foremost, among Jewish scholars.

Thus, for instance, Prof. Mark Cohen of Princeton University defines anti-Semitism as "a complex system that is based, from a religious viewpoint, on stereotypical, mythical and irrational beliefs about the highly-powerful, malevolent and Satanic Jew . . . ", and explains that "such anti-Semitism did not exist in the shadow of the crescent in the Muslim world of the Middle Ages".[10] Similarly, the pre-eminent Islamic researcher, Bernard Lewis (a Jewish Zionist), wrote that "there is little sign of any deep-rooted emotional hostility directed against Jews, such as the anti-Semitism of the Christian world . . . [the new Muslim anti-Semitism] is a function of the Arab–Israeli conflict cynically exploited for propaganda reasons by Arab rulers and intellectual elites. It is something that came from above, from the leadership, rather than from below, from the society, as a political and polemical weapon to be discarded if and when it is no longer required". These and other researchers point to long time periods during which "the Jews enjoyed rather good relationships with their Muslim neighbors most of the time . . ."[11]

Indeed, it is noteworthy that from a wide historical view, Muslim–Jewish relationships in Muslim countries were in most places and during most eras tolerable and even fair. In this relationship, the Jews were mostly passive and obedient, as inferior subjects with no political rights or military power, and dared not publicly express anti-Muslim sentiments, which in any case were rare. During certain periods, Jews were persecuted by Muslim rulers, and the illiterate and incited rabble at times massacred the Jews and forced their conversion to Islam (such as in Yemen, Persia and North Africa at different periods). However, most of the time and in most countries, Jews lived among the Muslims in a satisfactory manner, and were even integrated into the commercial and economic life and participated in many dialogues with Muslims in the cultural and creative spheres. The eras recognized as positive were from the 7th century (the Umayyad Khalifate), and the

"Golden Age" in Spain and Egypt (10th to 13th centuries), as well
as the Ottoman period (end of the 15th century after the expulsion
from Spain) up to World War I. Hence, despite the hardships that
befell the Jews in Islamic lands from time to time, their condition
was incomparably better than that of their brethren in Christian
lands, and usually also better than the Christians in Islamic lands.

The Muslims' ambivalent and complex attitude towards Jews, in
various places and to different degrees, continued also after the
dissolution of the Ottoman Empire. Following the establishment of
Arab states, severe manifestations of hatred of Jews surfaced (and
later was followed by the hatred towards Israel), mainly in reaction
to the appearance of the Jewish national movement – Zionism – in
the Holy Land/Palestine. For example, the mufti of Jerusalem, Haj
Amin al-Husseini, leader of the Arab-Palestinian national movement, was the first to begin the process of integrating and using
radical Islam in this movement. His anti-Semitic and pro-Nazi
positions were well-known; he incited Muslims to massacre Jews,
and provoked the pogroms against Jews in Iraq in 1941 (the *Farhud*)
and in Hebron and Jerusalem in 1929.

In contrast, in various Arab countries and especially in Iraq,
Egypt, Syria, Morocco and Tunisia, the Jews continued during
different time periods and especially prior to the Zionist influence,
to lead a tolerable or even satisfactory life, and were integrated into
the economic and cultural life, even holding political positions. The
Zionist movement in the Holy Land also experienced at times cooperation from prominent Muslim Arabs, such as: Faisal I, King of
Syria (1918–1920); his brother, Abdallah, King of Transjordan,
1921–1946; and the King of Jordan, 1946–1957; Muslim
Palestinian parties (such as the Nashashibi family during the British
mandate), and additional Egyptian and Syrian pragmatic Muslim
personages. However, the United Nations Partition Plan Resolution
in November 1947, and the creation of the State of Israel several
months later, incited waves of anti-Jewish (and anti-Israeli) violence
in Arab countries and to the uprooting of ancient Jewish congregations in the Middle East and North Africa.

Nonetheless, even after the establishment of the State of Israel, a
considerable number of Muslim states conducted public or secret
ties with Israel (especially Jordan), thanks to political, economic and
security-related interests and motives, and even out of moderate
Islamic approaches. Thus for example, as early as 1949 two

(secular) Muslim regimes in the region recognized Israel – Turkey and Iran – mainly out of strategic considerations; later, during the 1950s, a line of African Muslim countries, with a moderate and pluralistic Islamic viewpoint, followed suit, out of economic considerations. From the mid-1960s a secret military-strategic connection was created between the Kurds (Sunni Muslims) in northern Iraq and Israel. In the 1990s a considerable number of Muslim countries from central Asia and the Balkans officially recognized Israel, after having been freed of the Soviet occupation.

Following the War of June 1967: Muslim Ambivalence – Animosity and Dialogue

After the war in June 1967, two central trends developed or gradually strengthened in the Arab and Muslim world, towards Israel and Jews; these continued after the Arab Spring uprisings as well (from 2011 and on). On the one hand, the ideological-religious current, mainly among radical and conservative leaders and populations that were harmfully affected by Israel's control of Islamic holy sites in East Jerusalem in 1967 war, and the occupation of Palestinian territories by Israel. On the other hand, from the end of the 1970s, a strategic-pragmatic current developed that was ready to recognize Israel and accept it in the region on condition that it retreats from the territories occupied in 1967 and agrees to the establishment of a Palestinian state alongside Israel, with East Jerusalem as its capital.

Indeed, among the fanatical Muslim factions the animosity towards Israel and the Jews grew progressively deeper and contained harsh anti-Semitic elements – in speeches, publications, video films, as well as many terrorist attacks against Jews and Israel. It is noteworthy that a massive anti-Israel and anti-Western wave which ensued after the Islamic revolution in Iran (1979), impacted mainly on Shi'ite communities and, inter alia, contributed to the rise of the extremist Hizbullah movement in Lebanon (1982). The leaders of Iran and of Hizbullah continue to call for the destruction of Israel (yet are careful not to harm the Jews still remaining in their countries, to differentiate them from "the Zionists"). Among radical Sunni Muslims, the al-Qaida movement was prominent in its anti-Western and anti-Israel positions, and was responsible, for example, for the mega-terrorist attack on September 11, 2001 of the

9

Twin Towers in New York and the Pentagon building in Washington, DC, which claimed the lives of nearly 3000 people. Other Sunni groups that harmed Jews and Israel via incitement and violence are the extremist Muslim organizations such as the Salafi-Jihadists and the radical groups of the Muslim Brotherhood in Arab countries, and the Hamas movement in the Gaza Strip.

On the other hand, since the war of June 1967, and later in October 1973, the strategic-pragmatic trend increasingly widened among Arab and Muslim regimes and elite groups that were aware of Israel's power (and the United States' massive support of Israel). They were prepared to accept Israel's existence and to recognize it within the pre-June 1967 borders, on condition that Israel retreat from the territories occupied in 1967, including East Jerusalem with its holy Muslim sites. This significant trend developed gradually and under various circumstances. Prior to that, Hussein, King of Jordan, conducted a "de facto" peace with Israel for many years (except during the wars of 1948 and 1967), and in 1994 he signed a formal peace treaty with the Jewish state. Egypt as well, the largest Arab-Muslim nation, that initiated and/or participated in five wars against Israel, signed peace treaties with her in 1978 and 1979. Syria, the extremist Arab country, nearly signed a political agreement with Israel in the year 2000. And above all, the PLO, Israel's arch-enemy – changed its hostile position in 1988, recognized the 1947 UN Partition Plan and reached agreements with Israel in 1993 and 1995. This led to the formation of economic and other ties with Israel, also with Morocco and Tunisia, Qatar and Oman; and in 2002 all the Arab and Islamic countries – 57 in number – supported the Saudi peace initiative that offered Israel peace, security and normalization in their relationships, on condition that it retreats to the 1967 lines and agrees to the establishment of a Palestinian state beyond those lines with East Jerusalem as its capital, and to the solution of the Palestinian refugee problem as per UN Resolution 194, passed in 1948 (which does not indicate the "right of return" and proposes the return of refugees on an individual basis and with Israel's consent, and compensation payments to refugees who don't return). This decision is still secure and valid, but Israel so far has not responded to it officially (see too further on).[12]

At the same time, large Muslim countries formed secret strategic ties with Israel, such as Indonesia and Pakistan (as well as Jordan and Morocco whose kings are perceived as the descendants of the prophet Muhammad). Senior religious Muslim figures as well related to Israel and to Judaism with amity, and even visited Israel and the Muslim holy sites in Jerusalem. Among them were muftis and imams from various African and Asian countries. Thus, for example, the former Indonesian president, Abdurrahman Wahid, who headed a large Muslim movement (*Nahdatul Ulama*) visited Israel several times, participated in Muslim–Jewish dialogues and lectured at various forums. The grand mufti of Egypt, Ali Jadd al-Haqq, issued a *fatwa* (a religious opinion) in 1979 that supports the peace treaty with Israel, on condition that Israel returns to the Muslims the territories occupied in 1967, including East Jerusalem. King Abdallah of Saudi Arabia and the Jordanian Prince Hassan held in the last few decades (each separately) a series of inter-religious dialogues between Muslims, Christians and Jews.

Following the Arab Spring uprisings that began in 2011 and brought to power Islamic regimes in Tunisia, Libya and Egypt, the Muslims' former dichotomous attitudes towards Jews and Israel did not change: On the one hand, Islamic extremists – Salafi-Jihadists – continued expressing their anti-Israel and anti-Semitic views; on the other hand, newly established (and old) Muslim regimes expressed pragmatic and even positive positions towards Jews and Israel, but emphasized Israel's obligation to promote a settlement with the Palestinians. This for example was the stand taken by Muhammad Mursi, former Egyptian president (2011–2013), representative of the Muslim Brotherhood, despite his past anti-Jewish remarks. He did not revoke the peace treaty with Israel, he appointed a new Egyptian ambassador to Tel Aviv, and mediated between Israel and Hamas to achieving a cease-fire after Operation Pillar of Defense (in Hebrew: *Amud Anan*) in 2012. The new president Abdel Fattah al-Sisi (2013–present) is a strategic ally with Israel. In December 2012 the new Egyptian constitution was ratified which, inter alia, granted equal rights to Jews (and Christians) in Egypt. Also former prime minister of Libya, Ali Zaidan, after the revolution in 2011, called in Davos for a solution to the regional conflict, to peace with Israel and to the reintegration of Jews in Libya (but since then Libya has been in political and military chaos). In comparison, the new Muslim regime and public in Tunisia continue their traditional positive attitude towards the Jews. In February 2011 a mass demonstration took place in Tunisia against the extremist anti-Jewish and anti-Christian Salafi Muslims, who were labeled a "cancer" by the

11

new liberal president, Munsif Marzuki. He even paid a royal visit to the synagogue in Jerba on Passover 2012 (since then the Tunisian government has changed, becoming more liberal and secular). Finally, an emergency conference of Islamic countries was held in Saudi Arabia in August 2012, which expressed renewed support of the Arab peace initiative and the Roadmap for Peace of the Quartet (both in 2002). The Saudi King Abdallah reconfirmed his peace initiative in February 2013, in March 2013 and in March 2017. The Arab League reconfirmed the initiative with certain changes to Israel's benefit (as did a senior Saudi prince, Turki al-Faisal, in July 2014).[13]

In conclusion, in contrast to the pessimistic evaluations of researchers, interpreters and politicians, both Jewish and otherwise, mentioned above, the majority of the Muslim elite echelons and regimes (but not significant parts of their populations) are not fanatic, are not anti-Israel or anti-Semitic, but rather are pragmatic and realistic and are guided by security-related, strategic, political and economic interests. In comparison, the Salafi Jihadist groups, including the Sunni ISIS and the Shi'ite Hizbullah (and of course Iran) maintain anti-Semitic and anti-Western positions that embody a threat not only to Israel, but to pragmatic Arab regimes as well. However, these extremist groups are not united and are given to harsh rivalry amongst themselves, especially with the Shi'ite Hizbullah. The latter maintains an ideological and strategic alliance with the extremist Muslim regime in Iran (and the Alawite regime in Syria) that threatens the Sunni countries of the region – Saudi Arabia, Jordan and Egypt, and Israel as well. Hence, the potential exists for a strategic alliance between these Sunni Muslim countries and Israel – in coordination with the United States – in order to fight this shared danger. To promote such a strategic alliance, Israel must act to resolve the Palestinian and East Jerusalem issues, for these are at the very heart of most Muslims' concern in the region and throughout the world, both within the populations and their regimes. Following the Arab Spring uprisings and the founding of elected governments by these populations, the Palestinian issue gained even greater significance in the Arab (and Islamic) countries, and has become the major acid test of Muslim–Jewish relationships. Non-resolution of this issue will worsen the attitudes of many Muslims against Jews and Israel and will strengthen the fanatic Muslim movements.

In contrast, a resolution of the Palestinian problem and the issue of East Jerusalem by consensus will decrease, or negate, the motives and excuses of the extremist Muslims – including Hamas – to fight Israel and the Jews, and will help improve Muslim–Jewish relationships and strengthen Israel's position in the Arab and Muslim world.

It may also be expected that resolving the Israel–Palestinian problem and minimizing the phenomenon of Islamic Judeophobia will also help decrease Jewish Islamophobia in Israel and the Diaspora. At the same time, we can hope that the educational systems and the media on both sides will mark not only the difficult periods in the relationship between Muslims and Jews, but will also highlight the shared values in Judaism and Islam, the dialogues and cultural cooperation between Muslims and Jews throughout history.

1

Duality and Dialogue
Muhammad, the Qur'an and the Middle Ages

The words of the Prophet Muhammad, founder of Islam, the Qur'an and the Hadith (traditions credited to the Prophet), shaped to a great extent the history of Islam and the relationships between Muslims and Jews till this day. These relationships can be defined, especially from the aspect of the Muslim rulers, as dualistic: On the one hand – tolerance, dialogue and cooperation; on the other hand – confrontation, animosity and violence.

In Muhammad's lifetime, in the Qur'an and the Hadith, greater emphasis is found on the negative attitude towards Jews, despite the fact, and perhaps because, Muhammad was significantly influenced by Jews and Judaism, and tried in vain to bring them into the new Muslim community. For example, he called upon his followers to pray facing Jerusalem (*Qibla*), in order to draw Jews to Islam, but after they refused, he instructed the Muslims to pray facing Mecca. At the time, the Jewish inhabitants and tribes of the Arabian Peninsula enjoyed political, military, economic and cultural power and constituted a serious challenge (more than the Christians) to Muhammad's ambitions; hence his emphasis on confrontation with the Jews, rather than a common denominator and dialogue with them. (Appropriately, the anti-Jewish Hamas continues to glorify Muhammad's military victory over the Jews of Khaybar: "*Khaybar, Khaybar, yah yahud, jaysh Muhammad sa-yaud*" – "Muhammad's army is about to return" and be victorious.)

Following the surrender of the Jews in the Arabian Peninsula and the conquest of wide areas of the Middle East and beyond, most

14

Arab rulers treated their Jewish subjects fairly, and at times even supportively, more so than towards the Christians; and not just for theological reasons – the pure monotheism of Judaism and Islam against the "Holy Trinity" of the Christians. Mostly, it was because, unlike the Christians, Jews did not pose a security threat or political challenge to the Muslim kingdoms. and sought to integrate as much as possible as inferior, obedient subjects who maintained dialogues and cooperation in the economic and cultural domains. Only very few voiced low-keyed, minimal criticism of the Muslim rulers' oppressive steps and enforced Islamization, as opposed to many more who praised and glorified the tolerance and moderation of Islam in the Middle Ages. Explanations of these dual positions will be detailed further on and in the final Summary chapter.

An Historical Perspective: The Middle Ages

Prior to the spread of Islam in the Arabian Peninsula during the third decade of the 7th century AD, Jews had been living there for many generations (following the destruction of the Holy Temple), in two regions: Yemen in the southern peninsula, and further north, in Hijaz, especially in the vicinity of Medina (Yathrib) and Mecca.

Like their neighbors, mostly Arab pagans (during the *Jahiliyyah* – the Age of Ignorance), and Christians in various places, the Jews too were assembled into tribes: In the south – under the Judaic king, Yosef Dhû Nuwās; and in the north – the tribes of Nadhir, Qurayza and Qaynuqa. Some worked in agriculture, others in interior and regional trade, and as silversmiths. Equality-based social, economic and political relationships prevailed between them and the Arab tribes, void of any religious or ethnic distinctions. Political and military alliances were created between Jewish and Arab tribes, even in warfare, when at times Jewish tribes were engaged in both sides of the tribal coalitions and fought one another. Nonetheless, the Arabs viewed the Jews as educated and cultured (a prominent Jewish poet of the time was Samuel Ben Adaya), and some Arab families sent their children to be educated by Jewish families; there were those who even adopted the Jewish religion. Apparently, Muhammad, the prophet of Islam, was impressed by Judaism and the Jews (and Christianity as well) insofar as regarding Abraham's monotheistic perceptions. Abraham (Ibrahim), who in Islam is admired as the

15

first monotheist (*Hanif*), appears in the Qur'an many times, also as the father of Isaac and Ishmael. Following in his footsteps, the first Divine revelation was given to Moses (and the second to Jesus), whereas Muhammad, in his full revelation, saw himself as the seal (the last) of the prophets. He demanded of the Jews to join him, and at first determined the direction of prayer (*Qibla*) towards Jerusalem, for he expected them to be part of the new Muslim nation. However, the Jews refused to accept his religion, perceiving it as denial and heresy, and even insulted him. In response, Muhammad accused the Jews of forgery of the Bible, and fought them through trickery and military power, which he recruited from among his followers and supporters. At first, he succeeded in driving out two Jewish tribes – Qaynuqa and Nadhir, then massacred the Qurayza tribe, and finally overpowered the Jews of Khaybar. The outcome was that all the Jews of Arabia accepted the patronage of Islam, and Jews from outlying regions then followed in their footsteps. The tradition that Muhammad left behind vis-à-vis the Jews was negative.[1]

After Muhammad's death, his successors, the Khalifs of the House of Umayya and the House of Abbas, continued to enforce Islam through widespread conquests, i.e., in Iraq and Persia (from the Sassanids), Syria, the Holy Land (Jerusalem was conquered in 638 AD), and Egypt (all were conquered from the Byzantines); later, parts of Central Asia, North Africa and Spain were also conquered (in the 8th century). From the 9th century, the rule of Muslim countries gradually passed from the hands of Arab rulers to local dynasties, amongst them the Persians, Turks, Kurds, Fatimid, Berbers, Mamluks and Ottomans. At the same time, and later, Islam expanded to widespread areas in southern Asia and southeastern Asia, such as India and Indonesia, as well as parts of Eastern and Western Africa. At different periods of time, Jewish communities had lived in some of these regions, which later came under the rule of Muslim regimes – Sunni and Shi'ite, both moderate and extreme (the rift between the Sunni and Shi'ites began in 685 CE and has continued throughout Muslim history, with the Sunni constituting the majority of Muslims worldwide).

Generally speaking, the Muslims' stand vis-à-vis the Jews in most places and through most eras was not unequivocally negative, as some writers claim;[2] their attitude was more complex, ambivalent and perhaps contradictory: On the one hand – patronization,

16

contempt and rejection, and on the other hand – tolerance
("Religion cannot be instilled by force"), acceptance and cooperation; this occurred to different degrees in different eras.[3] These dual
positions were basically formulated by Muslim law, sacred scripts
and Muslim traditions, primarily the Qur'an. Thus, for instance, the
verses that are positive in regard to Jews (and Christians) are:
"Those who believe [the Muslims], and those who are Jewish, and
the Christians . . . any who believe in God and the Last Day, and
act righteously – will have their reward with their Lord; they have
nothing to fear, nor will they grieve . . . ", as well as: "Say, We believe
in God . . . and in what was revealed to Abraham, and Ishmael, and
Isaac, and Jacob, and the Patriarchs; and in what was given to Moses
and Jesus; and in what was given to the prophets – from their Lord.
We make no distinction between any of them . . ."[4] In "The Nation's
Contract" that Muhammad wrote at the beginning of his activity in
Medina, the following was said, inter alia: "You have your way and
I have my way").[5] To this we must add that according to both
Muslim and Jewish tradition, Arabs and Jews are the descendants of
Abraham, and upon his death he was buried by his sons Isaac and
Ishmael at the Cave of the Patriarchs [Tomb of the Patriarchs] in
Hebron; and that the Jews have an affinity to the Land of Israel and
Jerusalem.

On the other hand, in the Qur'an and the Hadith a significant
number of negative expressions regarding the Jews can be found,
which perhaps also reflect Muhammad's disappointment at their
refusal to accept his religion. For example: "We made a covenant
with the Children of Israel: 'Worship none but God . . . and pray
regularly, and give alms. Then you turned away.' Also: 'They were
struck with humiliation and poverty, and incurred wrath from God.
That was because they rejected God's revelations and wrongfully
killed the prophets. That was because they disobeyed and trans-
gressed.'"[6] The Qur'an also maintains a more severe attitude
towards the Jews than to the Christians: "You will find that the
people most hostile towards the believers [the Muslims] are the Jews
. . . ; and you will find that the nearest in affection towards the
believers are those who say, 'We are Christians'."[7] This is probably
linked to Muhammad's rivalry with the Jews and his good relationship with the Christians; and even though, or because, Judaism is
closer to Islam – in pure monotheism – than to Christianity and the
"Holy Trinity", which is considered a basic heresy both in Judaism

and Islam. Indeed, as we shall see further on, in many time periods, Muslims preferred Jews over Christians, not only out of theological considerations, but also out of strategic, political and security considerations as well. Additionally, there were reciprocal influences and cooperation between Muslims and Jews (and Christians) in the fields of economy, culture, science and religion (for example, the Jewish influence in all that is related to prayer, the *Shahadah* – a declaration of belief in the oneness of God, fasting, laws such as the Shari'a and the Fiqh (law), halal, circumcision, charity, Sabbath and the Bible.) However, as with the Qur'an and its impact, the Muslim rulers who came after Muhammad treated the Jews (and the Christians) with ambivalence: On the one hand, they perceived them as inferior politically, legally and socially; on the other hand, they enjoyed ethnic-religious autonomy and the freedom for economic, social and cultural activities, and even appointments to positions in government administration.

In principle, Jews and Christians were considered by Muslims to be non-believers and even heretics of the true religion, Islam, and the prophet Muhammad, the messenger of Allah. It was therefore mandatory to treat them as inferior and demeaned subjects, who are obligated to pay a poll tax (the *Jizya*), and to enforce political, legislative and social limitations, as stated in the Qur'an: "Fight those who do not believe in God, nor in the Last Day, nor forbid what God and His Messenger have forbidden, nor abide by the religion of truth – from among those who received the Scripture – until they pay the due tax, willingly and agree to submit". They were also labeled in the Qur'an "apes and pigs".[8]

Furthermore, additional restrictions were placed upon the Jews and Christians that weren't always enforced (as opposed to the *Jizya* tax), such as the ban on holding senior political positions, the ban on military service, and bearing witness against Muslims in Muslim Shari'a courts; and according to the stipulations set by the Khalif Umar Ibn al-Khattab (717–720) they were forbidden to build or to renovate houses of worship, or to wear Muslim garments (of the color green); but they had to wear clothing items of a specific color – the Jews had to wear honey-colored (yellow) garments or patches of fabric of that color on their garments (also as stipulated by the Khalif al-Mutawakkil, 847–861). These ritualistic and social decrees were mainly implemented in the times of extremist Muslim rule, but not during many other periods of moderate and more liberal rulers. On the other hand, as believers in the Divine revelation in part, and in return for payment of the *Jizya* and as per the contract with them, the Muslim state and Muslim law accorded patronage (*dhimma*) and security of life and property to Jews and Christians (*ahl al-dhimma*), and granted them autonomy of worship, ritual, jurisdiction in matrimonial issues, culture and education, and usually without forced Islamization – perhaps based on the verse from the Qur'an, "There shall be no compulsion in religion".[9] Jews were also permitted to work in a variety of occupations, almost without restrictions, and a significant number of Jews worked (also in partnership with Muslims) in trade, as silversmiths, in traditional banking, financial consultancy, science and medicine.

Indeed, although their status was inferior, and at times they were persecuted, the conditions of the Jews in Islamic countries over long periods of time were far better than their brethren in Christian Europe of the Middle Ages (and after that), who suffered brutal anti-Semitism that included blood libel, religious persecution, expulsion and pogroms – for example, under Byzantine rule, during the Spanish Inquisition and the Crusades (and even later, in Czarist Russia and Nazi Germany).

An expression to some degree of the Jews' preference of Islamic rule over Christian rule is found, for example, at the start of the Islamic conquests, as stated in the *Midrash* (Talmudic legend): "The Lord does not bring about the rule of Ismael but to save you from the rule of the evil . . . " (Byzantine) . . . and further on "The rule of Ismael is moderate" and is "a benevolent rule". Similarly, Rabbi Shimon bar Yochai, in the 2nd century CE, in his vision prayed for the release of the Jews by the "rule of Ismael". Jews cooperated with the Muslim army in its war against Byzantium and in return were allowed to return and reside in Jerusalem, from which they had earlier been expelled; according to both Muslim and Jewish sources, Jews helped build the Al-Aqsa Mosque and the Dome of the Rock.[10] A significant number of Jews converted to Islam thanks to Islam's moderate attitude and to its cultural impact.

In this regard, it may be said that during most of the periods and in most of the countries the condition of the Jews was satisfactory, from fair to tolerable, especially under enlightened and liberal rulers and in periods of political and economic stability. However, under the rule of extremist Muslim rulers, and during periods of unrest, including the invasions of the Crusaders and the Mongols, the Jews were persecuted and at times suffered murderous attacks. Thus, for instance, the Umayyad Khalifs, such as Muawiya, Ibn Abi Sufyan and others who ruled at different time periods during the 7th century, as well as rulers from the Abbas dynasty (from the 8th century) who, amongst other things, bestowed significant authority upon the exilarchs and the heads of the *yeshivas* (Jewish academies) in Iraq.[11] From the mid-10th century and on, over a long time period, the Jews enjoyed the "Golden Age" in Muslim Spain, North Africa and the Middle East, and attained important cultural achievements, political and economic influence and relative security. It was a period of unique cultural relationships – "A wonderful mixture of two cultures" (Yehuda Ratshabi), or "a Jewish–Muslim symbiosis" (Goitein), of the monumental Jewish intellectuals such as Ibn Ezra, Samuel Ibn Naghrillah, Alharizi, Ibn Pakuda, Maimonides, Saadia Gaon, Yehuda HaLevi, Ibn Gvirol, and more. They wrote in Arabic and delved in philosophy, medicine, astronomy and the various natural sciences. At the same time, the *yeshivas* continued to flower in Iraq (Sura and Pompedita), in Egypt (Fustat) and in the Holy Land (Tiberias and Jerusalem). These Jews and others were significantly influenced by the Islamic culture in its many forms, including the Sufi-Muslim mysticism that influenced the doctrine of Jewish Kabbala in the 12th to 13th centuries. The "Golden Age" was manifest in Tunisia and Egypt as well, for example during part of the Fatimid Khalifate (a Shi'ite dynasty), and mainly during the Ayyubid era (Kurdish dynasty) led by Saladin, who conquered Jerusalem from the Crusaders, increased its importance to Islam and returned the Jews who had been expelled from the city by the Crusaders. Not many Jews lived in Jerusalem and for many subsequent periods, even though nearly all Jews in exile prayed daily facing the Temple Mount. Muslim rulers permitted the Jews to pray at the Western Wall, but not on the Temple Mount. In other regions as well Jews enjoyed religious freedom, especially during the Middle Ages.

The American Jewish historian, Mark Cohen, wrote that "the convivencia of Jews and Muslims in Muslim Spain and elsewhere in the Medieval Islamic world was real . . . the cultural achievements . . . the political influence . . . the apparent security of the Jews amongst the Muslims". And according to the British Jewish historian, Martin Gilbert, "The social interaction of the Jews of Baghdad developed over four hundred years of coexistence between Jews and Muslims", from 762 CE.[12]

Similarly, Jewish Israeli researchers and historians, such as Goitein and Ashtor; and Muslims, such as Maqrizi, and lately also Hawary wrote in a positive vein about the Jews of Egypt in that time period, basing their work also on the Cairo *Geniza* – a collection of historical manuscripts of the Jewish communities. For example, according to the Egyptian researcher, Muhammad Hawary, "The Jewish community of Egypt in the high Middle Ages was affluent, influential and on the whole stable and secure". Its members worked in agriculture and handicrafts, nurtured vineyards, dealt in the production of wine, cheeses and sugar, and dying fabric; they held senior positions in the government, even as doctors of the sultans (Maimonides, for example). An Egyptian poet of that era describes (with some exaggeration) the Jews' condition thus: "The Jews of our time have attained the goal of their aspirations. The honors are theirs and so are the riches. Counselors . . . are taken from their midst; Egyptians, I advise you become Jews, for Heaven itself has turned Jewish." Prof. Miriam Frankel defines this period, based on the research by Prof. Goitein, as "democratic, liberal, open, rational and aesthetic".[13]

However, there was also the flip – and difficult – side of this coin that in part stemmed from the fanaticism of the rulers, and in part from their envy of the Jews' success and show of power. Hence, at various time periods, restrictions were placed on building synagogues, and decrees on dress codes were passed. Jews were physically attacked as well. For example, in Granada, Spain, a Muslim mob in 1066 CE murdered a Jewish vizier ("a man of influence and arrogance"), and thousands of other Jews as well. The renowned Jewish historian of the Middle East, Bernard Lewis, explained that this was "a rare occurrence in Muslim history", as "Jews had broken the conditions of the contract with Islam and the Muslim state, and were seen to be getting too much wealth and too much power".[14] In Egypt and Syria the Fatimid khalif al-Hakim Biamr Allah (996–1021 CE), who during his early rule was tolerant and fair towards the Jews, changed his attitude and turned fanatic – he destroyed synagogues (and churches) and imposed various restrictions on Jews (and Christians). During the era following the Fatimid period – the extremist-Muslim Mamluk era (1250–1517 CE) – Jews and Christians in Egypt and Syria continued to suffer at times from discrimination, financial extortion and various harassments. Other extremist Muslim dynasties at different periods that persecuted the Jews and imposed, inter alia, forced conversion edicts, were: the Berber al-Murābiṭun Khalifates and the al-Muwahiddun dynasties in North Africa from the 11th to the 13th centuries; the Safavid Shi'ite dynasty in Persia, from the 16th to the 19th centuries; the Shia Zaidiyyah in Yemen in the 17th century; and the Sudanese Mahdiyya at the end of the 19th century.

Thus, for example, in Shi'ite Persia the Jews were considered impure (*najes*), and at different times were forced (especially in Mashhad, 1839) to convert to Islam, and were the victims of massacres and blood libels. On the other hand, the Jews in Persia also lived through better times. In Yemen as well, during the Shi'ite-Zaidiyyah dynasty, the Jews of San'a were forced to convert to Islam in 1648, or at least to go into exile; they refused to convert to Islam and many of the exiles died along the way. But, in contrast, the Muslim residents of San'a pressured the governor to dismiss the edict, claiming that the Jewish craftsmen were vital to the city's welfare.

As to the position taken by the Shi'ites (who today comprise 10–15% of the Muslims), it is noteworthy that "alongside the theology of isolation and distancing from the (defiled) Jew . . . there is a tendency amongst the Shi'a to identify with the Jewish people and perceive them as an ancient wonder . . . as a persecuted minority that in future will fulfill an important place in history" (see also Chapter 4).[15]

In conclusion, the persecution of Jews in the Middle Ages, mainly by the al-Muwahhidun (Almohad) Khalifate in North Africa and Yemen, led Maimonides to reach the sad conclusion in his "Letter to Yemen" that "Never has a nation risen against the Jewish people that is a more hateful enemy than the nation of Ismael". Less blunt, yet rather hostile was Rabbi Chai Ben-Sharira from the Pompedita Academy (*Yeshiva*), who wrote in the 11th century that "all Muslims should be viewed as extortionists and thieves and that in the Bible the Arabs are mentioned in a negative way."[16] In contrast, many other rabbis held that living in exile amongst Ishmael [the Muslims] was one of the acts of grace that God had bestowed upon His people, who were able to sustain themselves, compared to their neighbors, and were able to express themselves freely.

Prof. Haim Zeev Hirschberg, a distinguished researcher on Jews in Islamic lands, holds that: "A general review of the Jewish, Christian and Arab sources shows us that the condition of the Jews in the Middle Ages under Arab rule was generally better than that of the Christians, and far better than the condition of the Jews in Christian countries in Europe . . . the Jews were less harmed when oppressed; their behavior did not arouse feelings of animosity and jealousy to the degree the Christians felt, who were arrogant and authoritative; nor were the Jews suspected of political ties with Christian kingdoms . . . Within the framework of tolerance towards 'protected populations' based on the Qur'an and the prophet's tradition, there appears a wide spectrum of colors and shades – from almost total equality with the Muslims in whatever has no clear affinity to religious matters, and up to the circumstance of being citizens of inferior status that are tolerated out of indifference to their very existence. The sectarian Islam (mainly the Shi'a) was more fanatic than the Sunni Islam . . . "[17]

Another Jewish researcher, Prof. Wasserstein, goes even further than the aforementioned and other researchers, when he recently claimed that "Islam saved Judaism . . . the Jews and Judaism were on the brink of falling into the abyss of oblivion (in the Byzantine and Persian eras). The coming of Islam saved them by offering them a new environment in which they could not only survive, but also prosper. Under Islam, their condition improved from all aspects: legislative, demographic, social, religious, political . . . economic, linguistically, culturally . . . the cultural flowering of the Jews in the Middle Ages was . . . to a great degree the result of the cultural flowering . . . .of Arab Islam."

As to the economic aspect, this is addressed by professors Zvi Ekstein and Maristella Butticini in *The Chosen Minority: How Studying Formed the Economic History of the Jews 1470–1490*. In reviewing this book, the economist Manuel Trachtenberg said, inter alia, as follows: " . . . in the mid-7th century, an historic meeting took place between the Jews and rising Islam . . . The impact of these changes on the Jews was dramatic: in the years 750–900 nearly all the Jews in Mesopotamia and Persia – about 75 percent of all world Jewry which then numbered only 1.2 million – abandoned agriculture, moved to the big cities of the Abbasid Khalifate and specialized in professions based on literacy and education, which earned far higher revenues than did agricultural work . . . This process (endowing every Jew with literacy) enriched the Jews in the awakening economy of the Muslim empire in key positions . . . whilst their cities transformed them into . . . being in high demand in Yemen, Syria, Egypt and the Maghreb countries . . ."[18]

2

The Ottoman Empire
Tolerance and Cooperation in the Balkans

Of the three Muslim empires that ruled concurrently for centuries in parts of Asia, Africa and Europe from the 16th century (and prior to that), the Turkish-Ottoman Empire was the most significant in regard to Muslim–Jewish relationships. The other two empires that developed at that time were: the Shi'ite–Safavid empire in Persia (from 1501), whose attitude towards the Jews was generally hostile (see Chapter 4), and the Mogul empire in India (from 1525), which at various time periods treated its Jewish communities well.

The Ottoman Empire was the largest and most enduring of the three empires and represented the Muslim-Sunni world via the grand mufti, *Shaykh al-Islām*, who held the highest religious-spiritual authority. This empire also imposed its authority, both practically and nominally, at different time periods over the holy sites of Islam in Mecca and Medina, and for 400 years in Jerusalem over the holy sites of Islam, Christianity and Judaism. It ruled for centuries over the greatest number of Jews, compared to all other Muslim countries. The attitudes taken by the Ottoman rulers towards their Jewish subjects were for most of the time typified by pragmatic tolerance, and even positivity.

Among the major causes for this phenomenon were: (a) The Ottomans' Muslim tradition of the Muslim-Sunni-Hanafi school of thought, in contrast to the more extreme Shi'ite position in Iran, and the strict Sunni-Wahabi school of jurisprudence in the Arabian Peninsula. (b) The superiority of the political-Ottoman rule vis-à-vis the Muslim-Sunni *ulama* (religious scholars) who were part of the establishment, in comparison to the Shi'ite religious clergy in Iran, who were independent and more radical and perceived themselves as the country's supreme leaders (*wilayat al-faqih*, rule of the religious scholar).

Subsequently, except for certain periods when the *ulama* had influence over the Ottoman Sultan (such as Bayezid II, 1481–1512, who treated the Jews severely, yet also absorbed the expelled from Spain), most sultans showed decent treatment towards the Jews. They influenced their religious-ethnic and socio-economic systems significantly, including instilling the position of the "Hakham Bashi" (Chief Rabbi) both in Istanbul and in Jerusalem. The Ottomans also permitted the Jews to emigrate to the Holy Land and pray at the Western Wall, though not at the Temple Mount.

However, at the end of the 19th century, Sultan Abdul Hamid (1876–1908) placed harsh restrictions on the emigration of Zionist Jews and at the same time took steps to increase the Muslim ambiance of Jerusalem, the Holy Land and the region. For example, he told Zionist dignitaries that al-Ḥaram al-Sharīf in Jerusalem was initially established by Islam and that he would not sell the Holy Land to the Jews and betray the Muslim nation that trusted him to protect it. In this regard, it is noteworthy that following the Muslim Ayyubid dynasties (led by Salah-a-Din who conquered Jerusalem in 1187 from the Crusaders) and the Mamluks (1250–1516) who took action at the time to restore Jerusalem and Islamize the Temple Mount again, the Ottomans in the 16th century invested great efforts in these missions. For example, building the massive wall surrounding Jerusalem, restoration of the mosques of al-Aqsa and the Dome of the Rock, and expanding Islamic activity in the city and on the Temple Mount. The Ottoman efforts to fortify Jerusalem also came in response to the activities of the powerful Christian countries in Jerusalem and the Holy Land in the 19th century.[1]

Supportive Attitudes towards the Jews

The Ottoman era was the longest running period in history, nearly 500 years of Muslim rule (1453–1917), over a large Jewish population (nearly 400 thousand in 1900); in part a very early population, but the majority descended from the Jews expelled from Spain and

Portugal (1492), as well as from central and Western Europe. (Prior to that time, there was also Turkish rule over parts of Anatolia for 150 years.) Hundreds of thousands of Jewish refugees were received with open arms by the immense Muslim empire that had gained control over expansive regions of the Middle East, North Africa and southern Europe. The Ottoman sovereigns imposed on their Jewish subjects political and jurisdictional limitations stemming from Islamic laws and traditions, and at times did nothing to prevent physical and economic harm to the Jews, executed by local rulers and illiterate, incited mobs, especially in distant provincial areas. Basically, however, the Muslim state treated its Jewish subjects with tolerance, and even sympathy at times, integrating many of them into various financial branches and government administration. The Muslim regime allowed them to conduct religious rituals, gave them jurisdiction over marital issues and educational and cultural activities, with little interference. This multi-cultural and pluralistic empire was "one of the most tolerant Muslim states that existed" in "constant interaction" with their Jewish subjects, to the point of creating a "significant and distinct Jewish-Ottoman or Jewish–Muslim heritage, no lesser than that called 'Judeo-Christian' or 'Western'; the Jews called it a 'Kingdom of Grace'".[2]

Moreover, as in earlier periods, the condition of the Jews in the Muslim Ottoman Empire continued to be better than that of the Jews in the Christian European countries, and at times was even superior to that of the Christian subjects throughout the empire. Both Jews and Christians enjoyed autonomous frameworks which the Ottomans called *Millet* (congregation, nation), with each Christian community headed by patriarchs (Orthodox, Armenian and Catholic) and a Chief Rabbi at the head of the Jewish community (the Hakham Bashi, and prior to that, Shaykh al-Yahud), all of whom held a formal position in the country. (This position continued after the dissolution of the Ottoman Empire as well, in the persona of the Sephardic Chief Rabbi, "*Rishon Le-Zion*", and is part of the Ottoman legacy in modern-day Israel.) Jews (and Christians) also held senior positions in the central Ottoman government, in the courts of the sultans and in the provinces, as treasury directors, advisors, translators and doctors. For example, Don Yosef Nassi served as advisor to the sultans, and Moshe and Yosef Hamon were physicians in the royal court (all in the 16th century).

27

In the 19th century two Jews were appointed as members of the "State Council", and a number of Jewish physicians worked in the courts of the sultans. In the same century, Jews held senior positions as financial advisers to the regional governors, such as Haim and Raphael Farhi in Damascus and Acre, and Yaacov and Ishak Huja in Baghdad and Basra. These and others contributed greatly to their communities as well. However, at times, due to the caprices of a cruel ruler, they risked a downfall and reversal of fortune. This was the fate of Haim Farhi, for example, who served as financial adviser to the governor of the Acre region, Sulayman al-Adil (the "Honest", the "Just", 1804–1818). A contemporary Christian historian wrote at the time (with envy and exaggeration): "Haim the Jew had control of all the ruling institutions and did as he pleased. It was said that a Jew has unlimited control over the Muslims and Christians, those of the lowest and highest positions, both near and far." However, prior to that, the region was under the rule of Ahmad Pasha al-Jazzar (the "Butcher"), who treated his advisor Farhi with cruelty: He commanded to gouge out one of his eyes, and cut off the tip of his nose and his left ear. The governor who followed Sulayman, Abdallah Pasha, ordered to execute Haim and confiscate his property. Perhaps in the spirit of the times the Swiss traveler Burckhardt wrote as follows: "There is scarcely an instant in the modern history of Syria or a Christian or Jew having long enjoyed the power of riches which he may have acquired. These persons are always taken off in the last moment at their greatest apparent glory."[3]

However, this time period and these cruel deeds were quite the exception, and as the 19th century progressed, the condition of the Jews throughout the region improved and stabilized. Jews (and Christians) continued paying the poll tax (*Jizya*), denoting their inferior status, but also serving as a guarantee of the patronage and security provided by the Muslim state. This tax was nullified in 1855 and was replaced with the Bedel tax – as ransom for military service. In 1869, Jews and Christians were proclaimed as equal subjects of the Empire; and in 1909 military service became mandatory for Jews. During World War I, Jews from the Holy Land, amongst them David Ben-Gurion and Yitzhak Ben-Zvi, served in the Turkish army. Other Jewish notables supported the Turkish war effort against the allied forces, Britain and France.

In the judicial field, theoretically discrimination against Jews (and Christians) continued, as they were not eligible to bear witness in

Muslim-Shariyya courts (*Mahkama*) against Muslims. However, in fact there were numerous cases in which Jews testified against Muslims in the *Mahkama*, and even won their cases. In addition, many Jews turned to these courts in trials against Christians or other Jews, and for the religious *awkaf* (endowment) of sacred properties.[4] Moreover, many Jews turned to the secular Ottoman courts of law that passed judgment in criminal, financial and social issues. For centuries, these courts were administered as per the Sultans' canon; and in the 19th century, within the framework of civil criminal and commercial courts that were administered according to European codes, a few Jewish judges were also appointed. (These European codes were included in the Ottoman civil code, called *Majalla*, traces of which have remained in current Israeli law, such as the word *Tapu* = *Tabu*, in land registries.)

In other fields as well differences were apparent between Muslim tradition and Ottoman reality, namely: The government did not always enforce the ban on building new synagogues or renovating old ones, or special dress codes. Enforcing these regulations depended on the position taken by the regional rulers and sultans – conservative or liberal – as well as the degree of power and fanaticism of the Muslim religious establishment; or the degree of closeness to the centers of government and the behavior of the Muslim masses. During periods of weak or cruel governance in regions that were distant from the center, Jews suffered violence at the hands of the masses, harassment and extortion by rulers and officials, and even blood libels, mainly from Christians. But in general, the Jews (mostly city dwellers) lived in relative security (also via "protection payments") and worked in various branches of finance, commerce and crafts, separately or in cooperation with their Muslim neighbors. They were even members in joint professional guilds with Muslims, and at the same time continued to manage educational-religious and cultural activities of their own. In the 17th and 18th centuries, some Jews were prominent in commerce and banking, and as military suppliers, goldsmiths, etc. Many were involved in the life and general culture of their city along with the Muslims. In addition to the 16th century, the first century of strong, flourishing and liberal Ottoman rule, and later on for long time periods, especially from the mid-19th century, the Jews' condition in the empire was fair, quite secure and at times relatively good, certainly when compared to the Ottoman Christian subjects. This was a period of modernization in the administration and the military, and of significant reforms (*Tanzimat*) in the status of Jews and Christians, reforms that were supported by the Western powers, yet also encountered obstacles and acts of violence.[5]

Thus, for example, Jews and Christians were given representation in the mid-19th century in the administrative councils (*Majlis-Idara*) of the *vilayets* (the provinces) and in the city councils (*baladiyya*, towards the end of the 19th century); in the general councils (*majlis umumi*) of the *vilayets* (at the start of the 20th century); and in the Ottoman parliament. It was established in 1876 (with four Jewish delegates, and later six), and was renewed with the rise to power of the 'Young Turks' in 1908. In some of these representative bodies, the Jewish delegates did not carry any weight or influence; some exhibited passivity or indifference; others feared expressing independent opinions and served as a rubber stamp for decisions taken by the Muslim majority; in some cases, Jewish delegates were removed from the representative bodies or neutralized by their Muslim colleagues. In contrast, there were Jewish delegates who acted with relative independence and represented with honor the issues of the Jewish communities. In any event, the very phenomenon of Jewish personages participating in the State's representative bodies served as a kind of significant positive change of the Jews' judicial-political status in the Ottoman state. In other areas as well that were under the rule or the influence of the regime, important steps were taken to equalize the status of the Jews and Christians to that of the Muslims: Jews were accepted into civil service in increasingly greater numbers – including the ministries of Foreign Affairs, the Treasury and Education; and the official documents of the Empire no longer included derogatory names for non-Muslims. Both Jews and Christians were given permits to build or renovate houses of worship and other ritual venues, and the dress code edicts were no longer valid.

Nonetheless, it is worth noting that the Ottoman Empire in the 19th century did not become secular according to Western European norms. It continued to be, up to the start of the 20th century – and especially under the rule of Sultan Abdul Hamid – a Muslim state in its essence and in its policies, and as such, neither Jews nor Christians were able to be full and equal partners in the political community.

The Muslim nature of the Ottoman Empire was apparent not only during the era of the extremist Muslim Sultan Khalif Abdul Hamid (1876–1908), but also under the sultans before him, including the liberal Sultan Abdul Majid (1839–1861). Those elements that fanatically maintained the Muslim character of the State were the religious leaders (the *ulama*) who held official positions in the administrative network. These, along with political leaders with conservative-Muslim leanings, great numbers of religious clergy and the majority Muslim population, adamantly opposed giving equal rights to non-Muslim subjects throughout the 19th century.

Indeed, the reforms in the status of non-Muslims, mainly those included in the 1856 royal decree of reforms, aroused great anger and opposition among the Muslim masses throughout the empire, towards the Christian subjects, the European delegates and the Ottoman ruling bodies. Many attempts were made by the *ulama* and the masses to prevent the implementation of these reforms, and in some places anti-Christian and anti-European riots broke out. In the city of Marash in southern Turkey, for instance, a Muslim mob murdered the British consul – a local Christian – and his family, following the announcement of the 1856 royal decrees. In the port city of Jedda in the Arabian Peninsula, the British and French consuls were murdered in 1858 by Muslim inhabitants; and in 1859 in Istanbul, a conspiracy was uncovered against the Sultan and the leaders of the reform, planned by high-ranking military officers and senior *ulama*, who opposed the increasing influence of the West and the granting of equal rights to Christians.[6]

In cities throughout Syria and in the Holy Land, riots of especially severe nature broke out. In Aleppo, in 1850, a Muslim mob attacked the Christian Quarter, massacred its residents, plundered and burnt churches and private homes. In Nablus, in 1856, Muslims murdered the Prussian consul – a local Christian, injured members of his community and destroyed homes and Christian places of ritual. In 1860 in Damascus, the worst anti-Christian massacre in the Empire occurred, in which thousands of Christians were slaughtered – men, women and children; many were forcibly converted to Islam and churches and houses in the Christian Quarter were plundered and destroyed.

During all these riots, and other anti-Christian outbreaks from the start of the *Tanzimat*, hardly any Jews were harmed, though –

like the Christians – they too were granted the new equality rights by the Ottoman reform.

A Triangular Relationship:
Muslims–Jews–Christians

In 1859, a Jewish traveler wrote: "The Ishmaelites (Muslims) and the Jews do not hate one another, but rather they like one another, but the uncircumcised (the Christians) are hated by the Ishmaelites."[7] In truth, Jews throughout the Ottoman Empire continued to serve as targets of attacks and injury during the era of reform, both by their Muslim neighbors and local rulers. However, these attacks were sporadic and light when compared with the pogroms led by the Muslims against the Christians. The motives that led to these attacks were religious and economic – the Muslims' sense of scorn towards the Jews, and their greed for the Jews' property – as compared to the motives for the Muslim aggression against Christians, which were mainly political and security-related: the opposition to political equal rights for Christians, which they perceived as a security risk to the Ottoman State. Indeed, the Christian subjects of the Empire, whose number was rather large, did not settle for the limited privileges granted to them. Some took advantage, publicly and provocatively – from the Muslim viewpoint – their rights of religious worship; others demanded assertively full and immediate political equality with the Muslims; there were those who even fought for full national independence. All were linked to or identified with various European countries that were helping them acquire independence or equality, and hence were suspected of being a 'fifth column' by many Muslims.

In contrast, the Jewish subjects, who constituted a smaller population, continued perceiving themselves in general as a religious minority, made due with the rights of ritual and the civil rights that were granted to them, and did not nurture political ambitions or interests, except for an "interest in the present and future welfare of the [Ottoman] country". Thus, for example, a senior Ottoman clerk wrote in the mid-19th century:

> [...] this tranquility (of the Jews) under Ottoman rule, so opposite
> to the agitation and convulsion of other Raiahas (non-Muslims),

especially of the Greeks [. . .] is explained partly by the peaceable habits and disposition of the Jews, which cause no umbrage to the Porte (high gate) [. . .] patient, industrious, and resigned to their fate, they wore – without an apparent sense of humiliation – the coloured beneesh [Jehoudane . . .] as a mark to distinguish them from the Musulman.[8]

Furthermore: the majority of the Jews identified with the Ottoman State and helped in difficult times. For instance, during the Crimean War (1854) and the Turkish–Russian war in 1877, Jews contributed financially towards the Turkish war effort. In 1892, marking 400 years of the settlement of Spanish exiles in the Ottoman Empire, the Jews held a prayer of thanksgiving for Turkey and published in the Jewish newspapers a song of praise of the Turkish Empire. In 1915, when the Turkish army sunk four British ships in the Dardanelles Straits, David Yellin – a member of the General Council in Jerusalem – published a proclamation praising the Turks' victory over the enemy.

Other means by which the Jews expressed their identification with the Ottoman state included moral support, passive – and at times active – help to Muslims in times of anti-Christian outbursts. Thus, for example, in 1821, a Jewish mob in Istanbul abused the corpse of the Greek patriarch, Gregory, who was put to death by the Ottoman government on charges of conspiracy of a Greek uprising. After Turkish rule returned to Syria in 1840, Jews helped Muslims who attacked Christians. In 1860 they were accused of helping Muslim and Druze rioters, who had carried out a great massacre of Christians in Damascus.

Yet, it must be emphasized that these hostile acts against Christians did not stem only – or mainly – from the Jews' identifying with the Ottoman state; actually, these acts were clearly connected to a line of deep motives and important interests that were inter-twined:

A response to and even revenge on the Christians' multiple harassments of the Jews, and especially the 'blood libels' that the Christians falsely accused the Jews of, throughout the empire, during the 19th century, and at times prior to that as well:
The competition between Christians and Jews on positions in the Ottoman administration and in various financial branches;

The struggle between two rival minorities to win the backing or support from the Muslim majority and the authorities against the rival minority;

Reaction to the traditional loathing between Christians and Jews against a theological-religious background.

The last three of the above factors in the rivalry between Christians and Jews were not new phenomena in the history of the Ottoman Empire. The economic competition between both minorities, which was charged with religious-cultural antagonism, was conducted for centuries in various places throughout the Ottoman Empire, according to 'accepted' rules of the game: Influence, lobbying, subversion and other non-violent political means. In the 19th century, manifestations of violence and delegitimization were added, when the Christians flourished a new/old weapon: accusing the Jews of anti-human crimes in an attempt to undermine, if not destroy, the moral basis of their existence and mark them as fair prey. This was done by spreading dozens of 'blood libels', which began in Aleppo in 1810 and continued throughout the 19th century, surfacing every few years, in Syria, Turkey, the Balkans, Rhodes, the Holy Land and Egypt. The most prominent 'blood libel' took place in 1840 in Damascus. The thematic motif of this phenomenon, which was new in the Middle East, was apparently supplied via the cultural process of transferring concepts from Christian Europe to Christians in the East, through European missionaries who were active in the region, or through local clerical apprentices that had been trained in Europe. The actual need to use blood libel grew not only from the increased competition between Christians and Jews for managerial posts and economic positions, but also from the worsening political hostility of Muslims against Christians against the background of the Ottoman reforms. Christian leaders sought ways to deflect Muslim animosity from them – towards the Jews, and accused them of murdering Christian and Muslim children and using their blood for baking the Passover matzos. These accusations were well absorbed, not only by the Christian masses, replete with religious-historic animosity, but they also caught the imagination of the Muslim masses, who were inundated with prejudice and ignorance. It may be assumed that the Christians' objective was to present the Jew as a satanic figure, an enemy of mankind – Christians and Muslims – and turn him into the scapegoat and the object of the Muslims' fury. Indeed, not a few Muslims, and with them Christians, joined together in violent anti-Jewish riots resulting from the blood libel; there were also Muslims in Turkey, Syria and Egypt[9] who used this weapon of blood libel against the Jews independently, in order to take revenge on personal enemies, and for extortion purposes as well. In some cases, these anti-Jewish accusations were supported by European consuls (French, British and others) and Ottoman rulers. However, for the most part, the Ottoman government protected its Jewish subjects from the blood libels and even punished its perpetrators. Thus, for instance, in September 1840, following a blood libel in Damascus, the sultan Abdul Majid published a royal decree that refuted the accusations against the Jews and acquitting them of any crime.[10] At a later period, this decree also served the Ottoman rulers as a judicial basis for refuting additional blood libels, declaring them as ground-less. In this regard, it is also noteworthy that the Ottoman rulers in the metropolitan areas and the provincial areas took action to protect their Jewish subjects from the harassments and attacks by both Christians and Muslims; Muslim dignitaries demonstrated from time to time a sympathetic attitude towards the Jews and tended to support them at times of dispute between Christians and Jews. This too was the stand taken by the conservative sultan Abdul Hamid who, amongst other things, instructed to absorb Jewish refugees in Turkey who had escaped from the horrors of the pogroms in Russia and the Ukraine in the1880s.

Based on what has been said above, it can be concluded that in the Christian–Jewish struggle for the support of the Muslim majority, most times the stakes were in favor of the Jews, despite the Christians' use of the blood libels. Throughout wide areas of the empire, a gradual closeness between Muslims and Jews developed, leading to the improved status and security of the Jews. In contrast, as mentioned above, the Muslim–Christian polarity increased, which led to pogroms and the massacre of Christians in Syria and Turkey, and to a large Christian emigration outside the borders of the empire.

However, in this Muslim–Christian–Jew triangle, in some areas such as Egypt, Syria and the Holy Land, a change began to take place towards the end of the 19th century and the start of the 20th century. A new basis for building relationships and cooperation between Muslims and Christians was formed within the framework of the Arab nationalist movements. In some areas, the Jews became the target of a joint Muslim–Christian struggle, be it because they did not take an active part in the local nationalist movement – as in Egypt and Syria – or because they established their own nationalist movement, i.e., Zionism in the Holy Land. The latter presented a challenge, if not a threat, to the nationalist Arab movement in Syria and the Holy Land, as we shall see further on. In contrast, in Turkey, Jews identified with the Turkish nationalist movement, begun by the "Young Turks" movement in 1908, and even took part in the activities of the movement's "Committee for Unity and Progress", before the revolution, and after.[11] Among the Jews who supported the new Ottoman regime were representatives of the Jewish-Zionist movement, with many young members, including David Ben-Gurion, Yitzhak Ben-Zvi and Moshe Sharet, who represented the Ottoman affinity amongst the Zionists in the Holy Land. The latter studied at the University of Istanbul and even enlisted more Jews to join the military in Turkey's service during World War I (Jews also took part in the Balkan Wars of 1912–1913 on Turkey's side). At the time, the Zionist movement requested of the new regime of the "Young Turks" to allow free emigration of Jews to the Holy Land (which had been previously forbidden by the sultan Abdul Hamid), and there establish an autonomous cultural center within the empire. These positions were in direct conflict with the religious leadership and the socio-economic bourgeois elite (including parliament members) of Jews in Turkey and the Empire, who sought to integrate more fully and dissociated themselves from the Zionist movement.

However, following the British and French conquest of Turkey in 1918, the Zionist Jews developed a pro-British, anti-Turkish nationalist orientation, whereas the chief rabbi and the community leaders maintained their loyalty to the Ottoman Empire, opposed the Zionist movement and developed pro-French leanings. The regime of the "Young Turks" treated the Jewish community, including the Zionists, sympathetically and took steps to integrate them into the country. However, when the Zionist movement in Turkey and in the Holy Land emphasized its nationalist and pro-British aspirations, the regime acted against it and supported the non-Zionist Jews whose desire was to integrate into the new Turkish country (see Chapter 5).

Before discussing developments in Muslim–Jewish relationships in modern-day Turkey, it is appropriate to first review the state of

the Jews in other Muslim countries – the Balkans, Sunni North
Africa and Shi'ite Iran.

Muslims and Jews in the Balkans

Historical Background

The Jews in the Balkans – Greece, Turkey, Bulgaria, Macedonia,
Serbia and Bosnia – were brought under Muslim Ottoman rule from
1430 till the 19th century or the early 20th century. The majority
were the expelled Jews of Spain (1492) who were well absorbed, and
a small minority that had come earlier (Greek-speaking Romaniote
Jews); and Jewish refugees from other European countries. Like
their brethren in other parts of the empire, the Balkan Jews were
treated mostly with tolerance and even positively by most of the
Ottoman rulers. As Jews from Saloniki wrote to their persecuted
brethren in Europe in the 17th century: "Come, join us in Turkey
and live like us a life of peace and freedom . . . and this city (Saloniki)
received them with love and warm-heartedness, as if it were our
esteemed mother Jerusalem."[12] Indeed, for a very long time,
Saloniki was one of the two Jewish centers in the region – after
Istanbul, with whom it competed to be the first, with "Saloniki
claiming the crown, a metropolis for the Jews . . . Jerusalem of the
Balkans . . . the city of the Torah and of erudition".

The Jews controlled the city's economy and held other important
positions. Alongside times of harassment and violence from rulers
and the masses, there were also times of tolerance, dialogue and
cooperation between Muslims and Jews, especially in the cities
throughout the Ottoman Empire; as noted by the scholar, Ben-
Naeh: "From a social and religious viewpoint, though the Jews were
secondary groups in the surrounding society, they in fact embodied
an integral part of the metropolitan population and integrated into
city life; everyday life in the city was a scene of constant, ongoing
negotiations in the commercial areas, surrounded by the life of the
guilds and entertainment venues . . ."[13]

The Growth of Zionism

Unlike some countries in the Balkans, such as Bulgaria, that were
freed of the Ottoman yoke (in 1878), Jewish leaders in other places,

37

such as Saloniki, Sarajevo, Istanbul and other cities, refrained from supporting the Herzlian Zionist movement (1897), for fear of insulting the Ottoman government and its sovereignty over the Holy Land; though some intellectual circles and Jewish newspapers actively spread the Zionist idea, at times with Zionist funding.

Following the dissolution of the Ottoman Empire at the end of World War I, Zionist activities amongst the Jews in the region greatly increased, especially in Saloniki, under the rule of Christian Greece; however, Greek rulers found it difficult to prevent anti-Jewish Christian activities. In World War II, many of the Jews of Greece were murdered by the Nazis, "and, as to the Jews, Saloniki turned into a barren desert . . .".[14] In Bosnia as well, with a Muslim majority, the Spanish Jews developed a non-Zionist Jewish identity; but in the 1950s several Jewish movements were active there (as in Saloniki): Socialist, Communist, religious and Revisionist. During World War II, under a pro-Nazi fascist regime, most of the Jews of Sarajevo (about 10,000) were arrested and sent to concentration camps, where many of the men were killed.

After the war, many of the Jewish survivors immigrated to Israel, Italy, Switzerland and the United States, and only several thousand remained; and till the end of Tito's Communist regime (1945–1980) – only several hundred were left. Most of the (secular) Jews, especially during the Communist era, were non-Zionist or anti-Zionist, whereas the religious Jews immigrated to Israel.[15]

The Dissolution of Yugoslavia

During the civil war in Yugoslavia (1991–2001), the Jews of Bosnia identified with the Muslim majority, emphasizing the long era of tolerance and security they had enjoyed during the Muslim Ottoman period; they provided humanitarian help to the Muslim fighters, though many Jews suffered during the war and immigrated to other countries.

During World War II, the small Jewish community of Kosovo was incorporated into the large (secular Muslim) country of Albania, which at first was under the rule of Fascist Italy, and whose population protected the Jews, with many local Muslims saving a significant number of Jews. But when Nazi Germany ruled in Kosovo, the Albanian pro-Nazi militia, supported by the Mufti Haj Amin, murdered Jews in that region; other Jews were handed over to the Germans by the Italians and were sent to the death camps.

After the war, only a part of the Jewish community of Kosovo (then part of Yugoslavia) immigrated to Israel, and following the civil war the Jewish community there reorganized itself and enjoyed the support of American Jewry. Kosovo (Muslim) developed good relations with the United States and Israel. However, to date, Israel has rejected requests from the Kosovo government (that declared its independence unilaterally in 2008) to recognize it and open an embassy there. The refusal stems from concern over angering (Christian) Serbia, which sought to continue its rule over Kosovo; and because Israel feared that the Palestinians in the territories might copy the Kosovo model and declare their independence from Israel's occupation.

The foreign minister of Kosovo wrote in October 2013 that the Jews and Albanians in Kosovo had enjoyed peaceful coexistence for centuries; Jews worked in trade, and as doctors and craftsmen, and were part of the society. During World War II the Albanians of Kosovo helped to save Jews, based on ancient Albanian tradition – a code of honor, "besa", and even provided shelter for Jews fleeing from other regions of Yugoslavia and Greece. King Zog of Albania in the 1930s invited the Jews to settle in his country; the same occurred in Kosovo, where many Jews were saved during World War II. In 2013 Kosovo erected a memorial to commemorate the Jewish victims of the war, upon the ruins of the synagogue that had been demolished by the Communist regime in 1963.[16]

The small Jewish community in Albania consisted mainly of exiles from Spain and Portugal who had reached the Ottoman Empire in the 16th century. This community was officially recognized in 1937 by the Albanian regime, which before World War II absorbed Jewish refugees fleeing from Germany and Austria and other European countries. During the war the Albanians protected the Jews from the Nazis, and many of them were awarded the honorary title of "Righteous Among the Nations" from the Yad Vashem Holocaust Museum in Jerusalem and the Holocaust Museum in Washington, DC.

The Communist government, which was atheistic, forbade any religious activity, including that of the Jews, but did not harm them, even after the dissolution of the Soviet Union. In 1991 most of the Albanian Jews immigrated to Israel out of economic considerations and not because of anti-Semitism. Today only a few dozen Jews live in the capital city Tirana, and they have a new synagogue at their disposal. In 1991 Albania and Israel established diplomatic ties, including embassies in Tirana and Tel Aviv in 2012; and in June 2017, Albania beat Israel at a soccer game, scoring 3:0 in the World Cup qualification games.[17]

Extremist Muslim Influences

With the dissolution of Yugoslavia and the outbreak of the civil war in Bosnia in the 1990s, Muslim countries – such as Turkey, Iran and Saudi Arabia – became involved in providing logistic and military aid to Bosnia and Kosovo; these two countries had to defend themselves from the cruel attacks by Christian Serbia in its goal of ethnic cleansing and the murder of Muslims. At the same time, Muslim areas in the Balkans – Bosnia, Kosovo, Albania and Macedonia – were penetrated by dozens of armed radical Muslim organizations, including the Salafi and Jihadists, such as al-Qaida; alongside numerous charitable and aid organizations.

In addition to their involvement in the civil war and the establishment of religious institutions, the radical organizations initiated terrorism against American institutions in the region (such as the American Embassy in Sarajevo in 2011) and similar targets in European countries. But significantly, harm towards the Jews who remained in the Balkan countries, or attacks against Israeli targets by these organizations, were not reported. However, several relevant references were heard. For example, in 1991 the National Muslim Council of Bosnia was established and its leader published an "Islamic Proclamation" calling for a new Islamic order, a universal Islamic community of believers (*Ummah*) that will include all Muslims, from Morocco to Indonesia. This proclamation, which did not call for violence, offered the minority groups freedom of religion and protection, on condition that they remain loyal to the Muslim regime. It praised the era in which Jews had lived under Islamic rule as legally protected subjects, yet were refused a national and independent status; it differentiated between Jews and Zionists; and expected that Arab and Muslim states will free occupied Palestine, especially Jerusalem that is foremost a Muslim city.

Another Muslim organization in Bosnia called for a Jihad in order to "push back the Jewish-Crusader attack on the lands of Islam".

Nonetheless, in general, the Muslim tradition of the absence of anti-Semitism in the Balkans continued amongst most of the Muslims in the region.[18]

Muslim Attitudes towards Jews and Israel in Western European Countries

Till now discussion focused on the attitude of Muslims towards Jews and Israel in countries of southern Europe – the Balkans and Turkey (part of which is in Europe). In these countries large Muslim and Jewish populations had lived together for centuries, when the relationship between them was good, tolerable and at times difficult, during different periods and under different circumstances.

In the Western European countries – France, Britain, Germany, Italy, Holland, Belgium and Scandinavia – nearly one million Jews reside today, mostly in France and Britain, some going back a long time and some as immigrants from North African countries, eastern Europe and the Middle East. In contrast, most of the Muslims – nearly 20 million – mainly in France, immigrated to the Western European countries from Africa, the Middle East, Asian countries and others. According to various studies, most Muslims – from a varied ethnic background – aspire to integrate into their new European countries, in the economy, society, culture and politics; not a few hold positions and roles in the governments, parliaments, city councils and public agencies.

A small number of Muslims, from various ethnic groups, are not integrated into the social life, and live in closed religious communities, and in part strive to impose Islam and the Shari'a in Europe. Among them are some radical groups that use violence and terrorism against non-Muslim institutions and targets, especially Jewish ones, in the name of the Muslim faith. But this response also stems from severe economic and social distress, such as unemployment, inadequate education, and exclusion and loathing from the surrounding populace.

The mutual relationships between Muslims and Jews in Western European countries have become very complex in the past few decades, and differ from one country to another, but are significantly impacted by Israel's policies towards the Palestinians. On the one hand, for decades dozens of interfaith groups and organizations have been active, and hundreds of dialogues on religion, society, culture and politics are held between Muslims and Jews, particularly in England. On the other hand, terrorist attacks by extremist Muslims were perpetrated against Jews, synagogues, Jewish shops and restaurants, alongside anti-Semitic and anti-Israeli propaganda and demonstrations. In some of these activities, non-Muslims participated as well, driven by fanatic Christian anti-Semitic views and identification with the suffering of Palestinians brought about by Israel. The reaction of many Jews is expressed through fear and alienation from Muslims and holding Islamophobic beliefs, whereas only a small number of Jews strive towards a dialogue with Muslims. Not many Muslims identify with the Holocaust of European Jewry, and today perceive themselves as the Jews had, fearing a similar fate. Yet, there are Muslims who compare the Palestinian *Nakba* to the Holocaust of the Jews, or claim that the Holocaust never happened.[19]

Besides a certain degree of solidarity round the issues of Kashrut-Halal, burial customs and attire, a significant number of Muslims and Jews, including religious and political figures, women and students, cooperate and initiate a great many dialogues on religion, society and culture in the aim to promote familiarity, education and mutual understanding, and struggle together against the manifestations of Muslim Judeophobia and Jewish Islamophobia that "may lead to the destruction of the human race".[20]

In Britain alone at least eighteen Muslim–Jewish organizations and forums (some with Christians as well) are proactive towards this objective, such as the Muslim–Jewish Forum of Greater Manchester; Alif-Aleph; the Council of Muslim–Jewish Leaders; the Sons of Abraham. In 2008, in Britain, Muslim representatives participated in a Holocaust memorial ceremony; in 2011 Muslim religious leaders accompanied by rabbis visited the Auschwitz death camp. Prior to that, Britain's Chief Rabbi Jonathan Sacks strongly condemned a caricature of the prophet Muhammad that appeared in a Danish journal in 2005, and called to respect and honor other religions; and in 2015 the Jewish leadership in Britain collected relief funds for refugees from Syria and several synagogues offered to absorb some of these refugees.

However, despite such gestures by Jewish leaders, and dialogues, proclamations and efforts at education in tandem with Muslim leaders, Islamic Judeophobia in Western European countries has increased in the past decades. It is manifested in anti-Semitic and anti-Israel attitudes among many Muslims, and in acts of violence and terrorism perpetrated by extremist Muslims against Jewish and Israeli targets in various countries. Thus, for instance, according to surveys carried out by the research institute, PEW, 49% of Muslims in Britain expressed anti-Semitic views in 2006, and 57% in 2016. Higher figures (67%) were registered in France, and according to a survey by the AJC (American Jewish Committee), about 55% of Muslims in Western Europe are anti-Semitic. Among the stereotypes of Jews held by Muslims in Europe: Jews have too much influence on world issues and on the world economy; Jews prefer Israel, that is harming Palestinians.[21]

Yet, it should be emphasized that the major motivation of Muslim anti-Semitism in Western Europe (and even more so in the Arab and Muslim world) is Israel's (supposed or actual) aggressive policies against Palestinians in east Jerusalem, the West Bank, the Gaza Strip, and also southern Lebanon. Thus, for example, the Muslim Imam in Malmö, Sweden, who took part in ceremonies opposing anti-Semitism, stated that 99% of instances of anti-Semitism amongst Muslims are related to the Israeli–Palestinian conflict. An Imam in Berlin called to kill all Zionists to the last one; whereas an Imam in northern Italy was expelled after having preached for the eradication of Jews in Italy. A Muslim politician in Sweden claimed that "our Palestinian brethren are being slaughtered by the Jewish pigs"; and other Muslims cried out: "Hamas, Hamas – Jews to the gas". In England, anti-Semitic Muslims accused Israel of killing children (during the IDF military actions in Gaza in 2014) and of "genocide"; whilst others said (in this regard) that "Hitler was right".[22]

Against this background of anti-Semitic exclamations, and the harsh events between Israel and the Palestinians, hundreds of acts of terrorism and violence were carried out by Muslim extremists against Jews and Jewish (and non-Jewish) sites in Western European countries during the past few decades (and many Muslims were also attacked in Europe by extremist Christians). The highest number of these terrorist acts occurred in France, such as: the attack of a Jewish restaurant in 1982 and a Jewish minimarket in 2015, the murder of Ilan Halimi in 2006 – all in Paris; the murder of four Jews near a Hebrew School in Toulouse in 2012. In neighboring Belgium the Jewish Museum in Brussels was attacked in 2014. Other similar events took place in Britain, Holland, Italy, Sweden and Germany.[23]

Finally, the words of the American ambassador to Belgium, Howard Gutman (a Jew), are noteworthy, which he eluded to at a Jewish conference to combat anti-Semitism (2011): Because of Israel's policies in the Israeli–Palestinian conflict, there is hatred of Muslims towards Jews, and stated that a peace agreement between Israel and the Palestinians will significantly diminish Muslim anti-Semitism. [24]

3

A Dual Relationship in Africa
The Northern and Sub-Saharan Countries

The North African countries experienced a continuity of relations and mutual ties between Muslims and Jews, starting with the Muslim conquest in the 7th century, when Jews comprised the major non-Muslim minority in the region (with few Christians, as in other Muslim countries). Under the governance of the Arab Muslim Umayyad Khalifate, the condition of the Jews improved, after having suffered under the earlier Byzantine rule. Even the Shi'ite–Isma'ili–Fatimid Khalifate in the 10th century treated the Jews with tolerance for a certain period of time (see also Chapter 4).

For centuries, Algeria, Tunisia and Libya came under nominal Ottoman rule (recognition of the sultan as the Khalif of the Muslims), but in fact were ruled by local dynasties over long time periods; the same occurred in Morocco that had no Ottoman affinity. France conquered Algeria in 1830, Tunisia in 1881 and Morocco in 1912; Italy gained control over Libya in 1911, which later won its independence in 1951. Morocco and Tunisia won independence in 1956 and Algeria in 1962. The Jews living in these countries, who throughout the centuries had experienced both good and bad relations with the Muslims, were forced almost totally (about 550,000 people) to immigrate to Israel and other locations after the 1948 war.[1]

The Northern Saharan Countries

Morocco

Morocco boasted one of the most ancient (after the destruction of the Holy Temple) and largest Jewish communities of all the Islamic countries. As noted in Chapter 1, the Jews of Morocco suffered during the 11th–13th centuries from the extremist Muslim rule under the Berber Al-Murabitun and Almohad dynasties. During the Marinid period (13th–15th centuries) the Jews' condition improved, as did their relations with the Muslims, some even holding senior positions in the courts of the Muslim rulers. During the Sa'adi dynastic era as well (16th–17th century) their condition was relatively stable, and some dealt in regional trade and were called *tuggar* (traders) of the sultan (among them were those who also immigrated to the Holy Land).

This was followed by the Muslim Alawi dynasty, starting from the end of the 17th century and till today. As did its predecessor, it referenced to the prophet Muhammad and was ambivalent towards the Jews – tolerance, dialogue and cooperation on the one hand; harassment and periodic oppressions (including the destruction of synagogues and pogroms), on the other hand. This fluctuated with the political, cultural and economic circumstances and the degree of religious Muslim influence over the rulers and their subjects.[2] Jews that were expelled from Spain that reached Morocco contributed significantly to the country's economic and cultural life and improved relations with the Muslims.

In the 19th century some changes took place – mostly positive, but some negative as well – in the condition of the Jews of Morocco, mostly due to European intervention, such as the occupation of Algeria by the French in 1830; and the French army's victory over the Sultan's army in east Morocco in 1844. At the same time, European circles increased their demands to improve the status of Christians and Jews, which included granting European passports to some of them. A further contribution came from the political and humanitarian activity of Moshe Montefiore, a British Jewish leader, for the benefit of the Jews of Morocco in 1864. Inter alia, he convinced Sultan Muhammad IV to negate the harsh accusations against the Jews and to publish a royal edict that commands treating his Jewish subjects well. This edict states, amongst other things, that

46

"his servitors, governors, cadis and other functionaries to treat with utmost benevolence the Israelites who are under the protection of our empire".[3]

However, during the first decade of the 20th century, Jews (as well as wealthy Muslims) were attacked by Berber tribes, who exploited the disintegration of the Moroccan rule with acts of plundering and theft. During the time of the French protectorate (1856–1912), the Jews of Morocco, most of whom were not granted French citizenship (in contrast to the Jews of Algeria), were relatively safe; many adopted the French culture, and among them were those who held senior positions in various fields. They enjoyed good relations, especially with the Berber Muslim communities (some of whom converted to Judaism at different periods). This stood in contrast to the tension that developed with the Arab Muslim communities against the background of the conflict between Arabs and Jews in the Holy Land under the British mandate; and especially following the Islamic Conference in Jerusalem in 1931, centering around the issue of al-Aqsa. During that time, and for centuries prior, Muslims from Morocco and neighboring countries went on a pilgrimage to Al-Aqsa Mosque on their way to the Haj in Mecca, while some of them settled near the mosque and established the *Ma'ghrabi* (Mugrabi) neighborhood.

During the time of the Vichy government in France (1942–1943), Jews suffered from established anti-Semitism, despite the attempts of Muhammad V to protect them as befitting their status of subjects of the protectorate Muslim state. But when American soldiers occupied parts of Morocco at the end of 1942, Muslims who were incited by French officials, attacked Jews in Casablanca and in other cities. Nonetheless, after World War II, the majority of Moroccan Jews (especially in the cities) continued embracing French culture, while only a minority rallied after the Arab Moroccan National Movement; yet others followed Zionism. After the 1947 United Nations' adoption of the Partition Plan and the establishment of the State of Israel in 1948, Arabs in Morocco viewed their Jewish neighbors as Zionists, despite attempts made by the Sultan (who was coronated as king in 1951) to call for Muslim–Jewish solidarity and to distinguish between Moroccan Jews and Zionist Jews in the Holy Land.

Apparently, in response to the emigration of Jews (mostly poor Jews) from Morocco to Israel in June 1948, Muslims murdered 41

Jews and led pogroms in the cities of Oujda and Jarada; in the 1950s wealthy Jews of high standing and of French identity were also murdered by Arab nationalists. These events, along with growing Arab nationalist sentiments among the Muslims and Zionist feelings among the Jews – led to a massive immigration of Moroccan Jews to Israel: 110,000 (40% of Moroccan Jewry) made *Aliyah* (immigrated) between 1948 to 1956; an additional 100,000 made *Aliyah* in 1961 (and there was also the drowning of a ship, organized by the *Mossad*, with its 42 passengers). Wealthy Jews chose to immigrate to France or Canada, and only several thousand remained in Morocco.

Yet, and uniquely so, the Jewish community remaining in Morocco was involved in the process of creating positive ties between Morocco and Israel and the Arab–Israeli peace process, while at the time some of its members also served in senior positions in the king's court. King Hassan II appointed Jews as financial advisors – David Amar and André Azoulay, while others served in the capacity of ministers. The king even encouraged Moroccan Israelis to visit Morocco and called them "my Moroccans". He also praised the "Golden Age" in Andalusia during the Middle Ages as a model of Jewish–Muslim relations in current-day Morocco.

From the early 1960s, intelligence and security relations were embarked upon between Morocco and Israel, including Israeli military aid to Morocco in its struggle against Algeria, and Moroccan intelligence aid to Israel prior to the 1967 war. King Hassan also mediated contact between Egypt and Israel prior to President Sadat's visit to Jerusalem in 1977. He was also proactive in advancing the Arab–Israeli peace process, and after the Oslo Accords (1993) he instructed to open an office of Moroccan interests in Israel, and permitted an Israeli ministry to operate in Morocco (Yitzhak Rabin, then Prime Minister, secretly visited Morocco in 1993, as did Shimon Peres in 1986). In 1985 King Hassan II proclaimed at a Paris conference: "The crisis in the Middle East is dividing the sons of Abraham, Jews, Muslims and Christians . . . and the future can exist only through dialogue. We have wasted too much time."[4]

However, as chairman of the Jerusalem Conference allying 57 Muslim countries, the King worked to protect the Muslim character of east Jerusalem, and especially of the holy sites of Islam, while emphasizing the religious aspects – and not the political – of this issue. His son, Muhammad VI, continued his father's pro-Israel policy, yet was hesitant regarding Israel and instructed the closing of the offices of interests in both countries, after the al-Aqsa Intifada broke out (2000).

Nonetheless, Morocco numbers among the 22 countries of the Arab League that confirmed the Saudi Arabian peace initiative of 2002, which recognized the borders of 1967 and is prepared to normalize relations with Israel, on condition that the latter agrees to the establishment of a Palestinian state alongside it, with east Jerusalem its capital. But the United States' proclamation of Jerusalem as Israel's capital and moving the American embassy from Tel Aviv to Jerusalem in May 2018, triggered angry mass demonstrations against Israel, especially in Casablanca. King Muhammad VI firmly objected to this move as well.

Tunisia

According to Jewish tradition, Jews had resided in the region of Tunisia even prior to the destruction of the first Holy Temple in Jerusalem, in 586 BC; and after the destruction of the Second Temple in 70 CE, many other Jews were exiled to these regions, where they engaged in agriculture and trade. In the 7th century they were joined by Jewish Spanish refugees who had escaped from persecution by the Visigoths, and had been involved in the struggles between the Muslim rulers in the region, but were persecuted by the victorious ruler, Imam Idris. In the 9th century, under different rule, their political and economic status was good, especially in the cities of Kairouan and Bizerta (where a Jewish governor ruled). However, in the 11th–13th centuries, like their brethren in Morocco and Libya, the Jews suffered greatly under the fanatic dynasties of the Al-Murabitun and Almohad, which included forced conversion to Islam and exile. After a short period of significant improvement in their lives, the Jews once more suffered during the 14th and 15th centuries, mainly from the taxes imposed.[5] However, under Ottoman rule that began in 1574 they enjoyed relative security and the freedom of religion and freedom of worship and the autonomous management of their community; this, despite a series of limitations on dress, as well as on extortion and harassment. During that time, wealthy Jews from Italy, descendants of the Jews expelled from Spain, reached Tunisia and dealt in trade.

49

At the start of the 18th century, the condition of the Jews in Tunisia improved following the increasing influence of European countries. In 1772, Mordechai Manuel Noah, the American consul in Tunisia, wrote: "With all the apparent oppression, the Jews are leading men . . . the principal mechanics . . . they are the head of the Customs House, they farm the revenues and the exportation of various articles and the monopoly of various merchandise . . . they keep the Bey's jewels and valuable articles and are his treasurers, secretaries and interpreters . . . matters of art, science and medicine are confined to the Jews . . . Every minister has two or three Jewish agents . . . possess a very controlling influence."

In 1855 the Jews' status of Dhimmi was nullified in Tunisia as part of the Ottoman reforms, and Jews were formally granted equality with the Muslims. A new constitution was instituted, under French influence (1857), which stated, inter alia: "No manner of duress will be imposed upon our Jewish subjects to forcing them to change their faith, and they willl not be hindered in the free observance of their religious rites. Their synagogues will be respected and protected from insult."[6]

In 1864 this constitution was annulled, but the government was cautious as to its treatment of the Jews for fear of European intervention. Nonetheless, the Jews were harmed by the constitution's annulment, yet others flourished in their trade with Europe. The Muslim elite was divided between the supporters and opponents of integrating Jews into the country's institutions. The French occupation and governance (1881–1946) brought great relief to the Jews of Tunisia (35,000 in number in 1881), and encouraged their assimilation into French culture and law, and their aspiration for emancipation under French supervision. Jews lived in peace and cooperation with Muslims, and were well-integrated into the economic, administrative and political spheres, especially the Jewish elite; their religious and cultural life improved as well.

During World War I, 500 Jews volunteered to serve in the French army. However, most Jews suffered from waves of anti-Semitism at the hands of the Muslims who had suffered from food shortages and the high price of basic food products. In an attempt to placate this embittered population and to channel its anger towards the Jews, the French government did not prevent the Muslims' attacks on Jews and on the synagogues. Yet, after the war, Muslim and Jewish intellectuals were active in the "Jewish–Muslim Unity" framework to improve the relationship between their two populations, or as stated by the Joint Committee: " To expose the desire of the Jews and Muslims and to find solutions acceptable to both sides, in order to work together towards building a new Tunisia of brotherhood under the French protectorate."[7]

Jews took part in the establishment and manning of senior positions in the national "Neo Destour" party (established in 1920); cooperation and dialogue between Jews and Muslims could even be found in writing Arabic poetry; and in 1935 both Jews and Muslims participated in rallies and celebrations commemorating 800 years of Maimonides' death. However, at that time too tension and violence developed again between Muslims and Jews vis-à-vis the Zionist-Arab conflict in the Holy Land/Palestine; and prior to that – because of the harsh economic crisis in 1932 as well.

During World War II, under the Vichy government and following that, under direct Nazi rule, the Jews of Tunisia suffered greatly from waves of anti-Semitism, oppression and imprisonment; 5,000 of them (out of 100,000) were sent to forced labor camps. (Some were saved by a Muslim named Khalid Abd al-Wahabi, who was later honored with the title of "Righteous Among the Nations" by the Yad Vashem Holocaust Center.)

During the 1950s most of the Jews of Tunisia supported the leader of the Tunisian Movement for Independence, Habib Bourguiba, who became the first president of an independent Tunisia in 1956. He appointed many Jews to senior positions and guaranteed the religious and civil rights of the Jews in his country. Later, however, Jews were discriminated against; the Jewish Community Council was annulled in 1958, and many Jews were arrested. This arose from the national institutions' policy that granted preference to Muslims to fulfill public service positions, as well as from the economic crisis.

Subsequently, 70,000 Jews left Tunisia, half of whom immigrated to Israel; 20,000 other Jews emigrated during the Israeli–Arab war of June 1967, during which Jews in Tunisia were attacked by Muslims in violent riots. Here it must be mentioned that Tunisian President Bourguiba was the first Arab leader to publicly propose in 1965 the establishment of a federation between the Arab countries and Israel, based on the borders as defined in the United Nations' Partition Plan of 1947. In 1987, following the military coup in Tunisia, the new military ruler, General Zayn al-'Ābidīn bin 'Alī, demonstrated kindness towards the remaining Jews in Tunisia, and despite some outbursts of anti-Semitism, Jews opened educational-religious-community networks. Tunisia also took part in the negotiations between Israel and the PLO on the Oslo Accords (1993, 1995). After the signing of the Oslo Accords, Israel and Tunisia opened offices of interest in each other's country, but with the outbreak of the al-Aqsa Intifada (2000), Tunisia closed its offices in Tel Aviv.

During the events of the "Arab Spring" that began in Tunisia in 2010, anti-Jewish voices were sounded by extremist Salafi Muslim demonstrators. However, Rāshid al-Ghannūshī, leader of the *Na'dah* party (Revival – under the auspices of the "Muslim Brotherhood") promised to protect the Jews from anti-Semitic attacks, after becoming prime minister. The new Tunisian President, Muncef Marzouki, even paid a royal visit to the synagogue in Djerba during the Passover holiday in April 2012, and promised to protect the Jewish citizens; this gesture was done to commemorate the terrorist attack on the synagogue in 2002. The leader of the Islamic *Tahrir* (Liberation) party, Ridha Balhaji, also said in 2012: "No one has a problem with Jews who live here for centuries . . . They are our neighbors, when they (the extremist Muslims) preach against Jews, they mean Israel – and not individual Jews in Tunisia." The reference is to "the Zionists", added a Muslim Salafi activist.

Nonetheless, in October 2013, Ms. Yamina Thabet, chair of the Society for the Support of Minorities, claimed that "the Tunisian Jews feel endangered. They are really afraid . . . a number of attacks against the Jewish community and harassment by the Tunisian security forces . . . (She) blamed the government, opposition and parties for the attack on Jews". In May 2018, a great number of Tunisians demonstrated against the transfer of the American Embassy to Jerusalem, and their president as well harshly opposed this move.[8]

Algeria

Like other communities in North Africa, Jews settled in Algeria after the destruction of the two Holy Temples, intermixed with the earlier Berber settlers (part of whom converted to Judaism), and struggled together against the Arab Muslim occupation in the 7th century, which was led by the Berber queen, Kahina. Following the Muslim occupation, when most of the Berbers converted to Islam, the majority of the Jews "Arabized" – blended in with the Arab culture and language.[9]

Following the Spanish Inquisition and the expulsion of the Jews (and Muslims), Jews settled in the area and empowered the existing communities demographically, economically and culturally – including use of the Ladino language as well. Later on, Italian Jews reached Algeria and they too contributed economically, especially through trade with Europe. As in other Muslim countries, the Jews of Algeria (who in 1871 numbered 30,000), were treated ambivalently by the rulers and the population: On the one hand, ethnic-religious, jurisdictional and cultural autonomy; on the other hand – payment of the *Jizya* poll tax, Islamization in the dress code and in the public domain, humiliations and at times violent riots.[10]

The Jews of Algeria suffered during the period of the extremist Muslim rule of the Al-Murabitun and Almohad Khalifates (11th–13th centuries), though the wealthy families (most Jews were poor) continued their trade relations with European countries. In the century that followed, the condition of the Jewish communities improved, despite the tension and the contrast between the expelled Jews from Spain who had reached the region, and the longstanding communities. Jews were appointed by the Muslim rulers to positions of advisors, financiers, doctors and diplomats. Jewish leaders were also appointed to the role of "Shaykh-al-Yahud" and possessed judicial authority, though many Jews had to turn to Muslim courts. Muslim–Jewish relations were generally good, and Jews who were persecuted at times found shelter in the mosques and protection from Muslim rioters by Muslim religious leaders.

It is noteworthy that the ruler (Dey) of Algeria got into an argument with the French consul over an old, very large monetary debt that the French government avoided paying to two families of Jewish traders who had supplied the French army with grains when it invaded Egypt (1798). The Dey slapped the consul's face with a fan in 1827, an act that served as one of the catalysts leading to the French occupation of Algeria in 1830.

The legal and judicial standing of the Algerian Jews was damaged and limited under the new French sovereignty; yet the Jews were granted French citizenship in 1870 in accordance with a decree introduced by Cremieux, a French-Jewish leader. They assimilated willfully and gradually into French culture and integrated into the local government. Jews from Tunisia and Morocco immigrated to Algeria to attain French citizenship; others maintained the Jewish tradition, established a Jewish educational network and set up Hebrew printing houses. On the other hand, these developments created political, social and economic tensions vis-à-vis the Muslims (who numbered 2.5 million), who refused to accept French citizenship.

The main opposition to the naturalization and integration of the Jews of French Algeria came actually from anti-Semitic French senior officials and settlers (also influenced by the Dreyfus Affair in France in 1894), who blamed the Jews for the failure of French policies and of accumulating money; they also opposed the Jews' participation in the elections. Among their arguments, they promoted points of significance such as: "The Jews are native Algerians, they are not French, but rather Arabs of the religion of Moses – their mother tongue is Arabic . . . their customs are Eastern and their manner of dress is Eastern . . . their singular profession is trade and their only passion is to accumulate money . . . Jews and Muslims are from the same origin; though they maintain different religions, they belong to one family . . . therefore any violation of the balance between them, by advancing the Jews to a higher status, will once again revive the Arabs' hostility towards them."[11]

In addition to the verbal attacks against Jews, the last few decades of the 19th century witnessed a line of violent events, including severe riots against Jews in different cities, in some of which Muslim soldiers in the French army took part, along with Arab Muslim citizens. This stemmed from incitement and financing by French anti-Semites, as well as fury at the Arabs' losing land to Jews who had loaned them money at high interest. But most Arabs were not anti-Semitic, and some even protected the Jews, as testified by Jewish leaders at the time: "In the Muslim quarter of Uran, not a single Jew was attacked; on the contrary, many Jews came there seeking shelter . . . there resided the greater part of the region's Arab population, no severe incidents were reported, as there is no anti-Semitism there. The Arabs fell upon the Jews only when they were recruited to do so." Yet, many Muslims had their doubts about the Jews, who "abandoned their long history in a Muslim land".[12]

Indeed, most Algerian Jews continued throughout the 20th century to identify themselves more as French than as Jews, and even highly disapproved of Zionism, which they viewed as "treason and shameful ingratitude" towards Algeria's society-at-large. The Jewish leadership in Algeria – wealthy and influential – strongly opposed Zionist activity in their country, which in any case was rather weak. On the other hand, local Muslim organizations demonstrated antagonism towards Zionist delegates and to Zionism in Palestine, and after the 1929 Arab riots in Hebron and Jerusalem, and the Arab revolt from 1936 to 1939, they called for a ban on "Zionist merchandise".

Muslim–Jewish tension was further fed by economic factors: the rural Muslim population's impoverishment, partly stemming from the Jews' loans at high interest; and the influence of rising Nazism in Germany in 1933. In August 1934, due to the provocation of a Jewish soldier in Constantine, Muslims led a pogrom against Jews, murdering 23, with many more injured; and vandalizing many private homes and shops. European residents weren't harmed at all in this pogrom.[13]

The Jews claimed that the pogrom was planned, and not at all spontaneous, and stemmed from several factors: the Muslims' envy of the Jews who were granted French citizenship; the impact of the rise of Nazism to govern in Germany; renewed anti-Semitic propaganda in Algeria and the denunciation of the Zionist idea in Arab propaganda and publications. To this, one must add the contention of nationalist secular Muslims – the Muslims' anger against the arrogance of the rich (and young) Jews, who had also attained political influence. Moreover, anti-Semitic French Christians residing in Algeria again incited the Muslims against the Jews, because of new regulations passed by the French prime minister, Leon Blum – a Jew – in 1936, which granted French citizenship to Muslims unconditionally.

Many Muslims, including the secular branch of the National Algerian Muslim movement, internalized and adopted this propaganda and incitement, leading to further attacks by Muslims against the Jews. Muslim leaders even presented the Jews as the enemies of Islam, basing their claim on the words of the prophet Muhammad; they also called for revenge against the Jews because of the Arabs of Palestine "who are collapsing under the Zionist yoke and struggling against British imperialism and its Zionist partner." Even the Nazi propaganda vehicles, and the Fascists (in Italy) incited the Muslims of Algeria against the Jews, with similar claims.[14]

On the other hand, moderate Muslim leaders condemned the anti-Semitic propaganda which, according to them, was meant to create riots between Muslims and Jews, in order to deflect the Muslims' hatred of France towards the Jews. Jewish leaders tried to cooperate with these Muslim circles, however following the Nazi occupation of France in World War II and the formation of the Vichy government, Muslim anti-Semitism in Algeria increased. Their representatives demanded that the Crémieux Decree that granted citizenship to the Jews, be rescinded and that harsh anti-Jewish regulations be introduced. This new development encouraged Muslim rioters to attack shops owned by Jews, in September 1940, in the city Algiers.

In the national struggle for Algerian independence following World War II (1954), only few Jews leaned towards the National Liberation Front (FLN), which promised them equal citizenship. Most Jews and the community institutions sided with the French settlers and a few even joined the secret military organization (OAS) that fought for a French Algeria. The Jews found themselves in an impossible dilemma and suffered from both sides. After the proclamation of an independent Algeria (1962), Jews were persecuted mainly by Muslims and the new Algerian government, and were accused of contact with Zionism and identifying with Israel. At this time, most of the Jewish population left Algeria; the majority immigrated to France and some to Israel (as early as 1948).

After the 1967 War against Israel (also called the Six-Day War), nearly all the synagogues in Algeria were confiscated and were transformed into mosques. Of the 120,000 Jews in Algeria in the 1940s, only 1000 remained in 1969, and about 50 in the 1990s. The Algerian governments since then have taken an anti-Israel and pro-Palestinian stand for many years. In May 2018 the Algerian rulers protested against the transfer of the American Embassy from Tel Aviv to Jerusalem and supported the Palestinians' demand for a country of their own, with al-Quds (east Jerusalem) its capital.[15]

Libya

As with Morocco, Tunisia and Algeria, Jews reached Libya after the destruction of the Holy Temple in Jerusalem, and their numbers grew later with the conversion to Judaism of Berber tribes, yet they remained the smallest Jewish community in Northern Africa

56

(around 20,000 in 1902). They resided mainly in the regions of Tripolitania and Cyrenaica. After the Arab Muslim occupation (642), the head of the Berber tribe, Kahina, who converted to Judaism, led a fight unsuccessfully against the Arab conquerors (693–688).

The ongoing Arab Muslim occupation led to prosperity among the Jewish communities in the 10th–11th centuries. However, as in other regions of North Africa, the Jews suffered under the rule of the Almohad Khalifate in the 12th and 13th centuries. In 1510 the Spaniards conquered Libya and ruled there for forty years, imposing the laws of the Inquisition against the Jews, via imprisonment, torture and being sold into slavery. Some of the Jews found shelter in the mountains. The Ottoman occupation of Libya (1551) enabled the Libyan Jews to make contact with their Jewish brethren in other regions of the empire and with their help to successfully develop social, financial, religious and educational systems – including the establishment of synagogues and study centers. Jews were also prominent in commerce in both the local and international arena, and in various crafts, and even held positions in the local Ottoman financial world.

But local wars at the end of the 18th and beginning of the 19th centuries brought great suffering upon the Jews (and Muslims) However, for the remainder of the 19th century, relationships of peaceful coexistence developed between Muslims and Jews, concurrent with the Ottoman rule of reforms that supported the Jewish community financially, allowed the appointment of a Chief Rabbi (Hakham Bashi), as well as widespread communal and religious activities. Nonetheless, at the end of the 19th century and the early 20th century, Muslim–Jewish relations worsened, accompanied by Muslim violence, due to economic competition, especially in trade. Consequently, many Jews welcomed the Italian occupation of Libya (from 1911 to 1943), hoping for a modern and reforming government. The good relations between Jews and Muslims indeed returned to their former level for a short time period.[16]

At this time, pan-Arab and pan-Muslim orientations and opposition to Italian rule flowered among the Muslims in Libya. The Jewish community was marked by a dichotomy with different leanings: On the one hand, assimilation into the Italian culture, with the encouragement of the new regime; and on the other hand, an inclination towards the Zionist movement, especially among the young people. As early as 1912, the first (but unsuccessful) Zionist organization was established in Tripoli, called *Ora Ve-Simcha* [Light and Joy], and later *Hevrat Zion* [Society of Zion]; emphasis was placed on learning Hebrew to renew Jewish identification and immigrating to the Holy Land. But despite the Zionist activities and the rather expansive study of the Hebrew language, only 500 Jews immigrated to the Holy Land up to 1943.[17]

At the same time, Muslim–Jewish tension grew against the background of the Arab–Jewish conflict in the Holy Land; and from the 1930s, various decrees were directed against the Jews by the Italian fascist regime that tended to support the positions taken by Muslims and Arabs against the Jews. During World War II, German military forces vandalized shops owned by Jews in Benghazi, and exiled 2000 Jews from Cyrenaica to the desert; some were sent to forced labor camps. Hundreds died, but many were saved by the British army that occupied the region at the start of 1943. Jewish soldiers serving in the British army helped promote Zionism amongst the Jews of Libya.

After the war, the previous well-established inclination towards coexistence and cooperation between Jews and Muslims, especially in Tripolitania, was renewed; most of the Jews residing there spoke Arabic and dressed as their Muslim neighbors did (except for a group of European Jews who lived in Tripoli). "Jews and Arabs also cooperated in institutions such as the courts and the police force, where Jews were allowed to serve for the first time. Following the war, some Jews expressed solidarity with Arab political groups and supported emancipation, self-rule, freedom and democracy." Others were concerned that Zionist activity would harm the normal relations with the Muslims.

Muslims expressed support of the Jews following the pogrom in Tripoli in 1945 (see below) and the city's Mufti even published a *fatwa* (a religious opinion) that called for friendship and cooperation between Jews and Arabs as was in the past. However, other Arabs condemned the Zionist activities in Libya and called for the dismissal of Jews from the police force.[18]

A short while after Libya's liberation from the yoke of Italy and Germany, the Jews suffered a terrible pogrom on November 4, 1945, at the hands of the Muslims, who were affected by news of Arab–Jewish conflicts in Palestine, and the desecration of the Dome of the Rock in Jerusalem, allegedly by Jews. Some 132 Jews were murdered in the pogrom and hundreds more were injured, synagogues and private homes were vandalized and destroyed; all this occurred while the British army was stationed in the area. However, other Muslims rescued Jews, and their leaders tried to halt the riots. But in June 1948, after the establishment of the State of Israel, Jews were again attacked by Muslims. From 1949, many Jews began immigrating to Israel, reaching 31,000 in number. Independent Libya (from 1951) took a stand that was anti-Jewish and anti-Israel; and during the June 1967 war Jews were again attacked and murdered, in response to a call for jihad against them from the mosques. The great synagogue in Tripoli was set on fire and Jewish homes and shops were vandalized by Muslim rioters; demonstrations were held and pro-Palestinian voices were sounded. Most of the Jews who remained were permitted by King Idris I to emigrate – most left for Israel and a significant number immigrated to Italy (and some were given protection by the ruling powers). The Libyan dictator, Mu'amar Qadhafi (from 1969), who was radically anti-Israel, proposed in 1993 to pay compensation to the Jews who had been forced to leave Libya, and also encouraged 200 Muslim pilgrims to visit the Al-Aqsa Mosque.[19]

After the Arab Spring revolution in Libya in 2011, some of the revolutionary leaders expressed their support for establishing close ties between Muslims and Jews. For example, Prime Minister Ali Zaidan announced at the Davos Conference in January 2013 that a solution of the Palestinian problem will bring peace with Israel and the integration of the Jews in Libya. In parallel, Israeli Jews from Libyan origin visited their country of birth at the invitation of government personages. The ongoing civil war in Libya that has continued for over eight years does not bode well for the Jews who have remained there. In May 2018, the Great Mufti of Libya, together with political leaders and many civilians, protested against the transfer of the American Embassy to Jerusalem.

Muslim African Countries South of the Sahara

In this chapter the relationships between Muslims and Jews were reviewed and examined, as well as the attitudes held towards Israel by the Muslim-Arab North African countries. In these countries significant, ancient Jewish communities resided that, since the Arab

Muslim occupation, experienced the sovereign rule of different Muslim dynasties and governments, including non-Arab and European rulers that held both positive and negative positions towards the Jews in different eras. The Jews who, for centuries, comprised practically the only non-Muslim population in the region (except for Christian French settlers in Algeria from the 19th century and on), were prominently involved in the Muslim economy and society, and developed their own religious and cultural life, as did their brethren in the Middle East.

In the 20th century, they became unwillingly involved in the Arab–Jewish conflict in the Holy Land/Palestine. They suffered harassments and riots at the hands of the Arab Muslim neighbors, and were forced to emigrate – the majority left for Israel – as the Arab Muslim regimes in their countries (with the exception of Morocco at different periods) hold hostile positions towards Israel, the Jewish State.

In contrast to these countries in North Africa, amongst the dozens of countries south of the Sahara, only five are Muslim Arab countries: (Northern) Sudan, Mauritania, Somalia, Djibouti and the Comoro Islands. They did not have authentic Jewish communities, except for Sudan – where a small Jewish community lived from the 19th century and up to 1970. The Muslim countries or those with a non-Arab Muslim majority in this sub-continent are: Senegal, Mali, Gambia, Guinea, Niger, Chad and Nigeria. In Nigeria, which boasts a large Muslim population, there are the Igbo (or Ibo) people (numbering close to 40,000) that claim they are Jews (descendants of the Ten Tribes). Such claims are also heard from other small groups in Mali, Ghana, Rwanda, Zimbabwe, Uganda and Kenya.

However, according to various studies, except for the Zakhor group in Mali (that was more ancient and converted to Islam in the past), most of these were communities that had formerly been converted to Christianity by missionaries, such as the Falasha (Beta Israel) in Ethiopia. These communities converted to Judaism and aspire to immigrate to Israel. In Kenya there have been for a long time more authentic Jewish and Israeli groups.[20]

Muslim attitudes towards the various Jewish communities south of the Sahara were ambivalent, similar to other regions in Africa and Asia. Thus, for example, Jews in Mali were persecuted by the fanatical Muslim ruler at the start of the 16th century; and at the end of the 19th century, Jews in Sudan (not many) were forcefully converted to Islam by an extremist Muslim ruler who called himself *Mahdi* (a messiah of sorts). However, during long periods of time, Jews prospered in these and other places, dealing in trade and other financial branches of activity.

The attitude of Muslim countries and rulers towards Israel – the Jewish State – since its establishment, and for many years after, was restrained, tolerant and even sympathetic. This stemmed from the moderate-pluralistic character of African Islam that was influenced by earlier traditional religions and by the secular life of its leaders and elite groups. Many of them made the distinction between African Islam and Arab Islam and opposed expanding the Arab–Israeli conflict into a Muslim–Jewish dispute. They even diverged from, or repelled, for many years the efforts of Arab countries such as Egypt, Saudi Arabia and Libya to break off relations with Israel and prevent its activity in their countries. Egyptian president Gamal Abdel Nasser was very proactive in this orientation based on his doctrine of the three circles – Arab, Muslim and African.

Saudi Arabia established mosques and other centers of religion and culture in an attempt to disseminate its favored principles and its anti-Israel and anti-Semitic sentiments. These sentiments were later spread throughout Muslim countries in Africa by Libyan ruler Muammar Gaddafi (from 1969) and the leaders of revolutionary Iran (from 1979) – distributing monetary bonuses while doing so.

In contrast, from the late 1950s, Israel began to be active in African countries south of the Sahara, as per Ben-Gurion's "Doctrine of Periphery" that states: "We must break the blockade that hostile Arab countries impose us, and build bridges to the liberated nations of black Africa."[21] Indeed in the mid-1960s there were already 30 Israeli diplomatic posts operating in African countries, including Muslim countries or countries with a Muslim majority, such as: Senegal, Mali, Guinea, Gambia, Niger and Nigeria. At the same time, many Israeli experts were working in these and other countries in the fields of agriculture, water, youth education; and later also in the fields of energy and health. Alongside that, meetings were held between Jewish Israeli leaders and Muslim African leaders, including religious leaders who had visited Israel and had prayed at the Al-Aqsa Mosque.

61

Yet, the occupation of the Al-Aqsa Mosque and additional Palestinian and Arab territories in June 1967 brought about a decline between Muslim (and other) African countries and Israel, and led to a manifestation of anti-Semitism. Thus, for example, Idi Amin, the Uganda leader (1971–1974) who was born to a Muslim father (an ex-Christian), turned anti-Israel and anti-Jews; he banned the Jewish community and instructed to destroy all the synagogues in his country. At the same time, and under the influence of Saudi Arabia, Egypt and Libya, most African countries, Muslim ones as well, broke off diplomatic relations with Israel; and in the war of October 1973 even increased the animosity of African Muslims towards Israel.

However, a significant improvement developed in the relations between Muslim African leaders and Israel after the latter had signed political agreements with Egypt in 1978–79 and with the Palestinians in 1993 and 1995; this, at the time that Arab Muslims became a significant factor in the ties between Israel and the Muslim African countries. Thus, as of the mid-1990s the diplomatic relations of Israel were gradually restored with most African countries, when in 1995 Mauritania, a Muslim Arab country, recognized Israel for the first time and established diplomatic relations. However, these relations were broken off when Israel attacked the Gaza Strip at the end of 2008. For that reason, additional Muslim countries also broke off diplomatic relations with Israel once again.

At the same time, extremist Muslim factions, including al-Qaida activists, began a line of incitements and attacks on Jews and Israelis in Kenya and Uganda (that renewed its diplomatic relations with Israel in 1995). In Kenya, for instance, a senior religious figure called for jihad against "the Jews and the heretics"; and in 2002 Muslim extremists attacked a hotel in Mombasa, where Israelis were lodging; and there was also an attempt to attack an El Al plane at the city's airport.

On the other hand, political and religious leaders in these and additional countries (and other Muslims as well) condemned these violent actions and took harsh steps against the extremist Muslim activists. Since then and till today, some of the Muslim African countries have leaned towards cooperation with Israel in a variety of fields, whereas other countries have severely criticized Israel, and even severed its diplomatic relationships due to Israel's policies towards the Palestinians.

A line of Israeli leaders and officials have visited in African countries in the past few years, including some Muslim countries, and took steps towards improved bilateral relationships. Foreign Minister Avigdor Lieberman visited in Nigeria and Ghana in 2010 with the aim of linking up to the economic organization of West African countries; and perhaps that step led to Israeli agricultural activity in Senegal, Mali, Niger and Guinea. In June 2016, Prime-Minister Netanyahu appeared and spoke for the first time at a conference of the economic organization of East African countries, in the hope of developing economic ties with Israel and enlisting pro-Israel support in response to anti-Israel activities in the United Nations' institutions.

The Egyptian regime led by General Sisi did not undermine, as in the past, these Israeli efforts, whereas Saudi Arabia, which lately has advanced its strategic relations with Israel (vis-à-vis Iran), influenced Somalia and Sudan – Muslim Arab countries in Africa – to draw closer to Israel.[22] In August 2017 a senior minister in the government of Sudan, Mubarak al Fadil al-Mahdi, leader of the Nationalist Party, expressed a most irregular position towards Israel and suggested to maintain normal relationships with Israel. This came after many years of Sudanese alliance with Iran, Hizbullah, Hamas and the Islamic Jihad against Israel. In the last years in fact Sudan has cooled its relationship with these allies and has drawn closer to Israel with the aim of obtaining American economic aid. Amongst other things, al-Mahdi noted that many Arab countries, even the Palestinians, are maintaining ties with Israel, yet also accused them of making many mistakes regarding the Palestinian–Israeli problem. In contrast, the President of Togo decided in September 2017 to cancel an Israel–Africa Summit (scheduled to be held in October), due to pressure from Palestinians and Arabs. In May 2018 the African Union condemned the transfer of the American Embassy to Jerusalem and once more supported the establishment of a Palestinian state with East Jerusalem as its capital.[23]

In conclusion, African Muslim leaders (including the king of Morocco, Muhammad VI) avoided maintaining diplomatic relations with Israel and voted against Israel in the UN institutions because of its policies regarding the Palestinians, Jerusalem and the Temple Mount/ al-Ḥaram al-Šharīf. It may be assumed that, like the Muslim countries in the Middle East and Asia, Muslim countries in Africa will improve their relations with Israel if it takes steps towards resolving these issues in a manner acceptable to both Muslims and Jews.

CHAPTER

4

The Shi'ite Positions of Iran, Hizbullah and Yemen

It may be generally said to some extent that in comparison with the Sunni Muslims, the attitude of the Shi'ite Muslims towards the Jews and Israel was for the most part negative and more hostile. Its basis is mainly a strict interpretation of Qur'an verses and traditional Islamic writings, that identify Jews as hypocritical, worse than Christians, inferior, downcast, cursed and impure (*Najes*, according to the Qur'an, Sura 9, verse 28), monkeys and pigs; hence a Muslim who kills a Jew is not punishable.

Alongside these harsh stereotypes, there are also a few (ancient) Shi'ite writings that reflect positive attitudes towards Jews who survived the edicts of Pharaoh and Haman, like the suffering of the Shi'ites at the hands of Sunni rulers. Shi'ite leaders at times called their kingdom the "New Israel", and Jews from time to time were treated well by Shi'ite Imams.[1]

Like the Sunni, the Shi'ite hostility towards Jews is not racist and deep-rooted as it is in Christianity, but rather is targeted against the Jewish religion (Judeophobia) and is influenced, be it harshly or lightly, by political, economic and social circumstances. It also depends upon the positions taken by rulers and religious leaders, who had supreme religious authority, as well as western European attitudes, Jewish-Zionist activities, and the balance of power and reciprocal relations between these elements.

In accordance with all the above factors, there were long periods of persecution and forced conversion of the Jews to Islam, by the Shi'ites in Iran, Yemen, and less so in Iraq. This, in contrast to the tolerable or reasonable periods for Jews in these countries; many years of moderate Shi'ite attitudes towards Jews and Israel, such as that of the secular Shi'ites in monarchist Iran, in Azerbaijan and in Lebanon. In the past several decades (since the revolution in Iran in 1979), the extreme and aggressive Shi'ite attitude towards Israel and Zionist Jews held by the Iranian regime and Hizbullah have become more prominent; mainly due to Israel's continued occupation of Palestinian territories and especially east Jerusalem and al-Haram al-Sharif. Every year Iran observes *Yawm al-Quds* (Jerusalem Day} with a major ceremony; and it has established a military corps carrying this name which calls for jihad, to liberate these sites.

For many years now Tehran has been active in establishing the "Shi'ite Crescent" to include Iraq, Syria and Lebanon in order to threaten Israel, with thousands of long-range missiles and rockets. A possible major motive for such a missile attack could stem from severe harm to the mosques on the Temple Mount that would be perpetrated by fanatical Jews, which, according to former heads of the General Security Services and the Mossad, could lead to a Muslim–Jewish Armageddon.

However, it should not be inferred that the Shi'ite Muslims alone are the enemy of Jews and Israel in an extreme and violent manner. There are also many Sunni Muslims who are no less hostile and violent, such as Hamas, the Islamic Jihad, Al-Qaida and ISIS. However, the ability of Iran and Hizbullah to cause damage to Israel and the Jews is very great. Additionally, there is also the deep-rooted religious-ideological motif that may produce a severe reaction to any harm to the holy places of Islam in Jerusalem. On the other hand, an agreed-upon solution to these issues and to the Palestinian problem may perhaps bring about moderation in the attitudes maintained by Iran and Hizbullah.

Attitudes of Shi'ite Dynasties towards Jews in the Region's History

At different historical periods, the attitudes of Shi'ite regimes towards Jews were, like the Sunni regimes, dualistic: On the one hand, tolerance, cooperation and dialogue; on the other hand, oppression, exploitation and harassment – which most of the time lasted longer and was of a more severe nature than those perpetrated by most Sunni regimes. Thus, for example, following a period of

Sunni oppression of the Shi'ites, Shi'ite dynasties gained control over some parts of the region in the 10th century and beyond, during which the fanatical Shi'ite–Persian–Buwayhid dynasty (945–1055) oppressed Jews, Christians and Sunnis in both Persia and Iraq. On the other hand, the Fatimid–Isma'ili–Shi'ite dynasty (969–1171) in North Africa (where it first emerged in 908), Egypt, the Holy Land, Syria, parts of Iraq and the Arabian Peninsula – was described by Prof. Goitein as the "liberal rulers of the Middle Ages". In most cases, they treated the Jews kindly, and appointed some of them to senior posts in their courts and governments in Egypt (the dynasty's center); whilst other Jews held important positions in various financial fields and were involved in widespread religious-cultural activities as well.

However, the Fatimid Khalif, al-Ḥākim bi-Amr Allāh (996–1021, also founder of the Druze sect), who at the start of his rule was called "Savior of the Jews from the fanatical Shi'ites", 'lost his mind' towards the end of his reign, and persecuted the Jews most cruelly, destroying their synagogues and homes, and forcing Jews to convert to Islam or emigrate.[2]

The longest periods of Shi'ite reign in Persia, and at times in parts of Iraq, were of the Safavid (1501–1736) and Qajar (1779–1924) dynasties. They were characterized by extreme hostility towards the Jews who were defined as *Najes* (defiled/impure); Jews were also excluded by many Shi'ite inhabitants; were forced to wear special garments; were expelled from many different places; were forbidden to leave their homes at times of rain (lest their impurity spread); and at times were forcibly converted to Islam. The most striking incident of forced Islamization upon Jews was in the city of Mashhad in 1839, after mass riots had occurred. Other cases of murder and the forced Islamization of Jews by Shi'ites occurred also in 1656 (in Isfahan), 1773 (in Basra), 1830 (in Tabriz) and 1820 (in Shiraz). In 1889 Shi'ite *ulama* issued a *fatwa* in Isfahan calling for jihad against the Jews in Persia, instructing to spill their blood and destroy their houses. However, the city's governor protected the Jews with his military forces and claimed that "the Jews are the strongest and most affluent people in Europe" and that killing them will lead to Russian and British invasion.[3]

On the other hand, there were also better periods in Safavid Persia between Shi'ites and Jews, especially under the rule of the Shah Abbas (1588–1629), and after the Safavid reign had ended.

During the short period under the rule of the Sunni leader Nadir Shah (1736–1747) Jews served in senior positions in his court and dealt in international trade. This ruler also asked to have the Bible translated into Persian and at the ceremony marking the completion of the translation work, he said: "I shall build Jerusalem anew and gather together the people of Israel." (The cities of Shiraz and Kashan were also called "Little Jerusalem" thanks to the religious and Bible-related activities of the Jews in those cities.)

However, during the rule of the Shi'ite Qajar dynasty, the oppression and humiliation of the Jews was reintroduced, and included forced conversion to Islam from time to time; although one of the rulers, Nasir al-Din Shah, took steps to protect the Jews from the incitements and aggression of Shi'ite religious leaders and mobs. Leaders of the Jewish community in Tehran referred to him as "a just king who loves the Jews as his very own". This manifestation of sovereign rulers protecting the Jews and standing up to fanatical mobs and Shi'ite *ulama* was characteristic of other periods as well, although the kings of Iran did not possess the religious authority that the Shi'ite *ulama* had.[4]

Thus, for instance, during the Shi'ite Pahlavi dynasty (1925–1979) the secular Persian rulers placed heavy pressure upon the Shi'ite religious clerics who incited against Jews and Israel, and forbade them to convert Jews to Islam and to call them *Najes* (impure). Indeed, during this time, the Jews in Iran enjoyed equal rights with the Muslims, great economic and cultural growth, positions in government, parliament delegates, Hebrew education in the schools, their own newspapers (such as *"Shalom"*), and extensive Zionist activity (mainly among the young generation).

Yet, the great secular reformer, Reza Shah (1925–1941), who had benefited the Jewish community, distrusted Zionism and forbade its activities (also due to its ties with Europe); he instructed to close the Jewish schools and to execute the Jewish leader, Shmuel Haim (1931) on the charge of conspiracy to replace the monarchic regime with a republic. The Reza Shah also drew closer to Nazi Germany due to his suspicion of British and Russian intentions, and because of the shared Aryan origin of both Germans and Iranians (in 1935 he changed the name of Persia to Iran). These factors, together with anti-Semitic Nazi propaganda, awakened concern in the Jewish community that was greatly troubled by the anti-Jewish (anti-Semitic) wave that had resurged among the Muslim Shi'ite population.[5] In order to fight this anti-Semitism, a considerable number of Jews joined the Communist Tudeh Party, where they fulfilled important roles in writing and publishing manifests.

The Judeophobic attitudes of the Shi'ite *ulama* and part of the population continued through the rule of Reza Shah's successor, Mohammad Reza Pahlavi (1941–1979), who oppressed the *ulama*, initiated secular reform and clung to Iran's pre-Islamic past. He even treated the Jews in his country with kindness, enabling their economic prosperity, with many holding positions in the academic and medical systems (the "Golden Age"). The Shah recognized Israel de facto in 1949 and built extensive strategic ties between them – both economic and security-related.

On the other hand, the establishment of the State of Israel in 1948 increased the anti-Jewish sentiments amongst many Shi'ites, which only increased after the war of June 1967, in which Israel occupied Palestinian territories, including East Jerusalem and al-Haram al-Sharif. Thus, the anti-Jewish and anti-Zionist feelings amongst the Iranian population blended together; although there were figures, such as Mohammad Mosaddegh (Prime Minister in 1953), who made the distinction between "colonialist" Zionism and the Jews of Iran (who numbered about 80,000 up to 1979). The latter, for the most part, continued to identify with their country, despite the difficult periods of their relations with the Shi'ite Muslims.[6]

The well-established and wealthy Jewish leadership allied itself with the ruling elite and neglected the Jewish education of its Jewish youth, and ceased cultivating national-religious values; this leadership sent its sons to be educated in Western countries, but not in Israel. The prosperous families chose to affiliate with the Iranian elite and neglected their poor brethren throughout the country.

There hardly existed any religious leadership in the Jewish community. Jews who had been active during the reign of Mohammad Reza Shah were young Communists, or educated leftist radicals that established the organization of Intellectual Jews in Iran. In 1978 they organized demonstrations against the Shah and supported Khomeini even prior to the Islamic revolution of 1979. They also supported the PLO and, together with Muslim clerics, attacked Zionism. They viewed the Jews of Tehran as part of the Iranian society that was fighting imperialism and Zionism.

Amnon Netzer, an Israeli of Iranian origin and professor of Iran Studies at the Hebrew University, said at a lecture given in 1980:

"The Jews of Iran have an affinity to Iran, to the country and its culture, and from a cultural standpoint, the assimilation of the Jewish community was more complete than the assimilation of the tribes, the ethnic groups and many religious minorities in Iran." They continued (outside of Iran as well) to be proud of the language, the poetry, music and literature of their Iranian homeland (and there was intermarriage with Muslims as well). Although among the young Jews in Iran there was an attraction to Zionism and Israel, this was not cultivated by the community leaders and the Jewish educational systems. Perhaps that is why the number of those who immigrated to Israel, which was great after 1948 (part of which was "immigration of distress"), decreased over the years. (There was also a period of time when Jews returned to Iran.) However, after 1979, 30,000 Jews left Iran – half of them came to Israel and the rest immigrated to the United States and Western Europe.[7]

Prof. David Menashri, also of Iranian descent, and a renowned expert on Iran, said at the end of Amnon Netzer's lecture: "My impression, after having recently been in Iran for two-and-a-half years, is that there is a very clear difference between an affinity to Judaism and an affinity to Israel. I met there Jewish youth with a deep affinity to Judaism . . . but when it comes to Zionism, these youth become impenetrable – their lack of interest in Zionism . . . I think that the image of Israel is very negative in the eyes of Jewish youth in Iran, and all that Dr. Surudi has said I agree with." Dr. Surudi, who was born in Iran and immigrated to Israel during the 1970s, spoke during a discussion of Dr. Netzer's lecture about the intermarriage between Jews and Muslims, with the main cause being "the assimilation process of the Jewish community within the local society, the expansion of ties, especially between Jewish and Muslim youth at the universities and work places . . . and it is true that thousands of Jews immigrated to Israel, not with the status of permanent settlers in the State of Israel . . . these people are sitting on their suitcases, and the moment things calm down in Iran, in my opinion these people may return there, if we do nothing about it."[8]

Prof. Haggai Ram, an expert on Iran from Ben-Gurion University, explained this phenomenon as it relates to Israel's ambivalent policy: On the one hand, it leans towards encouraging immigration to the Jewish State; on the other hand, it perceives the continued life of the Jews in Iran of the Shah "as a legitimate and even desirable existential option". But even after the Islamic revolution in 1979 and the exposure of its anti-Israel/anti-Zionist, and even anti-Semitic position, 25,000 Jews (out of 80,000) continued living in Iran; about 15,000 immigrated to Israel and thousands of others immigrated to the United States and Europe.

Ram claims that parallel to the blood libels and pogroms against the Jews, there were also "moments of cooperation, reciprocity and prosperity – moments whose power is no less forceful", and that there were "mutual influences between Jews and Muslims". He quotes from the memoirs of Meir Ezri, who was Israeli representative in Iran for many years: "As the descendant of an ancient Jewish-Persian family, I will note with pride that for over two thousand years, the Jews of Iran preserved with impressive success their devotion to the faith of Israel and the Jewish heritage . . . and unwavering loyalty to Iran and its national interests."[9]

Indeed, even after the 1979 revolution, Jews continued to identify with the Islamic-Iranian revolution and some contributed to the war effort and fought (and were killed) in the battles against Iraq (1980–1988), not because they wished to find favor in the eyes of the new regime, but out of loyalty to the country (as per Ram and Menashri). In 2014 a monument was erected in Tehran commemorating the Jews who had fallen in that war. The leaders of the revolutionary Islamic regime tried to distinguish between Zionists and Jews and emphasize that not all Jews are Zionists; and that the Jews are considered acknowledged by Islam and accepted into the Iranian family on condition that they demonstrate allegiance to the country.

The leader of the revolution, Khomeini, published a *fatwa* declaring that the Jews are a fully protected community, and added that the new regime did not expel Jews, as did other Arab countries after the 1948 war, and as Egypt did after 1956. The regime allowed them the freedom of religious ritual and religious education (though Jewish schools were directed by Muslims up to 2015). Iranian textbooks that promote unity and equality between religions, mention the Jews as a protected community, who lived before the time of the prophet Mohammad and the Imam Ali. Jews were allowed to teach according to their textbooks under the Ministry of Education's supervision; but Israel and Zionism in Israel are denounced as aggression, because of the occupation of Jerusalem and Palestine (anti-Jewish tones can also be found in the textbooks – see below).[10]

There is one Jewish member of the Iranian Parliament who declares allegiance to Iran and removes himself from Zionism and

Israel. Nonetheless, the regime executed the honorary leader of the Jewish community and 17 other Jews who were accused of ties with Israel and Zionism and spying against Iran. Rabbis from the anti-Zionist Neturei Karta sect have visited in Iran several times at the invitation of the regime, which has lately also allowed Jews in Iran and in Israel to engage in reciprocal family visits; Iranian Jews were also allowed to emigrate abroad and indirectly reach Israel as well.

Despite generous proposals made by Jewish organizations in the West, only several hundred Jews left revolutionary Iran, wherein most Jews claim they enjoy a comfortable life in Iran. In Tehran there are 13 synagogues, most with Hebrew schools, a Jewish library and one hospital. In Isfahan there are about 18 synagogues; and in Palestine Square in the city's center, stands a mosque called al-Aqsa, and next to it is a synagogue, on which, in 2009, a large placard was hung, with the Persian text, "Congratulations upon the 30th Anniversary of the Islamic Revolution – from the Jewish community in Isfahan". In 2003, the president of Iran, Khatami, visited the central synagogue in Tehran.

The American Jewish publicist, Richard Cohen, who visited there in 2009, heard the following from a Jewish antique dealer: "I have been in this store for 43 years and never had a problem. I have visited my relatives in Israel; but when I see something like the attack (by Israel) on Gaza, I demonstrated too (against Israel) as an Iranian . . ." An Iranian Jew, a former member of parliament, claimed that despite the harsh demonstrations against Israel – "I feel deep tolerance here towards Jews". Another Jewish parliament member (Majlis), who also served as professor of medicine at the Jewish Hospital in Tehran, declared in 2015 his enthusiastic support of the Iranian regime and his opposition to Israel's policies towards the Palestinians. A Jew living in Isfahan said in an interview with a journalist of the *Yediot Ahronot* newspaper (in 2015): "First of all we are Iranians, Iranian Jews, not Israeli Jews. We love Iran, our country." The journalist, Orly Azulay, reported that the Jews in Iran enjoy freedom of religious worship and pray every Friday together with the Muslims at the grave of the Prophet Isaiah located inside the mosque in Isfahan.[11]

On the other hand, Iranian leaders, the media, movies, caricatures and slogans express anti-Jewish/anti-Semitic attitudes, such as the publication of "The Protocols of the Elders of Zion" (in 1994 and 1999); discrimination also exists against Jews in areas of employment, education and housing; and clearly in the dictatorial regime's oppressive methods. But the ultimate enemies of revolutionary Shi'ite Iran are undoubtedly Zionism and the Jewish Zionist State of Israel[12] that must be destroyed, that "little Satan" (but not the bigger Satan – the United States).

The Israel–Palestine Issue

The major motive behind Iran's hostility in regard to the Israel–Palestine issue is ideological-religious – it is a struggle and a sacrifice against Israel's control over Palestine and especially Jerusalem (al-Quds) and al-Haram-al-Sharif (as mentioned above, every year Iran traditionally commemorates the *Yawm al-Quds*, the Day of al-Quds, and has established a military corps named "al-Quds"). These viewpoints lean on the Qur'an, Islam, Shi'ite principles, the Shi'ite revolution and the historical order. Khomeini and other leaders of the Iranian revolution have expressed themselves orally and in writing from time to time about the threat of the aggressive and racist Israel together with the Imperialist West against the Muslim world. Israel is presented as a "cancerous growth", "the enemy of Islam and of the human race". "Enemy Number One of Iran". These and similar statements, which are found in textbooks as well, are augmented by anti-Jewish/anti-Semitic elements stemming from both Islamic and Christian sources; and the distinction between Israel and Zionism ("the new crusaders") and Zionist and non-Zionist Jews is not always made. Israel's policy towards the Palestinians is compared to Nazi Germany's policies towards the Jews; claiming that the Bible of the Jewish people encourages the killing of Muslims; "and the thought processes of the Zionists and Hitler are one and the same".

In contrast, Iranian leaders and intellectuals have at times identified with the suffering of the Jews in the Holocaust, but have also compared this to the suffering of the Palestinians under Israeli occupation. The relatively moderate president, Khatami, and even the radical president, Ahmadi Nijad, and others of high standing, have said that they will not oppose a peace agreement between Israel and Palestine: "Why should Iran be more Palestinian than the Palestinians? Why should it oppose a peace process when Arab countries are partners to it and are ready for compromise? With that, our main concern is to protect the holy sites of Islam, despite

73

the economic burden, and in any event, we do not believe that a just agreement between Israel and the Palestinians shall really be achieved". President Khatami even supported an interfaith dialogue, and did not stand in the way of Iranian academicians meeting clandestinely with their Jewish-Israeli colleagues. Following his retirement from the presidency, he established in Geneva an institute for interfaith dialogue and in 2007 he intended to participate in the Muslim–Christian–Jewish conclave held at Harvard University (initiated by the author); but in the end he did not take part in the dialogue (be it for technical or fundamental reasons) and did not publicly include Israel as a partner in initiated dialogues between civilizations.[13]

Concurrently, some Iranian academicians from time to time voiced positive appreciation of Israel's achievements in the social and economic fields, and held dialogues with Israeli researchers at public academic conferences. And Israeli experts holding foreign passports also continued working in Iran in various economic fields. It is worth noting that during the Iran–Iraq war (1980–1988) Israel sold weapons to Iran, not out of love of Iran, but out of its hatred towards Iraq. Nonetheless, all Israeli prime ministers, and the greater part of the Jewish population in Israel, have emphasized the danger that Shi'ite Iran poses to Israel, especially against the background of Iran's nuclear weapons development; and have prepared Israel's military forces (Netanyahu in particular – as Prime-Minister, and Ehud Barak – as Defense Minister) for a preemptive strike against Iran's nuclear plants.

In conclusion, there is no doubt that revolutionary Iran poses a strategic threat to Israel, not only because of its potential nuclear power, but also because of the thousands of long-range missiles it possesses, and its terrorist activities against Israeli and Jewish targets (as in its involvement in the bombing of the Israeli embassy and Jewish community center in Buenos Aires, Argentina in 1992 and 1994 respectively). Moreover, for many years Iran has been helping its ideological ally, Hizbullah in Lebanon (and also the Sunni Hamas and Islamic Jihad),[14] to build an immense arsenal of missiles and rockets aimed at Israel; this, within the framework of a strategic Shi'ite alignment that also includes the Syrian Alawi regime and perhaps the Iraqi Shi'ite regime, and is designated to even take over or influence Arab Sunni countries in the region that are rich in oil deposits.

74

The critical questions are: If and under what circumstances might Iran and Hizbullah attack Israel? Perhaps in response to severe damage to the Al-Aqsa Mosque and the Dome of the Rock, perpetrated by fanatical Jews, thus turning into reality the worst-case scenario of a Muslim–Jewish Armageddon? On the other hand, can Israel's conventional and nuclear (according to foreign sources) deterrence prevent Iran and Hizbullah from attacking Israel under any condition? And will settling the Palestinian problem and the issue of east Jerusalem through a peace agreement remove the Iranian threat against Israel?

Shi'ites and Jews in Lebanon: Hizbullah – Iran's Spearhead vis-à-vis Israel

The large Shi'ite population in Lebanon, which for many years held only a marginal status, hardly showed interest in its small Jewish population, most of which did not reside in Shi'ite regions. Nonetheless, the Shi'ites perceived the Jews as part of Lebanon and did not demonstrate religious antagonism towards them; and in southern Lebanon good relations were developed between Shi'ites and local Jews and with the Jews living across the border in the Holy Land.

However, with the appearance of the Zionist movement in the Holy Land, a Shi'ite Lebanese journal reported (in 1921) that Muslims (and Christians) in Palestine began defending themselves via the "al-Quds revolt", against the Zionists-Jews (who are returning to their ancient homeland with the help of Western powers); Muslims even began collecting money for renovating the Al-Aqsa Mosque. Another article (in 1934) expressed surprise: "How come they (the Zionist-Jews) forgot the kindness of the Arabs and of Islam – and want to make Palestine – which they had left thousands of years ago – their national home in an entirely Muslim country . . . which more than 300 million Muslims venerate and honor."[15]

Even though many Muslims in Lebanon made the distinction between local Jews and Zionists in Palestine, the riots at the Western Wall in 1929, and the Arab revolt in 1936, led to anti-Jewish Muslim demonstrations and riots in Lebanon, including in the partially Shi'ite city of Sidon, which grew stronger after the mufti Haj Amin al-Husseini was expelled from Palestine to Lebanon. Towards the establishment of the State of Israel and because of that, Jews were attacked and killed in Tripoli, and in Beirut the central synagogue was set afire in 1950. On the other hand, Jews in different regions were given police protection from Shi'ites' attacks; while Jewish refugees from Syria and Iran found shelter in Lebanon. Jews from Sidon "contributed towards the Palestinian struggle against Israel". Yet, Shi'ite notables continued opposing Israeli-Zionist activities in the Holy Land (which they feared might even trickle into southern Lebanon), emphasized the Arab character of the land (Palestine) and the holiness of Jerusalem; and praised the Muslim holy fighters (*mujahiddun*), anticipating the defeat of Zionism at the hands of Arab unity.

Jamil Bayham, a Shi'ite leader of the "Association of Lebanese Parties for Fighting Zionism", wrote in 1948 that it is the aim of Zionism to enslave the Arabs. He claimed that when the Zionists were a small minority, they spoke of "our Arab brothers"; but after having gained power – they spoke of "our Arab neighbors"; and finally they began speaking of "our Arab enemy . . . ", and soon they will speak of "our Arab slaves".

Other Shi'ite intellectuals also expressed concern about the Zionist expansion and its (supposed) conquests in Arab states, and called for jihad to protect the Al-Aqsa Mosque; and Palestine, with its glorious heritage of 1400 years amongst the Arab nations and Islam. Anti-Zionist declarations were mingled with anti-Jewish declarations despite the fact that Jews in Lebanon had become integrated and had affirmed their loyalty to the country, and were not identified with Zionism by many of the Muslims.

However, with the passing of time, anti-Jewish/anti-Semitic expressions increasingly appeared amongst the Shi'ites, based on the Qur'an and the Hadith, and on Christian anti-Semitism. Yet, a distinction was also made between Jews and Zionism (in keeping with the viewpoint of Sayid Qutub, the theorist of the "Muslim Brothers" movement)[16]. Following the war of 1967 and the occupation of east Jerusalem and the Al-Aqsa Mosque, demonstrations against the Jews were renewed, and close to 3,000 Jews emigrated – leaving Beirut and Sidon (each with large Shi'ite populations). The Shi'ite view of identifying Zionism and Israel with the Jews continued also under the charismatic leadership of Imam Musa al-Sadr (who was born in Iran, reached Lebanon in 1959 and disappeared in Libya in 1978). He contributed greatly to the revival of Shi'ite community and the establishment of the "Amal" movement in Lebanon. He preached armed resistance against the Jewish State, and freeing Palestine and Jerusalem; however, he refrained from attacking the Jewish community in Lebanon out of tactic-pragmatic considerations.[17]

Another senior Shi'ite leader who, together with Khomeini, contributed to the formulation of the doctrines of Hizbullah – the opponent of the Amal movement – was Muhammad Hussein Fadlallah, who was born in the Shi'ite holy city of Najaf in Iraq. Even though he was a fierce opponent of Zionists and Jews, and saw them as one and the same, he proposed, in the spirit of the Qur'an, to hold a dialogue (*hiwar*) with them in a pleasant manner. However, he was of the opinion that with the help of the Fundamentalist Christians, the Jews (Zionists) aim to destroy the Al-Aqsa Mosque and build the Holy Temple in its place; that they are planning the Armageddon and are waiting for the coming of the Messiah to do so.[18]

The current leader of Hizbullah (since 1992), Hasan Nasrallah, sees the liberation of Jerusalem from Jewish occupation as a Jihad and a supreme *Shahada* (sacrifice); he expresses severe anti-Zionist and anti-Jewish attitudes, in line with the ideology and strategy of the revolutionary-Shi'ite regime in Iran. Hizbullah was established (1982) under the influence of the Islamic revolution in Iran in 1979 and also in response to Israel's occupation of southern Lebanon in 1982. At first, the movement broke off from the Shi'ite Amal (Hope) movement, which was national-social and anti-sectarian, and even had secret ties with Israel from time to time.

At first, Hizbullah adopted the doctrine promoted by Khomeini and declared itself an Islamic movement, part of the worldwide Islamic nation. However, with time and under the influence of Fadlallah, Hizbullah also presented itself as a Lebanese national movement.[19] However, it did not change its ideology and militant strategy towards Zionism, Israel and the Jews, preserving the Qur'an's viewpoint, the original Shi'ite doctrines and Khomeini's principles, but did not employ Christian anti-Semitism.

The outcome of the first Lebanese war (1982) led Nasrallah to boast that Israel is not invincible, and that it had suffered powerful attacks from Hizbullah in the second Lebanese war (2006). Since then, the organization has armed itself, with the help of Iran, with rockets and missiles – over 100,000, some of which are long-range and capable of targeting expansive areas of Israel. The same applies to Iran's long-range missiles and its nuclear option, which creates a strategic threat to Israel. This dangerous Shi'ite front (perhaps along with Syria, Lebanon and Iraq) may constitute the Muslim side in an all-out war (Armageddon), which might erupt in the event that fanatic Jewish elements harm Islamic holy sites in Jerusalem and that Israel will not resolve the Palestinian problem.

Tamir Pardo, former head of Israel's *Mossad*, said in regard to the Iranian threat: "The demographic problem is an existential threat to Israel – when there is no agreement between the residents of this land lying between Jordan and the sea, Jews and Muslims, whose numbers are nearly identical."[20]

And finally, as in Iran, Hizbullah is not consistent in its attitude towards Jews in general, and the Jews in Lebanon in particular. On the one hand, it accuses the Jews of being the enemy of Islam and does not hesitate to kill them, as it did with the bombing of the Jewish community center in Buenos Aires, and also with attacks against Jews in Lebanon. On the other hand, its leaders are still attempting (unsuccessfully), to distinguish between Zionists and Jews, especially in Lebanon. In 2015 Hizbullah helped reconstruct the *Magen Avraham* synagogue, which was (mistakenly?) bombed by the Israeli air-force in the first Lebanese war, 1982.

In May 2018, Shi'ite leaders in Hizbullah, Iran and Iraq condemned the transfer of the American Embassy to Jerusalem, and demanded a Palestinian capital in East Jerusalem. But in late 2019, Shi'ites in Lebanon and Iraq strongly protested against Iran's interference and influence.[21]

Relations between Shi'ites and Jews in Yemen

As in Iran, the Shi'ite Zaydiyyah dynasties that ruled in Yemen over a long time period, were hostile towards the Jewish population, excluded them and defined them as unclean (*Najes*). At times parts of these communities were forced to convert to Islam or were expelled. On the other hand, under Sunni rulers, the condition of the Jews in Yemen was more tolerant or fairer.

The Zaydi sect (named after the fifth Shi'ite Imam), which expanded in the 8th century, ruled in northern Yemen from the 10th century, and for long periods was characterized by its oppression of the Jews and discrimination against them in the 12th, 15th, 17th,

18th and 20th centuries. These oppressions also included regulations to convert Jewish orphaned children to Islam; to turn synagogues into mosques; to collect the Jizya tax; to enforce dress codes, to limit the Jews' ability to purchase and build homes; to concentrate them in certain regions and humiliate them.[22] In the 12th century, for example, the extremely distressful condition of the Yemenite Jews brought Maimonides – who himself suffered harsh oppression from the fanatic Sunni dynasty in Morocco – to write the "Yemenite Letter". In this letter his calls upon the Jews of Yemen to preserve their religion, but to refrain from irritating their opponents.

In the 13th and 14th centuries, under the Sunni Rashidi dynasty, the condition of the Yemenite Jews greatly improved – socially and economically. However, in the 15th century, at the time of the rule of the Shi'ite Tahiri dynasty, their situation once again turned for the worse; and in 1457, the ancient synagogue in Sanaa was destroyed. In 1546, Yemen was conquered by the Sunni Turkish Ottomans (up to 1635), who improved the legal standing of the Jews and allowed them to maintain contact with other Jewish communities in the Ottoman Empire, including the learned Kabbalists in Safed. However, the Shi'ite population, which objected to the Turkish–Jewish connection, induced the Ottoman rulers to worsen their attitude towards the Jews. Thus, for instance, the Jewish Yemenite poet, Shalom Shabazi (1619–1680), wrote about the harsh attitude of the Turkish ruler in southern Yemen towards the Jews, which included an attempt to convert Shabazi and his father, Yosef Avigad, to Islam.

After the Ottoman rulers were expelled in 1635, the Shi'ite Qasimid dynasty was very hostile towards the Jews in Yemen, as local Muslims took revenge upon the Jews for their relatively comfortable relations with the Turks, and "the claim that the Jews side with the Turks . . . ".[23] The legal status of the Jews along with their social and physical condition worsened greatly also due to the impact of the messianic ideas of Sabbatai Zvi (1665) in Yemen, and the Jews' defiant behavior towards the Muslims. Under the influence of Shi'ite religious leaders, Jews were arrested, others suffered humiliation and harassment, and many were exiled to distant places (the Mawza exile, 1679); their homes were confiscated and the synagogues were turned into mosques. But at the end of the 18th century, under the rule of sovereigns more pragmatic than the religious leaders, synagogues were restored and Jews were returned to their cities, but not to their homes; and they gained senior positions in the economic domain. This stemmed from the unique contribution of the Jews as monetary directors, silversmiths, merchants, builders, weavers and other craftsmen. The pragmatic rulers objected to the demands of the religious leaders to expel the Jews from Yemen.

Indeed, following the new Ottoman conquest of Yemen (1872), the Yemenite Jews' condition improved; a new Jewish neighborhood and new synagogues were built in Sanaa. However, the *Jizya* tax was not revoked (unlike in other regions of the empire), and the harsh attitude of the local Shi'ite population did not change. All this, along with drought and hunger, and a messianic longing for Zion, motivated Jews in Yemen to immigrate to the Holy Land. With the restored rule of the Shi'ite Zaydi Imam Yahyah (1905–1948 with a brief interim) the Jews suffered once again legal, public and social discrimination; Jewish orphans were forced to convert to Islam and Jews were not allowed to immigrate to the Holy Land. However, his successor, Ahmad, in 1949 allowed most of the Jews (around 45,000) to leave for Israel, following a period of incitement and violence (including pogroms in Aden in 1947) against the Jews, with the establishment of the State of Israel.

Despite the formal antagonism towards Israel of the Shi'ite Zaydiyyah government in Yemen, a logistic cooperation was formed between Israel and Yemen in the years 1962–1967, against the Republican Sunni rebels who were supported by revolutionary Egypt. In the early 1960s the Yemenite government permitted the remaining Jews (around 1800) to emigrate – the great majority left for Israel, but a small minority remained under the auspices of the ultra-Orthodox, anti-Zionist Satmar sect, or were moved to the United States by this sect. Since then, only several dozen Jewish families have remained in some villages in Sa'dah, Ra'daa and Sana'a. Some live peacefully with their Muslim neighbors, while others have suffered from radical Shi'ite Muslims, including Shi'ite Houthi rebels since 2012. The latter have spread anti-Israel and anti-Semitic statements as well in the past few years.[24]

So far, we have discussed the positions taken by Shi'ites towards Jews, Zionists and the Jewish State – in Shi'ite Iran, in Yemen with its large Shi'ite population and Shi'ite rulers, and in Lebanon with its prominent Shi'ite community and the militant Hizbullah at its center. Clearly we have learned that when compared to the Sunni Muslims, the attitude of the Shi'ite Muslims towards Jews and Israel was and has remained dualistic, with a clear emphasis on antagonistic, negative views, but also periods of tolerance and dialogue.

These ambivalent attitudes are linked not only to the extremist Shi'ite religious ideology (Jews – "unclean"), but also to existing circumstances and other important factors, such as: the balance of power between fanatical religious leaders and pragmatic rulers – both Shi'ites and Sunni (who ruled at different time periods); the character of the various regimes; strategic, political and economic considerations; the relationships between various ethnic groups and external influences. These factors also impacted on the relationship between Shi'ites and Jews in Iraq and in Bahrain, both with a majority Shi'ite population and Sunni regimes, and in Azerbaijan with a secular Shi'ite population and regime.

The Relationship between Shi'ites and Jews in Iraq

The relationship between Shi'ites and Jews in Iraq was influenced by the presence of the principal Shi'ite centers in Najaf and Karbala, and the deep affinity to other important Muslim sites in Qom and Mashhad (Iran), in Mecca and Medina and in Jerusalem (Al-Aqsa Mosque). Yet, despite that and the fact that the Shi'ites were the largest congregation in Iraq (over 50%), sovereign rule in Iraq (except for short time periods) was in the hands of Sunni Muslim dynasties for centuries (only after 2003 did the regime pass over to the Shi'ites through democratic elections). Even though Shi'ite notables held senior positions in the Iraqi governments and political parties, most of the Shi'ite population suffered political, social and economic discrimination and deprivation.

Against this varied, extensive background, the dual positions held by the Shi'ites in Iraq towards the Jews, Zionists and Israel are understandable: On the one hand, there was some tolerance and cooperation (especially in trade) between the rejected or deprived minorities; on the other hand, great animosity prevailed for long time periods. Thus, for example, economic cooperation between the Shi'ites and Jews in the 1930s was later replaced with envy and competition from the educated Shi'ites for positions held by Jews in public administration and the financial sectors. At the time, the Shi'ites were influenced by the anti-Semitic Nazi propaganda and the Zionist-Arab conflict in the Holy Land/Palestine. Even though Shi'ite notables and ministers made the distinction between Zionists and Jews, others incited against the Jews and attacked them. This occurred in the 1941 pogrom (*farhud*) against the Iraqi Jews and in violent actions linked to the establishment of the State of Israel (1947–1948).

A Shi'ite religious leader at the time published a *fatwa* forbidding the sale of lands to Jews throughout all Arab countries; and in 1950, another Shi'ite religious leader forbade Muslims to buy houses from Jews who were immigrating to Israel – declaring "a religious war" against Israel. On the other hand, against the background of anti-Jewish riots, the Shi'ite prime minister of Iraq, Muhammad al-Sadr, called in 1948 not to harm the Jews.[25] In 1967 as well, with Israel's occupation of east Jerusalem and the Temple Mount/al-Haram al-Sharif, and the harsh reactions of Muslims, the senior Shi'ite leader, Sayyid Muhsin al Hakim, published a *fatwa* calling not to harm the Jews (in Iraq).

Up to 2003, Iraqi rule continued to remain in the hands of Sunni regimes that demonstrated hostile attitudes towards Israel, including their participation in the 1967 and 1973 wars. In 1981 Israel demolished the Osirak nuclear reactor in Iraq. In 1991, during the war in Kuwait, the dictator Saddam Hussein launched 39 missiles at Israel, and at the same time continued supporting extremist anti-Israel Palestinian organizations. Following the United States' occupation of Iraq in 2003, the Shi'ite governments that were then established and were preoccupied with harsh internal disputes, expressed only moderate criticism against Israel, as did the Shi'ite religious leaders; whereas Kurdish-Sunni ministers and parliament members expressed sympathy towards Israel. The Iraqi government condemned, for example, the Israeli operation in Gaza (2008–2009) and the IDF's operation against the Turkish ship, *Mavi Marmara*, in 2010. The Shi'ite Dawa Party called upon the Muslim countries in 2008 to sever all relations with Israel. This took place only a number of years after the 2002 Saudi Arabian peace initiative had been accepted by Arab and Islam countries (including Iraq). The supreme Shi'ite cleric Ali Sistani condemned Israel's attack on Gaza, but also called to protect the citizens in Iraq, regardless of religious or ethnic affiliation. The senior Shi'ite leader Muqtada al-Sadr in 2018 called upon the Iraqi Jews to return to Iraq and receive full citizenship.

It may be assumed that the less extreme positions towards Jews held by Sistani and other Shi'ite (Arab) religious leaders in Iraq, compared to revolutionary Iran, stem also from the different status held by the religious leaders vis-à-vis the ruling powers: In Iran, the supreme power was in the hands of the religious leader – *Wilayyat al-Faqih*, whereas in Iraq, Sistani and other religious leaders acknowledge the supremacy of the political rulers. In late 2019 many Iraqi Shi'ites strongly protested against Iran's interference and influence in Iraq. The assassination of Qassem Suleimani, Iran's top general, in Baghdad on the third of January 2020 by the U.S. army may reduce Iran's influence in Iraq for some time.

Bahrain

Similar to Iraq, the majority of the Bahrain population (around 1.3 million) in the Persian/Arab Gulf are Shi'ites (about 70%) – from as early as the Shi'ite Safavid occupation (1602–1783). Since then, the Sunni Khalifa family rules the country, supported both militarily and politically by Saudi Arabia and the United States against the Shi'ite Iranian threat.

The members of the small and prosperous Jewish community (around 1500 in 1948, and only several dozen members today), were nearly all of Iraqi origin, and lived quietly and peacefully for many years under Sunni rule. However, around the establishment of the State of Israel, in 1947–1948, Jews were attacked in the capital city Manama (with a Shi'ite majority), houses were vandalized and destroyed, as was the only synagogue. Some Jews found shelter with Muslims, but many immigrated to Israel. During the June 1967 war, most of the Jews who had remained in Bahrain emigrated due to anti-Semitic propaganda, but those who stayed continue to enjoy the freedom of religious ritual and physical security. In 2007, the king appointed the Jewish Mrs. Huda Nunu – a member of the Upper House of Parliament – as Bahrain's Ambassador to the United States.[26] In her stead in the parliament, another Jewish woman was appointed, Nancy Khaduri (Kaduri); and in early 2015 the king attended Hanukkah celebrations along with other Muslims.

Bahrain officially supports the Palestinian positions and is agreeable to ties with Israel only after the establishment of a Palestinian state. However, in 2005 the king instructed that in public declarations, Israel is not to be called "the enemy" or a "Zionist entity".

Prior to that, he allowed an Israeli minister to attend a conference on environmental issues; and in 2007, the foreign minister of Bahrain met with Jewish leaders in the United States and with then-Israeli Foreign Minister Tzipi Livni at the United Nations assembly in New York. There are also reports of both secret and open ties between Bahrain and Israel, including a visit from a Bahrain delegation to Israel at the end of 2017, as well as visits by senior Israelis to Bahrain in 2019.

Azerbaijan

More than any other Shi'ite country or community in the region, with 93% of its residents Shi'ite Muslims, Azerbaijan holds the most positive attitude towards Jews and Israel, ever since its independence from Soviet rule in 1991. This results from the country's very long tradition of tolerance towards Jews, its secular regime and its security-related, strategic, political, cultural and economic interests.

Present-day Jewish communities in Azerbaijan number around 9,000 (out of 10 million residents), as compared to nearly 30,000 after World War II (many emigrated out of economic considerations). The majority – about 5,500 – are "mountain Jews" (in the north; some call them the "Tati"), whose roots are ancient (since the destruction of the First Temple). They consistently preserved Jewish tradition, though some of them were assimilated into the Muslim community – socially and culturally – and also included mixed marriages. There were also few Lovers of Zion at the end of the 19th century, but the vast majority continued identifying themselves with their country more than with Israel. As one of them said in 1992: "Yes, we are Jews, but when [Jewish] blood is spilled in Israel we feel pain for our brothers. But we are citizens of Azerbaijan and our homeland is here . . . we should protect our homeland."[27] Jews also participated in the war against Armenia over Nagorno-Karabakh in 1992. In 2003, a leader of the "mountain Jews" told a reporter: "Not only do we live as Jews, we also share our language, culture, music, traditions, and our life with our Azeri neighbors."[28]

The second largest Jewish group is that of Russian Jews who immigrated to Azerbaijan at the end of the 19th century, especially after World War II (since then, some Jews also arrived there from Georgia) – most of them are of Ashkenazi origin and preserved their Russian culture, and settled in the capital city of Baku. There were

84

few cases of anti-Semitism towards them and other Jews, initiated by radical Shi'ite Muslim circles who started to emerge in the last few decades. However, these radicals were forcefully excluded and oppressed by the secular rule of the presidents of the Aliyev dynasty. A report on worldwide anti-Semitism published in 2004 by the U.S. State Department states as follows: "Cases of prejudice and discrimination against the Jews in the country (Azerbaijan) were very limited, and in the few instances of anti-Semitic activity, the government has been quick to respond."[29] This government also forbids religious education in the schools and calls for separation of church and state and equality of all its citizens. The press, which is under the strict supervision of the autocratic government, nearly always expresses these positions.

According to a study done by Tural Ahmadov, most Shi'ite Muslims in the country are not extremists, and their religious identity is not favored over their national identity, but is part of it. Many of them do not see in the Palestinian–Israeli conflict a religious conflict, but rather a territorial dispute. Nonetheless, they support the Palestinians and their claim over east Jerusalem; yet, some of them side with Israel.

According to a survey conducted by Ahmadov at the universities, whereas many students blame Israel, others blame the Palestinians, as to how the conflict between them is managed. They feel their government must maintain a neutral stance in this conflict. Many uphold the two-state solution with Jerusalem divided as the capital of both countries. In response to the al-Aqsa Intifada in Jerusalem (2000) and the Gaza operation (2008/9), demonstrations were held and criticism of Israel was voiced in the media, yet the government did not express an opinion on these issues.[30] (In 2008 there was an attempt at bombing the Israeli Embassy in Baku, probably by agents of Iran and Hizbullah.)

The government of Azerbaijan not only has treated the Jews in its land well, but also continues to maintain meaningful security-related and strategic ties with Israel (including vis-à-vis Shi'ite Iran). Amongst the Israeli leaders who visited in Azerbaijan in the last decade were President Shimon Peres (2009), and Prime Minister Binyamin Netanyahu and Defense Minister Avigdor Lieberman (2016). Netanyahu then declared that "Israel and Azerbaijan enjoy excellent relationships and a warm friendship", and later also said: "Israel is a Jewish state and Azerbaijan is a Muslim state, and here we have an example of Muslims and Jews working together to ensure a future for us both." That same year, at a meeting with a delegation from the World Jewish Congress, President Aliyev emphasized "the excellent relations with the Jewish community and with Israel." A short while later, President Aliyev invited about ten Israelis to the international conference in Baku, amongst them six Nobel Prize winners.[31]

Finally, it is noteworthy that the relationship between Shi'ite Azerbaijan and Israel and the Jews is better than Turkey's relationship with the Jews and Israel, considering that Turkey has a majority of Sunni Muslims, but has an ethnic and cultural affinity to the Azeri people.

CHAPTER
5

Changing Positions of Sunni Turkey and Central Asia

After the fall of the Ottoman Empire and the establishment of the Turkish Republic in 1923, and up to the present, trends have developed within Turkish governments and the general public towards continuity and even change in regard to Jews, Zionism and Israel; against a background of internal, regional and international circumstances and influences.

On the one hand, various governments and sectors of the Turkish populace continued the longstanding Ottoman tradition of tolerance, dialogue and cooperation with its Jewish citizens, and even absorbed Jewish refugees from the Holocaust. In March 1949, Turkey recognized the State of Israel and was the second Muslim state to do so, after Iran. Turkey continued to maintain proper and even good relations with the Jewish state over long time periods, especially as to strategic, security-related and economic issues. On the other hand, some Turkish governments imposed various limitations upon the Jews, especially of an economic and educational nature, and were unsuccessful in preventing harsh anti-Semitic manifestations that included acts of violence and murder. Similarly, negative positions against Israel developed in Turkey after 1967. Senior Turkish leaders, especially, attacked Israel for its severe actions against the Palestinians in the Gaza Strip and the West Bank, and especially at the Temple Mount/al-Ḥaram al-Sharīf, going so far as to call these actions "genocide" and political terrorism. Erdoğan and a great number of Turks strongly condemned the transfer of the U.S. Embassy to Jerusalem in May 2018, and the Turkish ambassador was recalled from Tel Aviv.

Concurrently, the majority of Turkish Jews continued to express their loyalty and devotion to Turkey, even during the era of the Republic, recalling the past centuries and Turkey having absorbed Jews expelled from Spain (from 1492) and their successful social and economic integration. Other Jews emigrated from Turkey to Israel, motivated by Zionism and periodic manifestations of anti-Semitism, most of which occurred in Istanbul, Izmir and Edirne. Over the years, 280,000 Jews left Turkey and immigrated to Israel. Today 18,000 Jews reside in Turkey, out of a population of 80 million.

Up to the Establishment of the State of Israel

Even prior to the establishment of the Turkish Republic in 1923, Jews in western Anatolia and Izmir suffered from the battles fought between the Turkish army and the Greek forces that had invaded the area in 1919 in an attempt to annex it to Greece. Most Jews continued expressing their loyalty to Turkey and many were enlisted in its armed forces. With the battles' end, they were successfully rehabilitated with the help of international Jewish organizations, and even expanded their economic activities, replacing the Greeks and Armenians who had been expelled.

Jewish leaders noted that their congregations have lived in Turkey for five hundred years and enjoy religious freedom, justice and amity: "All we wish for is to see our sacred and beloved country progress in every field"; to integrate into the country's social and political life as Turkish citizens of the Mosaic faith. At the same time, representatives of the new Turkish government praised the loyalty and contribution of the Jews to the country and the homeland, and noted that "in the eyes of the homeland, there is no difference between Muhammad, Ahmad or Chaim Nahum [the Chief Rabbi]".[1]

In contrast to these affirmative positions, anti-Jewish sentiments were also proliferated and included accusations that Jews had cooperated with the Greeks during the war and then took possession of the assets of Greeks and Armenians who had been expelled from Turkey. Jews were labeled as ungrateful, as pimps and bloodsuckers; harming Muslim peasants and traders and taking control of the Turkish economy. In some cities in Thrace, Jews were violently attacked and banned. On occasion, Turkish governments protected the Jews, yet they also harassed them, and dismissed them from government and public positions and from Jewish schools, in which a Turkish curriculum was forced upon them (as part of the Kemalist regime's policy of Turkification). Moreover, during the Palestinian riots of 1929, Turkish Jews were accused of providing financial help to Jews in the Holy Land.[2] However, as time passed, alongside the tribute to Jews expressed by publicists, Turkish governments improved their outlook as well, helping the Jews financially and allowing them to build new synagogues, including the *Neveh Shalom* synagogue in Istanbul.

After the rise of Nazism in Germany (1933), Turkey absorbed scores of Jewish German lecturers and professors into the University of Istanbul (alongside the Jewish Turkish professors who continued teaching there). Financial institutions and banks hired hundreds of German Jews as well (who also helped to establish the Turkish Opera) along with Jews from other anti-Semitic European countries. At the same time, however, Jewish tradesmen (alongside Christian tradesmen) continued to control Turkish trade[3] and were condemned by the Turks for controlling the economy. Additionally, Turkish nationalist youth and intellectuals were being influenced by the Nazis and cooperated with them, publishing blatant anti-Semitic materials, such as "The Protocols of the Elders of Zion". For example, one of the leaders of the Turkish nationalists wrote in 1934:

> There is no one in the world who likes the creature called a Jew, except for the Jews themselves, a corrupt people . . . the Jew is an exemplar of inferiority, cowardice and evil . . . The Germans are the first nation to solve the Jewish problem . . . the world despises this cursed people . . . we are familiar with the destructive role that Jews play in the morality and economy of our country . . . we do not believe that Jews will become Turks, even if we so desired. Mud cannot convert into iron.[4]

By contrast, liberal Turkish prime ministers and government officials denounced anti-Semitic manifestations. Prime Minister Bayar declared in 1938: "In our country a Jewish problem does not exist . . . yet we have no intention of artificially creating a Jewish problem due to external influences. Another prominent Turk noted at the same time that 'there is no anti-Semitism in Turkey' and that the Jews 'have contributed greatly to trade and industry in the Republic . . . they are good and loyal citizens, they see their future in Turkey, they invest money in the country and contribute to economic growth.'"[5]

However, during World War II, in which Turkey was neutral yet sided with Germany, Turkish leaders ceased noting that the Jews were equal citizens; they discriminated against Jewish soldiers in the Turkish army and imposed heavy taxes on Jews (and Christians). But from 1943, with the approaching institution of democratic rule in Turkey and a developing pro-Western orientation, the status of the Jews greatly improved. Two of them – Prof. Avraham Galante and Shalmon Adato, were elected in 1946 as Parliament members from the Democratic Party. Turkey also helped save Jewish refugees coming from European countries and from Rhodes; some were absorbed, and many others were permitted to immigrate to the Holy Land. (An exception was the *Struma* disaster, when the ship carrying passengers was denied the right to disembark at Istanbul's port, under British pressure, and further events resulted in the sinking of the ship with all 781 Jewish refugees aboard.) The Jewish communities in Turkey recovered and reorganized; the Jewish educational system initiated religious and Hebrew studies; many Jewish newspapers were published; and Jews enjoyed the renewed economic prosperity.[6]

Establishment of the State of Israel: Duality and Dialogue, Pros and Cons

A considerable portion of the Muslim population in Turkey – especially the anti-Semitic right-wing parties and Islamist groups – supported the Arabs in the 1948 war against Israel, in contrast to other extensive groups that expressed support of Israel. The Turkish government, which voted against the partition plan in 1947, recognized Israel in 1949 and allowed its Jewish citizens to immigrate to the Jewish state. Even prior to 1948, more than 10,000 Turkish Jews immigrated to the Holy Land, mainly due to harassment and persecution; after the establishment of the State of Israel, tens of thousands more immigrated to Israel – nearly 40% of all Turkish Jewry, and over the years nearly 80% of them settled permanently in Israel and were well integrated.

90

Among the major reasons for the continued immigration of Turkish Jews to Israel were the increasing manifestations of anti-Semitism and violence towards Jews, especially by Arab-Muslim terrorists, in the context of the Palestinian–Israeli conflict. Thus, for instance, the *Neve Shalom* Synagogue in Istanbul was attacked twice – in 1986 and in 2003, leaving in its wake scores killed and hundreds (Jews and Muslims) injured. And after the *Mavi Marmara* affair, in which the Turkish ship was attacked by the IDF in 2010 as it made its way to Gaza, threats were sounded and economic bans were imposed on Jews in Turkey.

Indeed, alongside significant developments in the strategic-security-related and economic relations between Turkey and Israel over decades, anti-Jewish, anti-Zionist and anti-Israel trends grew stronger in the Turkish population, especially within the Islamic parties: The "National Rescue Party", headed by Erbakan (1972–1980); the "Welfare Party" (1983–1998); and the "Party for Justice and Development", led by Erdoğan, that has ruled in Turkey since 2002.

These trends reflected great hostility towards Israel, whose presence in the region and whose wars against the Arabs (supposedly) were harmful to Muslims and Islam and all of humanity. Furthermore, they held that Zionism was breeding anarchy in Turkey, controlling the world and aiming at rebuilding Solomon's Temple on Mt. Zion. These severe accusations were published in Muslim and nationalist books, journals and newspapers.[7] In the moderate mainstream newspapers as well, alongside certain praises of Israel, harsh criticism was written of the "Zionist" state that is supported by Western imperialism. Violent events against Palestinians were especially given prominence, such as the Dayr Yassin massacre in 1948; the Sabra and Shatila massacre (1982 – executed by the (Christian) Maronites, under cover of the IDF), which was labeled "genocide"; and additional attacks of the IDF on Palestinians, which were fiercely denounced by the Turkish governments as well (see below).

Menachem Begin and Ariel Sharon were defined (in 1982) as "the greatest criminals of international terrorism, barbarians and murderers, like Hitler and Eichmann". Ehud Barak too was compared to Hitler (during the Intifada in the year 2000), and Yitzhak Rabin was called "the murderer of Palestinian children" (after he himself had been assassinated in 1995). Moreover, while

91

the central press continued to support the Palestinians and their uprising in the Intifadas of 1987 and 2000, Islamic newspapers also expressed religious Muslim solidarity with the Palestinians – especially with Hamas – and defined their struggle as a conflict between Islam and the Jews/Zionists.

The recruited press emphasized the importance of East Jerusalem to Islam and the Palestinians, whereas the mainstream press recommended establishing an international administration for the Old City of Jerusalem. In contrast, against the Islamic anti-Jewish, anti-Israel and anti-Zionist public opinion, many from the mainstream supported Israel's right to exist alongside a Palestinian state – though within the pre-June 1967 lines. Some of them denounced Palestinian terrorism against Israel and praised Rabin's contribution to peace in the region. The Turkish military command for many years supported reinforcing the strategic-military ties with Israel.

This relatively moderate trend supported by certain populaces, senior army officers and various Turkish governments also found expression in the school textbooks. According to a study conducted by Dr. Giray in 2009, textbooks used in Turkish high-schools barely mentioned the Palestinian–Israeli conflict, whereas Judaism and the Jews were generally presented in a positive and factual manner. For example: That they established a strong country in the Holy Land; that King David began building the Holy Temple in Jerusalem and King Solomon continued its construction. On the other hand, it was noted that the Jews believe they are the chosen people and have even distorted the teachings of the Bible.

According to a more recent study on the textbooks in Turkey, carried out by Dr. Eldad Pardo, the Jewish bond to the Holy Land and Jerusalem is mentioned, including the desire to build the Holy Temple at the al-Aqsa site on the Temple Mount. In addition to the matter of distorting the Bible, the Jews are presented as traitors of the Prophet Muhammad. The new textbooks discuss the Israeli–Palestinian conflict in detail from a viewpoint sympathetic to the Palestinians and raises doubts as to the legitimacy of Jews in the Holy Land. Emphasis is given to the view that peace between Israel and the Palestinians depends on Israel's retreat from the territories it occupied in 1967, and the resolution of the issue of Jerusalem, the Palestinian refugees and the Jewish settlements. In addition, it is noted that Turkey absorbed many Jews who had been expelled from

Spain in 1492, and that today there is cooperation between Turkey and Israel due to regional strategic considerations (in some text-books, admiration of Israel's achievements is expressed).

In the past few years, probably influenced by Erdoğan's Islamic rule and Israel's actions against the Palestinians, new trends of Islamization are surfacing on the one hand, and anti-Semitism on the other hand. Thus, for example, after the IDF's military campaign in Gaza in August 2014 (*Tzuk Eitan*), once again a wave of anti-Semitism rose in the general public and the social medias, and included praise of Hitler for having killed the Jews, threats and violence against Jews, demonstrations and calling Jews "dogs". In a series of books for elementary school pupils, Darwin is presented as a Jew with a long nose, surrounded by monkeys; and Einstein is defined as "dirty", and as having missed being included in the Nazi gestapo's actions against the Jews.[8]

Position and Policy of the Turkish Government

It may be assumed that the changes in the school textbooks reflect to a significant degree the shifts in Turkey's position towards Israel, especially vis-à-vis the Palestinian issue and Jerusalem. These positions were in the past and remain to date ambivalent: On the one hand, sustained dialogue and strategic-security-related and economic cooperation; on the other hand, harsh criticism of the State of Israel's treatment of Arabs in general, and of the Palestinians in particular.

Only a number of years after its recognition of Israel (in March 1949), Turkey recalled its diplomatic delegate in Israel (in November 1956) in protest of the Sinai–Suez operation in October 1956; yet practically speaking, the relations between both countries remained intact. The same occurred following the 1967 war, when Ankara supported UN resolution 242, calling for Israel's retreat from the Arab territories it had occupied during the war.

In the aim of drawing closer to the Arab and Muslim world, Turkey joined the "(New) Organization of the Islamic Conference" (the OIC, in 1969), where discussions were held on the fire set to the Al-Aqsa Mosque (by a Christian Australian, Michael Rohan), and the status of Jerusalem. Turkey supported criticism of Israel on the Palestinian issue, on a "humanitarian basis". And following the

1973 war – in which it sided with the Arabs – Turkey increased its diplomatic support of the Palestinians in the UN and in the PLO as being the single and legitimate representative of the Palestinian people (1975). In 1979 Turkey granted diplomatic recognition to the PLO and allowed it to establish a delegation in Ankara – not an embassy – similar to Israel's status.

However, in 1980 in response to the decision of Israel's Knesset to annex East Jerusalem, Turkey lowered the status of the Israeli delegation in Ankara and closed its consulate in Jerusalem for a period of time. The Turkish justification was: "Israel's uncompromising policy regarding the conflict in the Middle East, and the fait accompli that it seeks to establish regarding the status of Jerusalem."

Both public and governmental support of the Palestinians increased following the eruption of the first Intifada (1987); and in 1988 Turkey recognized Palestine as an independent state, and this was followed by its denouncement of the Israeli settlements in Palestinian territory. With the outbreak of the al-Aqsa Intifada (2000) the (secular) Turkish president, Ahmet Necdet Sezer, announced: "The Muslim world is deeply concerned over the violent actions against our Palestinian brethren after the Friday prayers in Jerusalem on September 28, in a place Islam holds to be one of the most sacred of all sites. Israeli soldiers used firearms . . . our Palestinian brethren have rights . . . including the establishment of their own state."

Turkish prime minister, Bülent Ecevit, expressed himself more bluntly when he defined the IDF's operation in Jenin (*Homat Magen*, April 2002) as "genocide before the eyes of the world" (he later retracted his words).[9] However, it is worth noting that these secular Turkish governments, and in their footsteps even Islamic governments, mediated between Israel and Arab countries to reach a political settlement, and worked during many years towards reinforcing diplomatic, strategic, military and economic ties with Israel.

Thus, for example, in 1991 Ankara raised the status of the Israeli delegation to that of an embassy; and following the celebrations marking 500 years to the Ottoman Empire's absorption of Jews expelled from Spain (1492), reciprocal visits were held by political and military leaders from Turkey and Israel. Besides more diverse military cooperation, the economic-commercial ties were greatly expanded between Turkey and Israel during the 1990s, totaling 3.5 billion dollars in 2008, which also included extensive tourism from Israel and many flight connections.

The Rule of Turkey's Party for Justice and Development

Recep Tayyip Erdoğan, head of the Islamic "Party for Justice and Development" and ruler of Turkey since 2002, also continued to nurture the relations with Israel in various fields, but mainly in trade and economics. He visited Israel in 2005 and announced at the "Yad Vashem" Holocaust Center that "anti-Semitism is a crime against humanity", and was awarded a prize by the Anti-Defamation League (a leading American Jewish organization). He also offered to mediate peace talks in the region and to strengthen the commercial and military ties with Israel. Israeli President Shimon Peres attended the Turkish National Assembly in 2006 (close to the visit of Palestinian President Mahmoud Abbas) and defined Turkey as "an important player in the Middle East in everything relating to the United States, Syria, the Palestinians and us".

Indeed, in addition to negotiations to build a new level at the Gate of the Moors (known also as the Mughrabi Gate) to the Al-Aqsa Mosque, and establishing a joint Israeli–Palestinian industrial park under the auspices of Turkey, Erdoğan mediated in 2007–2008 secret talks between Israel's prime minister Ehud Olmert and representatives of Bashar al-Asad, president of Syria. However, before these talks could be (successfully) completed, the IDF attacked the Gaza Strip in 2008, in response to the kidnapping of three Jewish lads near Hebron by Hamas activists. Erdoğan severely denounced this military action and swore that "Allah will punish" Israel; even prior to that, in 2004, Erdoğan defined the IDF's actions against Palestinians and the murder of Hamas leader Sheikh Yassin as "state terrorism" by Israel.[10]

Since then, relations between Erdoğan and the Israeli government have greatly deteriorated, especially with Prime Minister Netanyahu (who stated that Turkey cannot be a fair mediator in talks with Syria). The continued military actions against Palestinians, mainly in the Gaza Strip and the Al-Aqsa Mosque, deeply hurt the feelings of many Muslim Turks, and strengthened

their identification with Muslim Palestinians. These actions espe-
cially insulted Erdoğan's feelings, as he sees himself the leader of the
Sunni Muslim world and, inter alia, is increasing Islamization in
Turkey and supporting the Palestinian Hamas.

On May 31, 2010, the IDF attacked the Turkish ship *Mavi
Marmara* that sailed to Gaza, and killed eight Turkish citizens who
were aboard the ship. Erdoğan once again labeled this action as
"state terrorism" by Israel and recalled the Turkish ambassador in
Israel (who several months earlier had been humiliated by Israel's
deputy Foreign Minister Dani Ayalon who offered the ambassador
to sit on a very low chair in his office). Erdoğan also lowered
Turkey's diplomatic status in Israel, expelled Israel's ambassador in
Ankara, cancelled the military (but not the economic) cooperation
with Israel, and demanded Israel's apologies and compensation for
the killing of Turkish citizens on board the ship.[11]

In March 2013 he defined Zionism as "a crime against
humanity" and denounced the manifestations of Islamophobia as
being similar to Zionism, anti-Semitism and fascism (later, Erdoğan
explained that his statements did not stem from anti-Semitism, but
rather from his opposition to the State of Israel). At the time, with
the intervention of President Obama, Netanyahu apologized for the
Marmara Affair and promised to compensate the families of the
Turks who died, but later reneged on this promise.

Only in March 2016, after additional talks, did Turkey and Israel
agree to sign a reconciliation agreement, which included the reciprocal return of the countries' ambassadors to their posts, the
removal of sanctions and Israeli compensation to the Turkish
families. In addition, agreement was given for Turkish humanitarian aid to the Gaza Strip, including the building of a hospital, a
power station and a water desalination plant (up to August 2019
none of this was implemented). Even earlier, in December 2010,
Turkey sent two firefighter planes to help put out the raging fire on
Mt. Carmel; and in October 2011 Israel sent tents and prefab struc-
tures to help the victims of the earthquake in the Van region
of Turkey.

Yet, despite the reconciliation agreement and the reciprocal
gestures, it appears that Turkish–Israeli relations have remained in
a state of deep crisis in the past few years regarding regional strategic
relations, the Palestinian issue and the problem of Jerusalem and the
Al-Aqsa Mosque. At the regional level, these two countries have

stopped being strategic allies and have become harsh rivals, while Israel has replaced its alliance with this important country, with military and security-related ties with Turkey's historic (Christian) enemies – Greece and Greek Cyprus (this included a state visit by Netanyahu to Thessaloniki on June 4, 2017).

In the Palestinian arena, Turkey appointed for the first time, in 2013 (before other Arab and Muslim countries), an ambassador to the State of "Palestine" (which in fact does not yet exist) and called to include Hamas in the negotiations with Israel – all of which lie in direct contradiction to Israel's positions. For many years, international conferences have been held in Turkey in support of Hamas and "liberating" Jerusalem and the Al-Aqsa Mosque from the Zionists and Israel. Turkey even invested extensive funding in many projects to strengthen the "Muslim heritage in Jerusalem". In early May 2017, after having been re-elected as president, Erdoğan delivered a speech at the *al-Quds Alwaqf* Convention ("For the protection of al-Aqsa"), in which he defined Israel as racist, attacked it for its *Muazzin* Bill, and called for Muslim masses to march on the Al-Aqsa Mosque. After the Palestinian terrorist attack on Israeli soldiers at the entrance to the Temple Mount on July 14, 2017, and a temporary shutdown of al-Aqsa to Muslim worshipers, Erdoğan denounced Israel for applying exaggerated force and its attempt "to take al-Aqsa from the Muslims". During this period, in Turkey and in many other Muslim countries, heated demonstrations against Israel were held, also in response to the US Embassy's relocation to Jerusalem in May 2018.[12]

Against the background of these critical developments, in the worst-case scenario of damage to the Al-Aqsa Mosque or the Dome of the Rock by Jewish extremists, Turkey may join other Muslim countries, and perhaps even Shi'ite Iran, in a military response against Israel. The best-case scenario, if Israel agrees to the establishment of a Palestinian state and an acceptable resolution of the issues of East Jerusalem and the Temple Mount (*al-Haram al-Sharif*), may be that Turkey is able to convince Hamas to enter into a political agreement with Israel and together to build a regional Sunni–Jewish strategic alliance against the strategic threat of Iran and the "Shi'ite Crescent".[13]

Muslim–Jewish Relations in Central Asia

Jews lived in Central Asia for long time periods, in Uzbekistan, Kazakhstan, Turkmenistan, Kyrgystan, Tajikistan and Afghanistan. The most ancient and most prominent among them were the Jews of Bukhara, in Uzbekistan – who numbered 2,500 in 1885 and reached their apex in numbers in 1939, numbering 50,000; this included 13,000 in Tashkent and 3,000 in Samarkand, and additional Jewish populations from neighboring countries.

Jews reached these regions after the destruction of the Second Temple in 70 CE, and later, and their numbers increased during Muslim rule from the start of the 8th century. They experienced political changes in this Islamic religious, cultural and economic center for centuries, including the Russian conquest in 1873 and the release from Soviet rule in 1991. As in other Muslim regions, they experienced dual treatment from the Muslim governments and populace: On the one hand, the enforcement of political-legal-social limitations as members of patronage groups (*dhimmi*), the *Jizya* poll tax, dress codes, harassments and forced conversion to Islam (in the 18th and 19th centuries). On the other hand, tolerance and cooperation, especially under the Muslim–Uzbek rule, as well as extensive activities in economic fields and regional and international trade, including the Silk Road; in a variety of crafts; medicine; the arts – poetry, music and Jewish culture; and religious and educational activities.[14]

After the Russian occupation, Jews in the region continued living as inferior citizens within autonomous frameworks under local Muslim rulers, yet with commercial ties to Russia and cultural ties with other Jewish communities, including the Holy Land. After the Bolshevik revolution and the Balfour Declaration in 1917, many Jews immigrated to the Holy Land from Bukhara at different periods and established a neighborhood in Jerusalem. After 1948, nearly 8000 Jews from Bukhara were living in Israel.

Uzbekistan and Israel established diplomatic ties in 1992, one year after Uzbekistan's independence; its first ambassador to Israel noted that his country had provided shelter to thousands of Jewish refugees from the Holocaust, and that "Jews have lived in Uzbekistan for over one thousand years. And although there were some unpleasant times during that era, in general Jews were not oppressed and were well-integrated into the mainstream, holding

98

senior positions in politics and the free professions . . . Uzbekistan has a rich Jewish tradition", and that there is "a strong political (and strategic) dialogue between Israel and Uzbekistan" and additional good relations in tourism, trade and medicine. To this, the Chief Rabbi of Uzbekistan added that "the President had excellent relations with the Jewish community".[15] Nonetheless, at the same time, extremist Muslim organizations have expressed anti-Semitic and anti-Israel positions in Uzbekistan and its neighboring countries.

In Neighboring Countries

Bukhari Uzbek Jews settled also in neighboring Muslim countries in central Asia at various time periods, and contributed to the development of Jewish communities in different cities. In Kazakhstan, for instance, today there is a Jewish population numbering 4000 (in 1972 their number was 17,000). Some of them came from Russia during World War II; they are aided by twenty organizations and maintain synagogues and Jewish education. Kazakhstan has diplomatic relations with Israel, along with security-related and intelligence ties, as well as oil trade. In 1992, around 7,000 Jews resided Kyrgystan, some of whom were Bukhari and others, Russian. Today only several hundred Jews still live there.

Israel and Kyrgystan maintain diplomatic relations and the relationship is developing well. The Jews' presence in Tajikistan goes back earlier (to the second century AD), when some of them came from Bukhara and for centuries were tradesmen along the Silk Road. In 1989 15,000 Jews lived here, including Holocaust survivors from Europe. Their number decreased in 1994 to 2000. The majority immigrated to Israel. Israel and Tajikistan maintain diplomatic relations. In Turkmenistan there currently reside very few Jews, who in the past were employed in the fields of medicine, music, administration and teaching. This country also maintains diplomatic and economic relations with Israel.

However, as mentioned, in some of these countries anti-Jewish and anti-Israel sentiments were promoted by extremist Muslims. Such manifestations and the longing for the Holy Land and Jerusalem motivated many Jews to leave these countries and immigrate to Israel, at various time periods.[16]

Afghanistan

Amongst the Jews of Afghanistan, the ties to the Holy Land were the strongest, also as a result of the Muslims' Judeophobia (anti-Semitism) at various periods. However, there were long periods of tolerance and even amity from the Sunni Muslims. Thus, for example, wrote the Jewish traveler, Ephraim Neimark in 1885, probably with some exaggeration: "The Afghan (Sunni) will hate the Persian (Shi'ite) and love the Jew, will protect and pity him and consider him his brother."

According to various traditions and documents, Jews reached Afghanistan after their expulsion from the Holy Land (by Nebuchadnezzar in 586 BCE and Shalmaneser in 720 BCE). They integrated into the local tribes – especially the Pashtun, or Pathan (who, according to various traditions and theories, are the descendants of the ten lost tribes of Israel). After the rise of Islam, many Jews converted to Islam and were assimilated into Muslim society.

In the 12th century the Jews numbered 80,000, but their numbers dwindled drastically under Mongolian and Persian rule. Jews who were forcefully converted to Islam in Persia (as in Mashhad, for instance, in 1839), reached Afghanistan, returned to the Jewish faith and developed a spiritual and economic life there, which included extensive trade along the Silk Road. The Persian conquest of parts of Afghanistan (Herat in 1857) introduced severe suffering for the Jews and forced conversion of some of them. The Jews expected the British (who ruled in India and conquered parts of Afghanistan in 1839–1842) "to rescue us from the Ishmaelite exile . . . that we may be granted to see the great redeemer and go up to Jerusalem the faithful city with the joy of the house of God speedily in our own days . . .".[17]

In 1927, the Jews of Afghanistan numbered only 5000 – mainly in Herat, Kabul and Balkh, as a result of the frequent Muslim oppressions and emigration to other countries. Some years later, under the rule of King Nadir Shah, the Jews' conditions improved greatly and they were granted equal rights as citizens. However, after the king was ousted and Nazi influence spread in the country, Jews were cruelly oppressed by Muslims and were stripped of their livelihoods. This trend continued after the establishment of the State of Israel as well; most Afghan Jews immigrated to Israel during the 1960s. Israel and Afghanistan have no diplomatic relations, yet

100

Afghan President Karzai said in 2005 that he would be glad to establish full diplomatic relations with Israel once the Palestinians have a state of their own. The new president, Ashraf Ghani, expressed deep concern over the United States' decision in 2017 to move its embassy to Jerusalem, a step "that would insult the entire Muslim world".[18]

The Positions of Muslims in India, Pakistan and Indonesia towards Jews and Israel

The Jewish communities in India were among the oldest and largest in the region and the majority of their members (around 70,000) immigrated to Israel after its establishment. These communities had settled in this subcontinent and included the Jews of Cochin, who apparently reached the region with the tradesmen of King Solomon; Spanish and Portuguese Jews who came following the expulsion from Spain (1492); Jews from Baghdad and Britain who arrived at different periods in the 16th century; and congregations of *Bnei Yisrael*, *Bnei Menashe* and *Bnei Ephraim* – some of whom resided in Pakistan and others who converted to Judaism in the past decades and later immigrated to Israel.

For long stretches of time, Jews lived in peaceful coexistence with their Indian neighbors and held a wide variety of positions in the country's economy, society, administration and military (for example, General Jack Jacob who in 1971 was commander of the military front against Pakistan). In those regions included in Muslim Pakistan (such as Karachi), Jews suffered due to the conflict in the Holy Land and the establishment of Israel. As early as 1917, with the publication of the Balfour Declaration, the "Muslim League" in India expressed its concern for "the safety and sanctity of the holy sites" in Jerusalem. This League, and its leader, Muhammad Ali Jinnah, who was a secular Muslim, opposed the establishment of a Jewish homeland on Muslim territory, though another leader of the league, Zafarullah Khan, met with Chaim Weizmann and even visited Palestine/the Holy Land in 1945.

Earlier, delegations of Muslims from India had visited the Al-Aqsa Mosque, after many Muslims had donated funds to renovate the mosque in response to the request of the Mufti of Jerusalem, Haj Amin al-Husseini.[19] Muslim Pakistan, which broke away from India

101

in early 1947, resolutely opposed the UN Partition Plan of November 1947, despite its similarity to the division of India. However, Zafarullah Khan, Pakistan's first foreign minister, continued discussions and meetings with Weizmann in 1948 and expressed pragmatic-realistic positions towards the State of Israel, thus reflecting the duality that typified his country later on.

Indeed, in 1952, at a press conference in Cairo, Zafarullah Khan declared that the Arab world must accept the Jewish state as part of the Middle East, within the framework of a peace settlement; he repeated these positions publicly in Baghdad and Karachi – his country's capital. At another opportunity, he noted that the Jewish congregation in Karachi had not been harmed during the times of anti-Israel incitements; that Pakistan is not anti-Jewish; and that he supports bilateral diplomatic relations and ties between Israeli and Pakistani experts and students. Despite the pro-Arab sentiments of Muslim populations in Pakistan, its government and senior diplomats shared a strategic common denominator with their Israeli colleagues, i.e.: opposition to the Egyptian government of Abdul Nasser that supported Nero's India and its war against Pakistan in the Kashmir region. At a public meeting with Canada's Israeli ambassador in December 1956, the Pakistani ambassador ('High Commissioner'), expressed amazement at the IDF victory in late October 1956 in Sinai against the Egyptian army (which his government had officially condemned), and added that "not all Pakistanis were pro-Arab or anti-Israel and some of them, like himself, realized quite well what a menace Nasser was". In July 1957 the Pakistani prime minister said during an interview on American television that "the Arab state ought to recognize Israel and make peace with her . . . (and that) Pakistan might eventually serve as mediator."[20]

However, in the mid-1960s, the stand adopted by Pakistani politicians took a turn for the worse in reaction to a growing closeness between India and Israel, the hostile positions towards Israel among the Pakistani population and the orientation of the country's leaders towards the Arab and Muslim world. The latter supported the Arabs in the war of June 1967; and in 1969, Pakistan initiated founding the "Islamic Conference Organization" (later called the Organization for Islamic Cooperation – OIC), under the leadership of Zulfikar Ali Bhutto. Pakistan has continued its anti-Israel policies since 1971, and in the war of October 1973 it dispatched sixteen pilots to fight alongside the Syrian air-force against Israel (and also sent doctors and medics to Syria and Egypt).

At the 1974 conference of the OIC, held in Lahore, Bhutto announced: "To Jews as Jews we can only be friendly; (however) to Jews as Zionists – intoxicated with their militarism and reeking with technological arrogance – we refuse to be hospitable . . . among the Arab territories occupied by Israel al-Quds (Jerusalem) holds a special place in the Muslim hearts . . . any agreement . . . which postulates Israeli occupation of the holy city . . . will not be worth the paper it is written on."

In 1977, Bhutto was removed by a military coup led by General Zia ul-Haq, who some years later improved his government's position towards Israel and Arab–Israel relations. For example, he acted in favor of returning Egypt to the OIC, after it had been expelled following the peace treaty it had signed with Israel. At the same time, he began initiating secret military ties with Israel, even though Pakistan had then developed an atomic bomb, or a "Muslim" atomic bomb. In public, ul-Haq compared the religious character of the Jewish state with Muslim Pakistan.[21]

After the death of Zia ul-Haq, and the return of democratic rule to Pakistan, and against the background of normalization of India–Israel relations (1992), a fundamental discussion arose in Pakistani society on the recognition of Israel. The new prime minister (from 1990), Nawaz Sharif, said that he "is keen to reexamine Pakistan's policy towards Israel and even contemplate recognition and normalization" with Israel. Pakistan's delegate to the United Nations spoke publicly of the need for dialogue with Israel. Following the Oslo Accords (1993) between Israel and the PLO and the establishment of ties between Arab countries and Israel, the ensuing debate in Pakistan increased round the issue of recognition of Israel, amongst senior officials, diplomats, the media, and even religious leaders. Politicians and senior experts claimed that Pakistan must adopt a realistic policy vis-à-vis Israel and recognize it, especially after the PLO and other Arab countries had done so. This positive development was temporarily disrupted in September 1994, when then Israeli Prime Minister Yitzhak Rabin refused to grant Pakistani Prime Minister Benazir Bhutto permission to visit Gaza without prior coordination with Israel; and also added a public rebuke: "The lady from Pakistan should acquire some manners." However, one month later, the Pakistani government sent an official representative to the peace-signing ceremony between Israel and Jordan. And in an interview to the Israeli newspaper *Yediot Ahronot*, in January 1996, Mrs. Bhutto sharply denounced the murder of Rabin (November 1995) and compared it to the execution of her father, Zulfikar Bhutto, in 1978. She further added that she is waiting to see other important countries in the Middle East progressing in their relationship with Israel, and then Pakistan will be able to come to a decision.

Nawaz Sharif, who returned to rule Pakistan in 1997, tended towards normalizing relations with Israel, and was supported by part of the Muslim religious establishment. Concurrently, senior Muslim religious leaders visited Israel and the Al-Aqsa Mosque, met with officials of Israel's Foreign Ministry and recommended recognition of Israel. General Mirza Islam Beg as well, who was commander-in-chief of Pakistan's army (1988–1991) and later leader of a political party, said in 1997 that "we have no conflict with Israel, therefore we should not hesitate to recognize Israel". Along with that, Israel's deputy Defense Minister, Sylvan Shalom, said about a year later: "We do not see Pakistan as our enemy; Pakistan has never been an enemy of Israel, and never threatened Israel" (even considering the fact that it has an atomic bomb).

The motives and reasoning of the rulers of Pakistan towards recognizing Israel are linked to their interest in weakening the ties between India and Israel, improving the relationship with the United States, and "serving the interests of Muslim Palestinians in the best possible way". The new Pakistani president, General Pervez Musharraf (who gained control through a military coup in October 1999), also sided with recognition of Israel when he said, inter alia (in 2002), "What is our dispute with Israel . . . should we be Catholic than the Pope or more Palestinian than the Palestinians themselves?" Nonetheless, after a meeting between Pakistan's and Israel's foreign ministers in Istanbul (2005), he claimed: "We will not talk about recognition of Israel until a Palestinian state is established."[22]

A public argument developed in Pakistan following the meeting of the foreign ministers; senior politicians, both secular and religious, supported this meeting and the recognition of Israel after a Palestinian state is established. However, some of them emphasized the need to continue the dialogue with Israel to promote the national interests of their country. All this was in conflict with significant Islamic circles who opposed the dialogue with Israel "because it occupies sacred sites belonging to Muslims" and "Palestinian lands". The latter also claimed that ties with Israel run contrary to "Pakistani ideology", to the values of Islam and the Palestinian issue.

President Musharraf continued the dialogue also with the Jewish community in the United States and held a public meeting with delegates of the American Jewish Congress (2005). He praised the similarity between Islam and Judaism and the historic times in which "Jews and Muslims lived in peace and harmony . . . through cooperation and coexistence". He repeatedly said that there is no direct conflict between his country and Israel, and that normalization between both countries will be reached only after a Palestinian state is established. In 2005, a Pakistani delegation of high-ranking representatives of political parties visited Israel and the occupied territories. The delegation included religious leaders as well, one of whom declared that normalization with Israel will be achieved only after the establishment of a Palestinian state, with East Jerusalem its capital. At the same time, additional dialogues were held between Israelis and Pakistanis, and a Pakistani–Israeli Society of Friends was founded in Pakistan; in New York a forum for peace was established between the two countries in a variety of fields. In Britain as well a similar forum was initiated with senior politicians and intellectuals.

In a number of school textbooks published in Pakistan after the rise of Musharraf to power, the question of recognition of Israel was discussed in a positive vein. In the Islamist textbooks as well, tolerance and freedom of religion, as well as Muslim–Jewish dialogue, are presented as having been granted to the Jews by the prophet Muhammad. Yet, in other books, Jews are portrayed in an anti-Semitic tone: "Greedy, cruel, deceitful . . . enemies of Islam . . . traitors . . . who plotted to kill the prophet Muhammad." Additionally, the Jews' struggle for establishing a homeland in 1948–49 was presented in a negative and twisted manner. In May 2018, Pakistan denounced the United States' decision to transfer its embassy to Jerusalem, and expressed its support of establishing a Palestinian state with the pre-1967 lines, with East Jerusalem its capital.[23]

The Positions Held by Muslims in India

The "Muslim League" in India continued expressing anti-Semitic stands whilst the Indian Congress party expressed its opposition to the Jewish national aspirations in the Holy Land. League members wrote, for example, of Shylock, the Merchant of Venice, and described the Jews as "spies, financiers and conspirators"; and as put by the leader of the Muslim Students Association in India: "The Israelis are many times worse than Nazis." Muslim Indian academicians described Israel as haughty, illegitimate, colonialist, stealing Arab lands, and carrying out ethnic cleansing among the Arabs. They and many others accused Israel, after 1967, of plotting to destroy the Al-Aqsa Mosque and build the Holy Temple upon its ruins.

However, these Judeophobic extreme views did not represent all of India's Muslims (nearly 170 million – the third biggest Muslim population in the world, after Pakistan with 190 million and Indonesia with 250 million). Even though most Muslims in India – both religious and secular – continued supporting the Palestinians, there were a significant number – mostly from the elite strata – who supported the full diplomatic recognition of Israel by India in 1992. This stemmed from a realistic-pragmatic approach and the decisions of Arab and Muslim countries to establish ties with Israel after the Madrid Peace Conference (1990–1991) and also after the Oslo Accords (1993, 1995).

Senior Muslim politicians and academicians, who at first had opposed relations with Israel, came on official visits to Israel throughout the 1990s. Nonetheless, at times of conflict between Israel and the Palestinians, senior Muslims and Hindus demanded of their government "to freeze all diplomatic relations with the State of Israel until such time as it recognizes the rights of Palestinians." The latter described Israel's activities in the West Bank as "atrocities"; similar to the barbaric anti-Muslim actions of the Jewish nationalist government, from 1998 to 2004, that was a "partner" in the Jewish conspiracy against Islam and Muslims. Despite this criticism, Israel–India relations (led by the Nationalist moderate Prime Minister Modi as of 2014), were greatly expanded and deepened in military and economic fields, and gained further momentum following the reciprocal visits of the countries' leaders in 2017.[24]

Positions of Muslims in Indonesia

Similar to the Muslims in India and Pakistan (about 170 million and 190 million respectively), the Muslims in Indonesia (about 250 million) hold dual positions towards Jews and the Jewish state. On the one hand, ideological religious hostility (Judeophobia) is widespread in the general public, in textbooks, political parties and religious organizations. This, as a result of the education and indoctrination by Muslim Arab religious leaders and writers, who emphasize the Israeli–Palestinian conflict and the issue of Jerusalem and the holy sites of Islam, the Temple Mount/al-Haram al-Sharif.

On the other hand, prominent government figures and political and religious Muslim leaders, and religious groups as well, continue expressing pragmatic and even positive views towards Jews, alongside ongoing secret strategic relations with Israel. Some of these leaders have visited Israel and led religious and cultural dialogues with Jews and Israelis, and are calling for an alliance between the Jewish, Christian and Muslim civilizations. However, it appears that as long as the Israeli–Palestinian conflict and the issue of Jerusalem and the Temple Mount are not resolved to everyone's satisfaction, the animosity towards Israel and Jews may grow deeper and more extensive.

Judeophobia Resulting from Israel's Actions against Palestinians

"Jews are clearly . . . the most hated people among Indonesian Muslims, because Israel as a state executed severe wrongdoings against the human rights of the Palestinians for sixty years, since the establishment of the Jewish state in 1948 . . . even though Palestine is geographically far away, it is emotionally close for Muslims . . . Antisemitism began here in the 1960s. Today, influenced by extremist elements, slogans can be heard, such as: 'Go to hell, Israel', or 'Jihad against Jews'."[25] These harsh words, written in 2008 by an Indonesian journalist, reflect the views held of many Muslims in Indonesia, and especially of conservative and extremist political parties and Islamic organizations, which are also reflected in the educational system and the media.

Today the Jewish community in Indonesia numbers about 200 people, compared to 3,000 in 1945. Most of them live in the capital city, Jakarta, in Surabaya, Bandung and Manado. Most are the descendants of Jewish tradesmen who had arrived at different periods in Indonesia, starting from the 16th century, mainly from Holland and Iraq. For centuries, the majority lived in coexistence and cooperation with the Muslims; some intermarried with Muslims, whilst others fully integrated into the general society. The Jewish religion was never officially recognized, and there was hardly any anti-Semitism in the country. However, the hatred of Jews developed later on amongst a significant part of the Muslim population due to Israel's policies towards the Palestinians. For example, in late 2008, following Israel's military actions in Gaza, fanatic Muslims demonstrated near the synagogue in Surabaya and led to its closing and destruction.[26]

However, the main opposition to Israel and the Jews stemmed from Israeli activity in Jerusalem and the Temple Mount, such as when Ariel Sharon (the "bloodthirsty butcher") went up to the Temple Mount in September 2000, leading to the outbreak of the Palestinian Intifada. This led to numerous demonstrations by Muslims in Indonesia, who perceived all of Jerusalem as a Muslim city, the "city of God". In relation to these events, and even to prior developments, harsh anti-Semitic and anti-Israel messages were disseminated via the press, textbooks, pamphlets, articles and books (some written by Muslim Arabs).

A major portion of these messages is based on "The Protocols of the Elders of Zion", claiming that the Jews desire to rule the Islamic world and that Israel is a threat to it. Therefore, Jihad must be proclaimed in Palestine, to "defeat the Jews". Another important source of the hatred towards Jews and Israel are the passages in the Qur'an and the Hadith that supposedly present 76 bad traits of the Jews – such as swindlers, provocateurs, antagonists, etc.[27]

In contrast to these significant anti-Semitic and anti-Israel movements, mainly amongst fanatic and conservative Muslim political parties and organizations, moderate and pragmatic movements are active among the political and social elite, as well as in important religious Muslim organizations. The latter criticize the generalizations and selective inaccuracies voiced by the conservative-extremist groups; and present more positive interpretations of the Qur'an's text on Jews. They also support good relations with Israel, on condition that it resolves the Palestinian problem and the issue of Jerusalem. They further claim that in the schools in Indonesia there is hardly any studying about Judaism and Jews.

Thus, for example, they point to Abraham as the common father in the Judeo-Muslim tradition; to the first revelation of Allah that was given to Moses; the status of "People of the Book" bestowed upon the Jews in the Qur'an; and the relations between Jews and Muslims that were far better than that of Muslims and Christians or Jews and Christians throughout history. Similarly, moderate factions promote the conjecture that the "Protocols of the Elders of Zion" is a fake text that does not represent an historical truth, nor has been properly researched.

Abdurrahman Wahid (or Gus Dur), past president of Indonesia and leader of the largest Muslim movement (*Nahdatul-Ulama*), which represents the majority of traditional Muslims, for many years expressed sympathetic positions towards Jews and Israel. Till his death (in 2009), he held that the relationship between Muslims and Jews is comparable to that between siblings, and stems from the adherence to the monotheistic tradition of Abraham. He supported the establishment of diplomatic relations with Israel (yet did not implement it during his term as president), also as a means to peace between Israel and the Palestinians, which he tried to promote. He visited Israel several times, took part in the signing of the peace treaty between Israel and Jordan, and in the March for Peace in Jerusalem (which he saw as a city shared by Israel and the Palestinians); he played an important part in the Muslim–Jewish dialogues held at the Hebrew University and at the Shimon Peres Center for Peace, and also emphasized his concept of a joint Muslim–Jewish civilization.

Prof. Azra, former rector of the Islamic University in Jakarta, and an important researcher in the international community, expanded this even further and supported the alliance of three civilizations – Jewish, Christian and Muslim – also as a means to peace between Israel and the Palestinians.[28] Indonesian president Susilo Bambang Yudhoyono (2004–2014) believed that such peace could not be attained, nor the sense of dissatisfaction removed, "without a solution of the Arab–Israeli conflict and the issue of Jerusalem". President Suharto (1967–1998) also claimed that this conflict was harming Muslim–Jewish relations worldwide. Even though he did not officially recognize Israel, he maintained military ties with Israel (from 1972);[29] and in 1993 he held a private meeting at his residence in Jakarta with then Israel's Prime Minister Yitzhak Rabin. In 2005, at the UN General Assembly, Israel's Foreign Minister, Sylvan Shalom met with his Indonesian colleague. Later, in 2012, Indonesia opened a consulate in Ramallah (under the Palestinian Authority), which also handled economic ties with Israel and the official visits of many Indonesian senior figures to Jerusalem. Indonesian journalists met with Netanyahu in Jerusalem in 2016; prior to that, a joint association for cooperation was established at the Bureau of Commerce, between Indonesia and Jerusalem, with an office in Tel Aviv (2009).

However, the factor that prevents the largest Muslim country in the world to establish normal diplomatic ties with the Jewish state is the absence of a resolution to the Palestinian problem, and especially the issue of Jerusalem. As was written in a popular Indonesian song some thirty years ago: "Palestine is the holy place for Jews, Christians and Muslims/ a symbol of peace for the three heavenly religions/ but now your destiny encourages pity/ your land got poured with embers/ murder and killing in every corner/ women and innocent children/became the victims of the raging war/ Oh, the World, do not tear Palestine off/ help Palestine to regain peace." In May 2018, thousands of Indonesian Muslims demonstrated against the U.S. intention to transfer its embassy to Jerusalem. President Widodo as well condemned this action.[30]

6

The Muslim–Jewish Relationship in the Holy Land/Palestine

From the last few decades of the 19th century, significant and even critical changes and developments occurred in Muslim–Jewish relationships in the Middle East, North Africa, Asia and other regions. It resulted from the disintegration of the Muslim Ottoman Empire; the involvement of the great powers, Britain and France, which created national countries in Turkey and the Fertile Crescent; and the growth of nationalist movements – Jewish-Zionist, Pan-Arab and Arab-Palestinian.

Islamic identification and the traditional ambivalent attitude of many Muslims towards Jews continued for a long time, while the new secular and intellectual elite embraced more and more anti-European and anti-Zionist ideas. Indeed, a blatant trend that developed within Arab nationalist circles, and especially Palestinians, was opposition to the Zionist movement and Zionist activities in the Holy Land (that began in 1881). These were considered by many Arab Muslims as European-colonialist incursions, not nationalist-Jewish, that were plotting to take over Palestinian lands and damage its Arab and Muslim character. However, there were other Arabs and Palestinians who welcomed the Zionist movement, especially out of economic considerations,

Concurrent to that, the Muslim–Jewish dialogue and cooperation that had prevailed in the Holy Land and in other countries in the region for many years were diminishing, along with a blurring for many Arabs in the distinction between Jews and Zionists. A significant number of Jews in these countries, including Palestine/ the

Holy Land, perceived themselves as "Jewish Arabs", as a religious-ethnic minority, and not as a national-political minority. Some identified with the nationalist movements and regimes in their countries, and even disavowed Zionism. Others were drawn to Zionism, and in the wake of incidents of violence and incitement against them from nationalist Arabs and radical Muslims, Jews from the regional countries tended to join the Jewish Zionist movement.

As time passed, the distinction between Zionists and Jews disappeared nearly completely among Muslim Arabs, especially the radicals, who related to Jews as the prime enemy of Islam and the Muslims. This anti-Semitic, Judeophobic attitude was prominent in the Palestinian National Movement, headed by the mufti Haj Amin al-Husseini in the 1920s. The mufti exploited the deep feelings of solidarity, shared by many Muslims in the Holy Land and throughout the region, with the Holy sites of Islam in Jerusalem (and with Palestine), in order to spread anti-Jewish and anti-Zionist ideas and promote Palestinian national causes along with Pan-Islamic objectives (whereas the leaders of the Jewish-Zionist settlement proposed political solutions for the Palestinians).

The use of Islamic motifs by Arab leaders in the struggle against Jewish Zionists grew stronger after the establishment of the State of Israel and the Palestinian disaster (the *Nakba*) in 1948. It worsened after the defeat (*Naksa*) in 1967, with Israel's occupation of Arab territories in Egypt, Syria and Palestine (from Jordan), and mainly – East Jerusalem and Islam's holy sites. Arab leaders called from time to time for *Jihad* – a Muslim holy war – to liberate the Al-Aqsa Mosque, *al-Haram al-Sharif* (the Temple Mount) and Palestine from the Jews. The elements that throughout many years consistently acted with violence and incitement against Jews in Israel and elsewhere were the radical Islamic movements, such as the Muslim Brotherhood in Egypt and elsewhere, Hamas in the Gaza Strip and the West Bank, the Islamic Movement of Sheikh Raad Salah in Israel, Hizbullah in Lebanon and the Muslim Iranian regime (as of 1979).

On the other hand, despite the extensive spread of antagonism towards Jews and Israel amongst Arab and Muslim populations, there appeared in different countries governments and leaders, both secular and religious, who leaned – and even took action – towards coexistence, dialogue and cooperation with Jews and Israel (but did not concede on the control of East Jerusalem and the Temple

112

Mount/al-Haram al-Sharif). Their motives were pragmatic: economic, political and security-related interests, and at times even ideological. Most prominent were Amir Faisal, King of Syria (1918–1920); the kings of Transjordan and Jordan (from 1920), all descendants of the prophet of Islam, Muhammad; the Nashashibi family in Palestine during the era of the British Mandate; governments of Turkey and Iran for many years, after 1949; the Moroccan kings, Hassan II and Muhammad VI; and for a long period – Egyptian presidents Anwar Sadat, Husni Mubarak and Abd al-Fatah al-Sisi; the president of Indonesia, Abdurrahman Wahid, and other Muslim leaders. In 1988 the PLO recognized Israel and in 1993 signed with Israel the Oslo Accords.

The height of the Muslim and Arab pragmatic approach came in 2002 when all the Arab states (22 in number), with the support of all the Islamic states (57 in number, including the Arab countries, with Iran's abstention), offered Israel peace, security and normal relations in return for its agreement to the establishment of a Palestinian state alongside Israel, according to the 1967 lines, with East Jerusalem (including the Temple Mount) its capital. Israel's governments so far have not officially accepted the positive Arab-Muslim program (except for Israeli prime minister, Ehud Olmert, who offered Mahmud Abbas a similar plan in 2008), thus creating asymmetry between right-wing Israeli governments and the pragmatic stands of Arab and Muslim countries since the late 1970s.

Zionist leadership, Israel's governments and the majority of Israel's Jewish (mostly secular) population defined their struggles and wars, up to 1967, as against the Palestinian national movement and Arab countries, in national, political, territorial and non-religious terms. For example, they did not attribute much importance to the Temple Mount (except for the Western Wall – which became a national cultural symbol), and East Jerusalem – that was under Jordanian rule from 1948 to 1967. The exceptions to this were Jewish nationalist circles (mostly secular) in movements such as *Beitar, Lehi,* and *Herut,* and parallel to them, a religious messianic Zionist movement (not of the ultra-Orthodox). The latter sought to remove the Islamic holy sites at the Temple Mount, and rebuild the third Holy Temple.

These groups, especially the religious Zionist movement, grew stronger after "liberating" East Jerusalem and the territories of Judea and Samaria (the West Bank) in 1967. With partial backing of the

Likud party that came into power in 1977, and the *"Bayit HaYehudi"* party as of 2008, Jewish radicals have drawn up a plan for rebuilding the Holy Temple upon the ruins of the mosques. (In 1984, for example, Yehuda Etzion attempted to blow up the Dome of the Rock.) Towards that purpose, till now 19 different organizations for rebuilding the Temple have been established and have won increasing support from the rabbis of the religious Zionist movements as well as from secular Jews. These actions, along with thousands of Jews going up to the Temple Mount (against the guidelines of the Chief Rabbinate), have been interpreted by many Muslims in Israel and throughout the world as an insult and a threat to the holy sites of Islam and an expression of hatred of Muslims (Islamophobia). On the other hand, it is important to note that Jewish religious and political leaders, among them ultra-Orthodox rabbis and former heads of Israel's General Security Service, have warned time and again against any damage to the mosques by radical Jews, which might lead to a Muslim–Jewish Armageddon.

So far, we have reviewed in general lines the central developments and changes in the mutual and dual relationships between Muslims and Jews in the Holy Land/Israel and in the region, from the end of the 19th century till now: The symmetry and asymmetry in these relationships at different time periods; the manifestations of Muslim Judeophobia and Jewish Islamophobia on the one hand, and trends towards coexistence and cooperation between Muslims and Jews, Arabs and Zionists, Palestinians and Israelis, on the other hand. Following is a detailed examination of Muslim–Jewish relationships and their development in the Holy Land and in Muslim Arab countries in the region, from the 19th century onwards.

Devlopment of Muslim–Jewish Relations in the Holy Land/Palestine

From the first half of the 19th century, (non-Zionist) Jews, mainly from Europe, settled in Jerusalem and in agricultural communities and new urban neighborhoods. This was done through the help of generous Jews such as Moshe Montefiore and Edmond de Rothschild (the latter even encouraged agricultural settlements of Arabs alongside Jews). European consuls, especially the British, also helped Jews reside in the Holy Land and even influenced the Ottoman rulers to allow Jews to settle and to protect them from the harassment of their Muslim and Christian neighbors.[1]

In 1882, in the Holy Land under Ottoman rule, there lived between 30–40 thousand Jews, compared to half a million Muslims (and 70 thousand Christians, mostly all Arabs).[2] Jews lived mainly in the four holy cities – Jerusalem (15–20 thousand), Hebron, Tiberias and Safed. There was also a Jewish populace in Acre, Haifa, Nablus and Peki'in, as well as in new Jewish settlements. There were Sephardic Jews (most of whom were long-time Ottoman subjects), Ashkenazi Jews (most of whom were subjects of foreign countries). Some were not Zionists, and most were religious Jews from Europe and from Asian countries – including Yemen, Iraq, Persia and Bukhara – who immigrated to the Holy Land, motivated by messianic religious longing for Jerusalem, the Western Wall and the Temple Mount.

For example, the Kabbalist Chaim Vital wrote in 1562 that in his dreams a religious figure of the Dome of the Rock is flying over the Temple Mount". And in 1884, Rabbi Rahamim Nissim Yitzhak Falaji from Izmir wrote allusively of the need to uproot the mosque that had been built on the site of the Holy Temple on the Temple Mount. In the mid-19th century a senior Ottoman official wrote: "United in an undissolvable tie of common faith and interest, which gathers strength from their isolation and contempt . . . the Jews cherish the hope of one day regaining possession of Jerusalem . . ."[3] This, in addition to the prayers of Jews in the diaspora during 2000 years to return to Jerusalem and rebuild the Holy Temple.

However, Ottoman rulers in the 19th century were mostly kind to the Jews and protected them now and again from their neighbors' harassment and violence. The rulers granted the Jews religious freedom and the building of synagogues, even allowing them to pray at the Western Wall, but not on the Temple Mount. Yet, this treatment changed for the worse from 1881, after the Zionist immigrations began, when the governing rulers set limitations on Jewish immigration, on Jews residing in the Holy Land and their ability to purchase land. However, following the uprising of the "Young Turks" in 1908, the attitude towards Jews improved for a short time (and the idea was even promoted of a Muslim–Jewish alliance between the leaders of the "Young Turks" and the Chief Rabbi of Istanbul).[4]

As to the position of Muslims towards Jews in the Holy Land prior to the Zionist immigrations: They were ambivalent – positive and negative in different populations – with different emphases at various periods, influenced by a variety of factors and circumstances. On the one hand, their negative attitude of contempt and humiliation, and at times animosity as well, in keeping with the traditional Muslim stand towards religious groups who were under Muslim protection. As the British consul in Jerusalem wrote in 1839: "The spirit of tolerance towards Jews is not yet known here to the same extent it is in Europe . . . Still, a Jew in Jerusalem is not estimated much above a dog."[5]

Even worse: At times Jews were attacked violently, were injured or murdered. For example: during the revolt of the Arab peasants in 1834 – by Egyptian soldiers who then had control in the Holy Land, and by local rioters. The same ensued after the Damascus Libel (1840), and the blood libel in Jerusalem (1847) by both Christians and Muslims. However, for most of the 19th century, Jews enjoyed tolerant treatment from their Muslim neighbors (but not from their Christian neighbors), and lived together in dialogue and economic and social cooperation. A Jewish visitor to the Holy Land in 1859 wrote (with exaggeration): "The Ishmaelites (the Muslims) and the Jews do not hate one another. On the contrary, they love one another. However, it is towards the uncircumcised (the Christians) that the Ishmaelites bear their hatred." A year later, a local Christian wrote: "As for the evildoing of the Jews and their hatred towards the Christians – this is not surprising; but, the surprise is that the Muslims prefer for the Jews to the Christians."[6]

Muslims preferred Jews over Christians throughout long historic periods, out of theological, political and security-related considerations, such as: The ties of local Christians to powerful Christian European governments that constituted a potential threat to the Muslim Ottoman Empire (see also Chapter 2 above). An exception to this was during the time of Muhammad Ali, Egyptian ruler of the Holy Land and Syria (1831–1840) – at that time the Muslim Egyptian government preferred the Christians over the Jews because of its desire to win the support of Britain and France against the Ottoman Empire.

After Zionism appeared on the scene, Arab Christians took action in the region to create a common denominator with the Arab Muslims in establishing a joint national Arab movement that would oppose the Jewish Zionist movement. As the Jewish Zionist leader, David Yellin, summed up in brief, in Jerusalem in 1911: "Fifteen years ago, the Muslims hated the Christians whilst their attitude towards the Jews was that of disdain; today their attitude towards Christians has changed for the better, and towards the Jews – for the worse."[7]

In contrast, the attitude of Jews towards Christians in the Holy Land was very hostile, due to the blood libels the latter initiated and the fierce economic competition between Christians and Jews. However, towards the Muslims the Jews showed great respect, at times even appreciation, in gratitude for their tolerance; though at times, also with ridicule (though not publicly), stemming from their historic religious arrogance towards the descendants of Ishmael.

It should be stated that during this critical period, at whose epicenter a struggle was raging between two national movements over control of the Holy Land/Palestine, mutual ambivalent relationships continued to develop, though they were asymmetrical, between Arab Muslims and Zionist and non-Zionist Jews in the Holy Land (and the region). The central and consolidated factions in both national movements led a fateful struggle, practically at zero-sum game; and, amongst other things, they severely damaged the frail fabric of coexistence and cooperation between Muslim Arabs and non-Zionist Jews in various places.

Indeed, for a substantial number of years, even after the appearance of Zionism in the Holy Land, Arab Muslims made a distinction between Jews and Zionists, between the "foreign Jews" and the "local Jew" or the "Arab Jew". But also those who did not make this distinction tended to cooperate with the Zionist movement or maintain a dual attitude towards it. For example, Yusuf Dhiya al-Khalidi, an honorable Palestinian Muslim, chairman of the Jerusalem Municipal Council and member of the Ottoman parliament, wrote in 1899 to the chief rabbi of France, Tsadok Kahn, as follows: "Who can challenge the right of the Jews on Palestine? O Lord, historically it is really your land . . . the Zionist idea was completely fine and just . . ." But he then continued to express concern regarding potential Jewish control over the (Muslim) religious sites in Jerusalem, and proposed that the Jews settle elsewhere in the world: "In the name of God, let Palestine be left in peace."[8]

The ambivalent Muslim Arab attitude towards the Jewish Zionist movement was conspicuous also at the time of the Balfour

Declaration (November, 1917) and subsequent to it. This declaration, in which Great Britain promised the Jews a "national homeland" in Palestine (apparently in parts of it) gave rise to severe opposition from Arab Muslims and non-Arab Muslims both in the immediate region and beyond – in Syria, Iraq, Egypt and even India (by the "Muslim League", headed by Muhammad Ali Jinnah – see Chapter 5 above).[9]

In contrast, other Muslim Arabs accepted the Balfour Declaration and even cooperated with the Zionist movement, out of strategic, political and pragmatic considerations and interests, and perhaps even out of a certain sympathy towards the Zionist undertaking. Most prominent among them was the Amir (and later king) of Syria, Faisal, son of Hussein, Sharif of Mecca, descendant of the family of the prophet Muhammad.

In an agreement signed by Amir Faisal in January 1919 with Dr. Chaim Weizmann, leader of the Zionist movement, it was stated, inter alia, that: "Mindful of the racial kinship and ancient bonds between the Arabs and the Jewish people, and realizing that the surest means of working out the consummation of their national aspirations is through the closest possible collaboration . . . necessary measures shall be taken to encourage and stimulate immigration of Jews into Palestine, on a large scale as quickly as possible, to settle Jewish immigrants upon the land . . . Arab peasant and tenant farmers shall be protected in their rights and shall be assisted in forwarding their economic development." And in a letter to Felix Frankfurter, an American Zionist leader, Faisal wrote on March 3, 1919: "We Arabs, especially the educated ones, look with deep sympathy on the Zionist movement . . . we wish the Jews a most hearty welcome home . . . ", " . . . we are working together for a reformed and revised Near East, and our two movements complete one another. The Jewish movement is national and not imperialistic; our movement is national and not imperialistic and there is room in Syria (extended, including the Holy Land/Palestine) for both of us, and neither can be a real success without the other."

Additionally, this agreement granted religious freedom to all religions, but did not mention the holy sites for Jews (and Christians) in Jerusalem, yet stated that the Muslim holy sites will come under Muslim control.[10] This perhaps indicates the allegiance of Faisal, the Arab Muslim, to the holy sites of Islam, in contrast to the secular

118

Zionist, Weizmann, who made no mention of the significance of the holy sites for Jews in Jerusalem.

The Faisal–Weizmann agreement was never implemented, yet for many years Muslims and Jews continued to maintain dialogue, to live in peace and even to jointly visit the holy sites of both religions (Jews were allowed to visit the Temple Mount as tourists). Jews publicly danced in the annual Muslim ceremony of the march from Nabi Musa to al-Aqsa, with waving flags of Abraham (Ibrahim) and Moses (Musa). According to comprehensive research done by Menachem Klein, in other cities such as Jerusalem, Jaffa, Hebron (and Haifa) a Jewish–Arab (Muslim) identity of sorts was created with a common language, similar attire and customs, and the publication of Hebrew-Arabic dictionaries and newspapers; partnership in cultural societies and periodic festivals. It was then said that the "Jews are children of this land".[11]

There was Jewish–Muslim cooperation along the political axis as well. For example: When Arab mayors were elected also by Jewish votes in 1927, such as Raghib Nashashibi in Jerusalem, and Hassan Shukri in Haifa, who was pro-Zionist. The Jerusalemite Nashashibi family in fact headed a large, but unconsolidated group of Muslim Palestinian Arab families that were urbanites, villagers and Bedouin, all of whom held pragmatic and even at times sympathetic positions towards the Jewish Zionist settlements in the Holy Land. This stemmed from considerations of economic and political benefit, ties with the Mandate government and, to a large degree, as opposition (*mu'arada*) to the Muslim Arab nationalist anti-Jewish-Zionist wing that controlled the Supreme Muslim Council (*majlisiun*), led by the mufti, Haj Amin al Husseini.

Other members of the opposition group included additional Jerusalemite families, such as the Khalidi and Dajani families, and mayors such as Umar Bitar of Jaffa, Sulayman Tuqan of Nablus, and village leaders from the Abu Ghush, Darwish and Zuabi families. To this, must be added the Muslim religious leaders, such as Asad Shuqayiri, the Mufti of Acre (and father of the founder of the PLO – Ahmad Shuqayiri) and Abdallah Tahbub, Mufti of Hebron; also, the Muslim Qadis of Jerusalem, Beer-Sheva and Beit-Shean.[12] They presented their moderate positions towards the Jewish Zionist enterprise as authentic Muslims and loyal Palestinian Arab nationalists. Thus, for example, some of the political frameworks they founded carried names such as the "National Defense Party", the

"National Muslim Association" and the "Congress of the Muslim Nation".

As early as the 1920s, the president of the National Defense Party and mayor of Haifa, Hasan Shukri, wrote (at the request of the Zionist administration and apparently influenced by the Faisal–Weizmann Agreement in 1919), as follows: "We do not consider the Jewish people as an enemy bent upon harming us; on the contrary, we see in the Jewish people a brother who is helping us build our shared country. We are convinced that without Jewish immigration and without financial aid, the country will not develop economically." And in 1930 Muhammad Tawil, a political activist and publicist, who perceived himself as "more nationalist than others", wrote that: "The Muslims want to live with the Jews in Palestine for the benefit of the country's internal condition." Alongside these economic motives, which included selling land to Jews as well and accepting Zionist financial support, there were Palestinians who viewed the cooperation with the Jews from an historical and ideological aspect, meaning: As a continuation of the historic coexistence between Arabs and Jews. Some expressed it thus: "Since the time of our common Father, Abraham . . . it is unworthy to harm our neighbors . . . such action goes against human morality and the command of the prophets . . ."

These Arab Muslim spokesmen also rebuffed being categorized by the nationalist religious Husseinis as traitors and collaborators with the Zionists; and in response, condemned the Husseinis' aggression towards Jews as "harming Islam and Arab nationalism". During the Arab revolt (1936–1939), "Peace Groups" of the Nashashibi family cooperated with the British and the Zionists against the Husseini rebels; and in 1937, Nashashibi leaders supported the recommendations of the British Peel Commission, which proposed dividing the Holy Land between Arabs and Jews and annexing some of the Arab territories to the Transjordan Emirate under the rule of Abdallah.[13] However, in the ideological-political struggle between the moderate Nashashibis and the extremist Husseinis, the latter had the upper hand, thanks to the Mufti's Islamic nationalist position on the one hand, and the increasing Jewish Zionist challenge on the other hand.

The charismatic mufti, Haj Amin al-Husseini, who presided as president of the Supreme Muslim Council from 1921, and led the Palestinian National Movement, fully exploited the deep devotion of Palestinian and non-Palestinian Muslims to Islam and its institutions, its Arab national ideas, and their fear of the political, social and economic dynamics of the Jewish Zionist *yeshuv* (settlement). He underscored the supposedly severe danger that Jews posed to the holy sites of Islam on the Temple Mount, and the Arab-Islamic nature of Palestine. In this regard, he was referring to the attempts of wealthy Jews, as early as the 1920s, to purchase the site of the Western Wall, which is considered a sacred Muslim site, and the Jews' ambitions to supposedly gain control over the Temple Mount/al-Haram al-Sharif, which includes the Al-Aqsa Mosque and the Dome of the Rock. The Mufti also made use of posters produced by Jews showing Theodore Herzl gazing upon the Temple Mount, and photos of the Dome of the Rock decorated with the Star of David.[14]

The Mufti mainly indicated the attempts by members of the *Beitar* group to gain control of the Western Wall in August 1929; these led to riots between Muslims and Jews in Jerusalem, Hebron and Safed, with many killed and injured on both sides, including amongst non-Zionist Jews as well. Haj Amin al-Husseini did not stop with the Palestinian Muslim Organization in fighting the Jewish *yeshuv*, but actively enlisted the Arab and Muslim world to help protect the holy sites of Islam in Jerusalem. In an all-Muslim conference held in Jerusalem in 1931, he succeeded in winning moral, financial and even military support from Arab and Muslim countries towards the struggle against the Jews and the British.

Among the most prominent Muslim volunteers was, for example, 'Izz ad-Din al-Qassam, a Syrian cleric who had reached Palestine in the early 1930s and organized an armed band that operated against the British and Jews in the Haifa area. He was killed by British soldiers in 1935 (the Hamas military organization, the 'Izz ad-Din al-Qassam Brigade, is named after him). After some time, committees for "the defenseof Palestine" were established in Arab countries by Pan-Arab circles, and an unofficial military force was organized, led by Fawzi al-Qawuqji, a former Syrian officer who had been involved in the Arab revolt in Palestine (1936–1939).[15]

At the same time, and influenced by the anti-Zionist struggle in the Holy Land (along with the rise of Nazism), the distinction between Jews and Zionists became blurred among nationalist and Islamic circles in Arab countries, such as Iraq, Egypt and Syria. Acts of violence were on the rise against Zionist and non-Zionist Jews, as will be examined further on. Violence against Zionist and non-Zionist Jews in the Holy Land had begun in the 1920s with the cries of *"Idhbah al Yahud"* (slaughter the Jews), and *"Nishrab dam al-Yahud"* (we will drink the blood of the Jews), as occurred in 1920–1921 in Jaffa and Jerusalem, and more extensively in 1929, following the riots at the Western Wall, in Hebron, Jerusalem and Safed.

In Hebron, Muslims cruelly massacred and injured scores of Jews – men, women and children, both Ashkenazi and Sephardi. Most were not Zionists. However, other Muslims rescued scores of Jews.[16] During the time of the Arab revolt (1936–1939) and after the UN Partition resolution in November 1947, Palestinian Arabs and non-Palestinian volunteers attacked Jewish targets.

The Mufti was involved in most of the Arab acts of violence, if in the form his leadership or by his inspiration – and used Muslim anti-Jewish/anti-Semitic language, especially against the background of the struggle over the holy sites. Thus, for example, he was involved in establishing the Muslim Palestinian military organization, *"al-jihad al-Muqaddas"* (the holy Jihad) that fought the Jews in the 1930s and in 1948. The Mufti defined the national struggle against the Jews as a Muslim–Jewish religious struggle, saying: "The primary impulse that motivated the Jews to think of transforming Palestine into a national home for themselves was religious – the religious idea that surges in their hearts and aims at rebuilding the Jewish Holy Temple of Solomon on the site of the holy aA-Aqsa Mosque . . . we must fight the Jews with their own weapon, the weapon of religion." At the same time, the Mufti was influenced by the rise of Nazism in Germany and their attitude towards Jews. During World War II (1941), the Mufti found shelter in Berlin; and in 1942 promises were made to him by Nazi leaders for the "destruction of the Jewish homeland in Palestine" and the battle against "worldwide Jewry".[17] The question that should now be addressed is, how did the Jewish population react, and what was the position of the Jewish population in the Holy Land towards their Muslim Arab neighbors and their many factions?

Positions of the Jews towards Muslim Arabs in the Holy Land/Palestine

First, it should be noted that many Zionist Jews ignored or denied the existence of Muslim Arabs and their long history of residence in and political affinity to the Holy Land. Other Jews, though not many, were aware of the presence of a majority population of Arabs. Yet, like the Muslim Arab political society and community, the Jewish Yeshuv in the Holy Land also held different, and even conflicting, views towards their Arab neighbors: From peaceful coexistence to military struggle; and in comparison, a certain asymmetry developed in the attitudes of the mainstream on both sides.

In contrast to the dominant Palestinian movement that was religious, anti-Jewish and aggressive, under the Mufti's leadership, the Zionist movement headed by Ben-Gurion was mostly secular and sought a political settlement with the Palestinians, similar to the position held by the Palestinian opposition groups. On the other hand, the (Jewish) Revisionist opposition, which also was mostly secular, yet nationalist and militant, upheld seizing through the force of arms control over the entire country ("the Iron Wall"), similar to the Palestinian religious nationalist movement. Also the messianic religious Zionist faction, such as the nationalist Jews, strove to control the Temple Mount and rebuild the Holy Temple.

In contrast, a small faction on the fringe of the Zionist movement strove for peaceful coexistence and social and political cooperation with the Arabs, even at the cost of relinquishing full political sovereignty. It included several groups, at whose center was *Brit Shalom* and the *HaShomer HaTza'ir* who were active during the Mandate era, but had no significant dialogue partners from the Palestinian side. In this regard, it is noteworthy that Zionist leaders and personages met with Arab leaders, mostly non-Palestinian, even prior to the Faisal–Weizmann Agreement (1919) and tried to reach understanding and agreements on Arab–Jewish coexistence in the Holy Land. Some of them lauded the closeness between Judaism and Islam, between Jews and Arabs and the existing friendship between Jews and Muslims.

For example, Nahum Sokolow suggested that Jews draw closer to Arab culture, learn Arabic and Arab literature and together with the Arabs build a "great Palestinian culture" while "reviving our

Semitic language". Ahad-Ha'am and Moshe Smilansky had similar views regarding culturally-based close ties with the Arabs.[18] The philosopher Martin Buber, who took part in establishing the "*Brith Shalom*" movement (1925) and the "*Ihud*" party (1942), wrote in 1924: "Islam is a much greater reality than we would wish to admit . . . It is our duty to get to know this reality . . . the Arab population is much more strongly conditioned by Islam than the Jews in general are by Judaism. Religion for the Arabs is also a matter of culture; hence we have been remiss in not acquainting ourselves with Islam . . . the prime necessity for personal contact is a knowledge of the Arabic language." And in 1939, in a letter to India's leader, Gandhi, Buber wrote that "we must fight to have the Jews seek true peace with the Arabs . . . both peoples should together develop the land's economy – and find new ways to reach compromise and agreement with each other . . . we wish to live alongside them, we don't wish to rule over them."[19]

Another partner to these ideas was Yehuda Magnes, president of the Hebrew University (1935–1948), which in 1926 established the Institute for Oriental Studies where professors, most of whom were German-born and sympathetic to Islam, taught the culture of Islam and initiated important research projects on Arabs and Islam. Another group that sought continued cultural, social and economic coexistence with the Muslims were the old-time inhabitants in the Holy Land, most of Sephardic origin, living in several cities; and the anti-Zionist Jewish-Arab Communist Party was the first to support a two-state solution for two nations.[20]

Mainstream Zionism

Supposedly, the mainstream of the Zionist movement in the Holy Land (the party of the Land of Israel Workers) led by Ben-Gurion and the Jewish Agency, aspired to reach a political agreement with the Arab National Movement, and at first even thought of establishing a bi-national Arab–Jewish state in the Holy Land, with equal status for both nations, through cooperation and contribution towards improving the economic conditions of the Arabs.

The Arab national leaders repudiated these suggestions in principle, not only because the Jewish *yeshuv* then formed a minority in the Holy Land, but also due to their fear of the Jews taking control over the land; and from their objection to Jewish arrogance. Thus, for example, Musa Alami, one of the prominent, moderate Palestinian leaders, replied as follows to Ben-Gurion's suggestions in 1933 to help the Palestinian economy: "I prefer to see this land poor and desolate for even another hundred years until we Arabs acquire the strength ourselves to develop it and bring it to bloom, and will not need your help."[21]

The Jewish Zionist leadership tried to form ties and understandings with the Muslim public in the Holy Land that constituted the great majority of the Arabs and traditionally was more moderate than Christian Arabs, who manifested anti-Jewish/anti-Semitic tendencies. The Jewish Agency initiated and supported the establishment of Muslim associations seeking "understanding and peace" with the Jewish *yeshuv*, such as the "National Muslim Association", and Muslim personages from among factions that opposed the Mufti. However, this association and its like, as well as moderate Muslim leaders, did not gain much public influence and were pushed to the fringes by the "Muslim–Christian Association" and other extremist groups that came under the Mufti's authority.[22] These Muslim leaders and others, as mentioned above, empowered their public status and the anti-Jewish sentiments among many Muslims by claiming that the Jews were aspiring to take over al-Haram al-Sharif – the Temple Mount – and rebuild the Holy Temple upon it. These claims leaned on the attempts by Jews to purchase the Temple Mount, and at least the Western Wall; and also upon statements made by Jews such as Alfred Mond (Lord Melchett) regarding the building of the Temple, and photos of Herzl with flags, a *menorah* and the Star of David over the Dome of the Rock.

In 1934, Ben-Gurion replied to Musa Alami, who had voiced these claims, as follows: "I told him that though Orthodox Jews believe, and it is no secret, that the Holy Temple will be rebuilt, this will happen only after the coming of the Messiah . . . by a miracle and not in a natural way."[23] Other Jewish leaders such as Chaim Weizmann explained to Muslim leaders that Jews want to pray at the Western Wall and not harm the holy sites of Islam. However, many Muslims were not convinced, and even opposed the Jews' praying at the Western Wall, which they considered part of the defined area of al-Haram al-Sharif/al-Aqsa (al-Buraq).

The Jewish Zionist leadership, which was consolidated and

dominant, was mostly secular and, unlike its Palestinian opponent, did not utilize religious Jewish motifs in its struggle against the Palestinian leadership. Thus, for instance, Chaim Weizmann refrained from noting the importance of Jerusalem for Jews in his agreement with Faisal (1919); the Zionist leadership also agreed to relinquish actual ties to Jerusalem when it accepted the Peel Program in 1937 and the Partition Program in 1947. Even in Israel's Declaration of Independence of 1948 no mention is made of Jerusalem; all this stemmed from the leadership's agreement to Jerusalem's internationalization.

However, in the end, the central Zionist leadership saw the Palestinian National Movement as an ideological, political and socio-economic threat, and in its struggle against it – a zero-sum game of sorts. With its European orientation and reliance on Britain (the Balfour Declaration), the Zionist movement strove with significant success to establish a national Jewish homeland; and further along the line, to establish a sovereign state; to build separate and autonomous institutions, including a military force and an educational system; to base itself on "Hebrew labor"; to purchase additional lands; to increase the number of immigrants from Europe and spread Zionism amongst the old Jewish population – Sephardi and Ashkenazi alike.

However, unlike most Sephardi Jews and few Ashkenazi Jews, many European Zionist Jews, both secular and religious, treated Arabs (Muslims) with arrogance, scorn and disrespect, and looked upon them as savages ("worse than the Russian hooligans in the pogroms"), and perceived themselves as "introducing civilization into this remote land".[24] According to Prof. Israel Bartal, researcher of the Zionist movement: "The leaders of the movements and of the Jewish *yeshuv* expressed their doubts regarding possible Jewish-Arab integration and tended to intentionally distance the Jewish *yeshuv* from social and cultural contact with the neighboring people . . . not only did they belittle the local Arab leaders . . . they also were patronizing in all cultural aspects and preferred ties with Europe." This attitude continued up to the establishment of the State of Israel and characterized the positions of the Labor Party leaders, such as Shimon Peres (see below).[25]

The Revisionist Position

This attitude of superiority was more prominent in the nationalist-secular revisionist movement (the "New Zionist Federation"). The founder and leader of the movement, Ze'ev Jabotinsky, claimed for example that "Ishmael isn't our uncle, thank God we belong to Europe and for 2000 years we helped create Western culture"; he further stated that Islam was a hollow and idolatrous religion (groups within the religious Zionist movement also repudiated Ishmael and perceived it as an idolatrous, negative and harmful figure). Prof. Yosef Klausner, one of the spiritual leaders of the Revisionist movement, called for linguistic-cultural isolationism from the Arabs. Prime Minister Benjamin Netanyahu, a scion of the Revisionist movement, also said in July 2017 that Israel is "part of the European culture", and that the Muslim immigrants to Europe are "barbarians", and years earlier he called the Arab Spring, the "Muslim Winter". In his book, *A Place Under the Sun* and in many speeches, he defined Israel as holding the front line of Western civilization in its struggle against Islam.[26]

Even prior to the central Zionist movement, the Revisionist stream was aware of an Arab movement in the Holy Land, but did not side with any political agreement with it; rather, it sought to control Palestine on both banks of the Jordan River via a Jewish majority and a strong military force ("Iron Wall"), while providing the Arabs with equal rights (as expressed in a song of the *Beitar* movement: "There, the son of Arabia shall enjoy abundance and joy, as shall the son of Nazareth . . . ").

Though they were secular, the political and spiritual leaders of this movement utilized a religious-Jewish motif out of ideological reasons, as well as the desire to enlist Jewish support in the Holy Land and from the diaspora, to "redeem" the Western Wall and even the Temple Mount. Some amongst them even called for violent attacks on the holy sites of Islam (this was certainly claimed by Muslim leaders). The Revisionist poet, Uri Zvi Greenberg, wrote in 1924 a poem about "dismembered Jerusalem", in which, inter alia: "Your head has been spattered, a mosque is attached to your neck, a glorious house for the Muslims, like a burial stone on a proud torso, and beneath it the blood is absorbed."

Other extremist Jews, like the members of *Beitar, Etzel (Irgun)* and *Lehi (the Stern Gang)*, planned or tried to explode the mosques on the Temple Mount, as in 1925 and 1947.[27] Others, Such as Abba Ahimeir, founder of *Brit HaBiryonim*, the Ruffians' Alliance (together with Uri Zvi Greenberg in 1929), advocated seizing control of the Western Wall by force. And, as noted above, the *Beitar* movement was the leading Jewish factor – along with Muslim extremists – that led to the eruption of riots at the Western Wall in 1929, resulting in scores of Jews and Arabs killed and wounded in Jerusalem, Hebron and other places.

Additionally, the *Etzel* organization, founded by Ze'ev Jabotinsky, killed and wounded many Arabs, including women and children (in response to the Arabs' killing of Jews), and also placed bombs in Arab markets (and carried out the bombing of the King David Hotel in 1946), and led the massacre of Arab villagers in Dayr Yassin in 1948. And, finally, the nationalist-secular *Lehi* movement, in its Declaration of Principles from 1940, listed the "building of the third Holy Temple as a symbol of full redemption."[28] (See also further on, Chapter 9.)

The Positions of Religious Zionist Jews

In comparison to the positions held by the Revisionist circles towards Arabs and Muslims and the issue of the Temple Mount, which were nationalist and secular with only a smidgen of Jewish religiosity, the positions held by the religious Jewish population were more complex and ambivalent, at different time periods. In part, these stemmed from nationalist-religious outlooks; in part, from messianic and historic religious beliefs; and there were some that aspired towards satisfactory or tolerable coexistence with the Muslims.

The longing for the Holy Land and Jerusalem and the belief in rebuilding the Holy Temple has remained so forcefully existent in the hearts of many Jews ever since the destruction of the two Temples. It is expressed in the daily prayers, in various ceremonies, and in the immigrations and settlements in the Holy Land and particularly in Jerusalem from the 16th century and on. And like many Muslims who mostly looked upon Jews with contempt as heretics and deniers of Islam, a substantial number of Jews perceived the sons of Ishmael (Muslims) as inferior and wild, based on the image of Ishmael in the Holy Scriptures and on homiletic exegeses. Rabbi Bahyah Ben-Yosef Ibn-Paquda wrote: "The sons

128

of Ishmael came from another place, another God . . . the Ishmaelites are our brothers in the flesh, and not in the soul and not in spirit . . ." However, as noted in Chapter 1, most Jews who lived in Muslim countries did not dare express such negative opinions, out of fear of the ruling bodies ("The law of the land is the law" – is binding).[29]

With that, many did believe and even stated that "The rule of Ishmael is moderate", "A rule of grace", and preferred it manifold over the "evil Edomite (Christian) rule". Most prominent amongst the few religious leaders who expressed themselves sharply against Islam and its holy sites was Maimonides, in the 12th century, most likely as he had been persecuted by the North African extremist Berber Muslim Almohad Khalifate, "*al-Muwaḥḥidūn*", and had been forced to convert to Islam for the sake of appearance. In his "Letter to Yemen" he wrote, "Never has a more bitter enemy risen against Israel than the Ishmaelite nation", and also, "The Ishmaelite nation increasingly harms us, to our misfortune, and no greater evil has ever threatened Israel as it has."[30]

According to a controversial conjecture of the Institute for the Holy Temple, Maimonides went up to the Temple Mount in 1166 (during the Crusader Era); however, no solid evidence supports this, nor his statements regarding the rebuilding of the Holy Temple and destruction of the mosques. Two references are found from the 19th century regarding this issue: The first, by Rabbi Rahamim Falaji of Izmir, who in his prayers expressed the destruction of the Al-Aqsa Mosque; and the second, by Rabbi Zvi Kalischer of Germany, who proposed renewing the ceremony of the Passover sacrifice on the Temple Mount.[31]

From the end of the 19th century, with the Zionist immigration to the Holy Land, different attitudes evolved within the religious circles towards Muslims (Arabs) and the issue of the Temple Mount: they were the religious Zionist movement, the ultra-Orthodox and the Sephardi Jews, all of which were organized in the *Mizrahi* movement, *Hapoel Hamizrachi*, the religious Kibbutz movement, the old-time *yeshuv* in the Holy Land, and the anti-Zionist *Neturei Karta* group. Many in the religious Zionist movement clung to the Messianic teachings of Maimonides according to which the Holy Temple would be rebuilt only after the coming of the Messiah. Yet, they added, now is the time to prepare for that by training *Cohanim* (Temple priests) and Levites (their

129

assistants). Towards that purpose, Rabbi Avraham Yitzhak HaCohen Kook established, in 1921, the *yeshiva* (religious college), *Torat Cohanim*, in Jerusalem, but forbade Jews to go up to the Temple Mount till the coming of the Messiah. His son as well, Rabbi Zvi Yehuda HaCohen Kook, shared these beliefs, but also advocated redemption of the land and use of force and messianic activism.

Other rabbis from the religious Zionist movement followed his teachings, especially the religious national faction linked to *Gush Emunim* (the Block of Faithful), that aspired to rebuild the Holy Temple on the ruins of the mosques, and thus also expressed their anti-Islamic opinions.[32] As to the attitude towards Muslim Arabs and the future of the Holy Land, there was deep disagreement between the extremists and the moderates in the religious Zionist movement. The extremists continued to identify the Muslims as the "savage" Ishmaelites, calling them "terrorists" and "Amalek" that must be destroyed: "Islam leads the abysmal and nationalist hatred of Israel – a culture that is forever attached to the religion of the sword"; "There is Arab and Muslim anti-Semitism . . . and the Holy Land does not belong to Ishmael, not even in part, but rather to Israel alone". Rabbi Shlomo Ben-Hamo, who studied under Rabbi Zvi Yehuda Kook, claimed that "It is God's will that Ishmael surrender to its master . . . the subjugation of the descendants of Ishmael and their inferiority and their recognition of the superiority of Judaism". Rabbi Goren wrote about Armageddon and the rebuilding of the Holy Temple as part of the process of the redemption of Israel.[33]

On the other hand, moderate groups within the religious Zionist movement, such as the religious Kibbutz movement, *Hamizrachi* and *Hapoel Hamizrachi* during the British mandate period, supported equality and peace with the Arabs, and the division of the Holy Land between Jews and Arabs (Muslims). Thus, for example, the journalist, Rabbi R. Binyamin, of the *Mizrachi* movement, wrote in the early 20th century: "The Arab nation resides in the Holy Land . . . it has fertilized many fields of wisdom and its name has spread throughout the world, and God has given them the prophet Muhammad, a prophet from amongst them . . . . God is the Lord God and Muhammad is His prophet, who has taught his people to discard foolish beliefs and to pursue charity and justice and cling to the Lord God of Israel, the God of Abraham and the prophets."

Moreover, other rabbis of the *Mizrahi* movement agreed to relinquish East Jerusalem as a part of the future Jewish state, meaning: An agreement to continued British rule in Jerusalem, as per the recommendation of the Peel Committee (1937), or the internationalization of Jerusalem, and the Partition Plan (1947). Their understanding was that "the Old City is a matter for the Messiah, we won't conquer it, it must occur by a Higher Power . . .".[34] In contrast, important circles within the *Mizrahi* and the *Hapoel Hamizrahi* movements radicalized their positions towards Muslim Arabs after the 1948 war, and especially after the 1967 war, as will be discussed further on.

The ultra-Orthodox *Agudat Yisrael* anti-Zionist movement strove for coexistence and cooperation with the Arabs and continued its opposition to the religious Zionists' aspirations regarding the Temple Mount and the Western Wall. In a letter addressed to the Muslim Congress in Jerusalem, in 1931, *Agudat Yisrael* stated as follows: "It is incumbent upon us to herewith proclaim that the Jews have no intention of harming the (Muslims') rights over their holy sites or to claim any right over these places . . . we spurn absolutely any suspicion to the effect that we desire to claim rights over your holy site, known as the Al-Aqsa Mosque . . . and as to the Western Wall . . . our one desire is that like our forefathers, we too shall be able to pour out our hearts in prayer undisturbed . . ." The *Aguda* even opposed the Jewish Zionist control of the Western Wall.

However, following the bloody massacres of 1929 and the rise of a Nazi government in Germany in the 1930s, and after the Arab revolt in 1936, *Agudat Yisrael*'s positions drew closer to those of the Jewish Zionist *yeshuv*, yet it continued supporting peace with the Arabs. The *Neturei Karta* faction broke off from *Agudat Yisrael* in the 1940s, took control of the ultra-Orthodox sector and expressed anti-Zionist, pro-Palestinian positions. At some stage, they even preferred the internationalization of Jerusalem or an Arab – not Zionist – rule of Jerusalem. In the 1980s the leaders of this sector drew closer to the PLO and requested religious autonomy under Palestinian rule.[35]

CHAPTER

7

Muslim Positions towards Jews in Iraq, Egypt, Syria and Lebanon

As was discussed above, the relations between Muslims and Jews in the 19th century were ambivalent: mostly the relations were that of coexistence and cooperation, but there were also years of persecution and harassment in a variety of circumstances. This ambivalence prevailed in the Arab countries in the Middle East and North Africa; and in Turkey – with a majority of Sunni Muslims. However, in Shi'ite Persia (Iran) and Yemen the positions held by governments and the Muslim public towards Jews were generally aggressive, though there were also more peaceful times (see Chapters 3, 4, 5).

Orit Bashkin, a researcher of the Jews of Iraq and the Middle East, and Daniel Schroeter, researcher of the Jews of North Africa, describe Muslim–Jewish relations in those regions in the late 19th century and early 20th century in a positive light:

> Jews living in Muslim countries were rarely seen as a threat. Jews and Muslims continued to intermingle in common urban spaces and to forge new bonds in the public sphere . . . changes also brought new patterns of Muslim–Jewish relations in the streets, shops, coffee shops and cinemas, clubs, sports stadiums and work places . . . and employment of many Jews in government and private offices . . . Jews worked as farmers, peasants, peddlers and traders, often in close ties with their Muslim partners . . . the idea of citizenship based on belonging to the national community rather than to a religious group appealed to many Jews, even though Islam was declared the official religion.[1]

However, at the end of the 19th century, after the appearance of the Zionist movement and its activities in the Holy Land, on the one hand, and the Arab National Movement in the region, on the other hand, positions held by Muslims both in government and society towards their Jewish neighbors, gradually changed, especially towards Zionists. Thus, the distinction increasingly faded between loyal Jews fully integrated in their countries of residence, and Jews identified with the Zionists in the Holy Land and with European countries; or Jews who supposedly were taking over Muslim Arab Palestinian land. This occurred despite the fact that Zionist activity in Arab countries was limited and did not attract many Jews, some of whom actually opposed it. Even the limited sympathy towards Zionism found in some small Muslim Arab circles encountered criticism and opposition from the Arab nationalist streams; such sympathy progressively vanished with the increasing development of the Zionist undertaking and the violent events between Palestinians and Zionists in the Holy Land during the 1930s.

Alongside that, there was increasing identification with the Palestinians from the region's Arabs and Muslims; "Committees for the Defense of Palestine" were established, which enlisted volunteer fighters, and collected weapons and money to fight the Zionist *yeshuv*. At the same time, intermittently, Jews and synagogues were attacked in Arab countries by Arab nationalists and Muslim extremists. These trends increased towards the UN resolution on the Partition Plan in November 1947 and the establishment of Israel in May 1948.

In that regard, it is noteworthy that at the session of the political committee of the UN General Assembly on November 24, 1947, Dr. Muhammad Husayin Haykal, the Egyptian delegate, warned as follows: "The lives of a million Jews in Muslim countries will be endangered as a result of the partition.... Partition may create anti-Semitism in these countries . . . the UN will bear responsibility for drastic riots and the massacre of a large number of Jews . . . if a Jewish state is established, no one will be able to prevent the riots; they will erupt in Palestine and spread to all Arab countries." Haykal also claimed that a million Jews are living peacefully in Egypt and in other Muslim countries, and they have no desire to migrate to Palestine.[2] Indeed, after the approval of the Partition Plan and the establishment of the State of Israel, many Jews were attacked and killed in Arab countries, their possessions were plundered and synagogues were set on fire; many others were expelled or escaped. Thus ancient Jewish communities were wiped out in Iraq, Syria, Egypt, Yemen, Morocco and Libya. This, for example, is the testimony of Shimon Sasson, a survivor of the Muslim attacks on the Jews in Aden (Yemen) in early December 1947, immediately after ratification of the UN Partition Plan: "Synagogues are burnt, schools are destroyed, stores are plundered; there are dead (and scores of) wounded . . . from the riots experienced by the ancient Jewish community in the port city."[3]

Syria

A discussion of Muslim–Jewish relations in Syria is highly significant because, amongst other things, of the geographic, political and cultural closeness of its Muslims and Jews to Palestine/the Holy Land. It was the nexus of the Zionist–Palestinian and Jewish–Muslim conflict, as of the appearance of the Jewish and Arab nationalist movements at the end of the 19th century.

In Chapter 2, we reviewed the triangle of relations between Muslims, Jews and Christians in the 19th century, which were characterized a Judeo-Muslim alliance of sorts (under Muslim Ottoman rule) against Christians. The latter, for many Muslims, were identified with the Christian European powers that threatened and impacted on the Muslim nature that characterized the Holy Land and the entire region. However, the growth of Arab and Zionist nationalist movements gradually led to an ideological and political affinity between Muslims and Christians, wherein the latter actively sought alliances with the former against Zionists and Jews. Nonetheless, Muslims in Syria did not change their traditional ambivalent stand towards Jews, while the Ottoman Muslim government, including the "Young Turks" (1908–1917), reflected sympathy towards the Jews (and even the Zionists) who continued to identify with the Ottoman rule.

During Faisal Bin-Hussein's semi-autonomous government (under British auspices) (1918–1920), this genuine Muslim Arab leader expressed a warm attitude towards Zionism, Jews, and Syrian Jews altogether. As we have seen before, Faisal, descendant of the family of the prophet Muhammad and leader of the Arab national uprising (1916), supported the Balfour Declaration (1917), defined the Zionist movement as "national and not colonialist", and called for Jewish immigration to the Holy Land and cooperation with the Arabs. He saw in the Jews of Syria citizens with equal rights and a part of the Syrian Arab national community.[4]

Like quite a few Syrian Jews, Eliyahu Sasson (who later served as minister in Israel's government) was a member of the Arab Syrian national movement and at the time declared: "I am a Jew in spirit and an Arab in my thoughts", "The Jews are Arabs . . . brothers are we as Syrians and cousins are we as Jews", "The Jews are ready for battle to fight with the Muslims to liberate Syria". Sasson was also active in the Zionist movement and sought to build a bridge between it and the Arab National movement, but failed in doing so. He blamed the Zionist leadership in the Holy Land (originating mostly from European countries) for having "abandoned the Jews of the Middle East and the Jews of Damascus especially", and for having failed, as Yaron Harel stated, "to draw the Jews of Damascus closer to the Zionist idea and use them as a bridge to the Arab National Movement". Yosef Yoel Rivlin, who taught in Hebrew schools in Damascus, testified to the arrogance of Zionist leaders towards Arabs, saying: "The important question is the Arab question, and had Weizmann and Ussishkin not thought the Arabs are worthless and had spoken with . . . Yosef Abadi who was then in Damascus and had close ties to Faisal I . . . they could have achieved a great deal."[5]

However, it should be noted that Amir (later King) Faisal did not represent the positions of the mainstream of Syria's Arab National Movement, the Syrian Congress and the Arab press, all of whom were nationalist, anti-Zionist and anti-Jewish. These trends grew stronger after July 1920, when French military forces expelled Faisal and his army from Syria and established a French mandate, which was anti-Zionist. Throughout the mandate period (up to 1946), two major streams continued their activities within the national movements: One was ideological, militant, Pan-Arab, anti-Zionist and anti-Jewish; the other held a pragmatic, positive view of Zionists and Jews. Additionally, religious Muslim circles took violent action against Jews in Syria at times of tension between Muslims and Jews in Palestine.

The pragmatic stream in fact continued the line held by Faisal, as national Syrian leaders maintained dialogues with Zionist leaders on establishing a Jewish homeland in parts of the Holy

Land/Palestine, but not in its entirety; and integrating it with the regional Arab Federation. These Syrian leaders also refrained from participating in the Islamic Conference, held in Jerusalem in 1931 at the initiative of the Jerusalem Mufti Haj Amin al-Husseini. His objective was to enlist Pan-Arab support against the Jewish *yeshuv* in the Holy Land that supposedly was intent on causing damage to the mosques on the Temple Mount. The Mufti also initiated and implemented violence against Zionists and Jews in the Holy Land. However, Jamil Mardam-Bey, prime minister of Syria, while visiting Paris in 1937, condemned Palestinian violence against the Jewish *yeshuv*, calling it "terrorism".[6]

The major waves of immigration to the Holy Land in the mid-1930s and the Arab revolt in Palestine against the Jewish *yeshuv* (and the British) empowered the ideological-nationalist and religious Muslim circles in Syria and their opposition to the Zionist undertaking. They led mass demonstrations, donated money and weapons and organized a military force numbering hundreds of fighters, led by Fawzi al-Qawuqji, an ex-Syrian officer who infiltrated Palestine/the Holy Land to help the Palestinian rebels.

This force was augmented, as previously stated, by Sheikh 'Izz ad-Din al-Qassam (whose name was given to the military arm of the Hamas from the late 1980s), who established in 1935 an armed Palestinian group in the Haifa area to engage in armed battle against the British; and Sheikh Muhammad al-Ashmar who headed another group of rebels in Palestine. In Syria, Muslims attacked Jews in 1935, 1938, and again in 1945 and 1949 (after the establishment of the State of Israel), and called for a boycott on the Jews. Scores of Jews were murdered or wounded, most of the synagogues and hundreds of homes and shops were set on fire, forcing many Jews to flee to Lebanon or the Holy Land (later Israel).

The Syrian government, which at first refrained from harming the Jews and even granted them representation in parliament in 1936, changed its position. It placed many obstacles before Jews who wished to emigrate, and later forbade it altogether and forced the Jews to carry identification cards marked with the word *"Musawi"*, meaning of the Mosaic faith (a Jew). Syria was also the first Arab country that imposed a strict economic boycott on the Jewish populace in the Holy Land in 1946, and in 1947 deployed military forces along its border with Palestine as instructed by the Arab League.[7]

At that time, in December 1947, Muslims led pogroms against the Jews of Aleppo, killing 75 people and wounding hundreds more; 200 homes, shops and synagogues were destroyed as well. In August 1949, Muslims bombed the synagogue in Damascus, killing 12 Jews and injuring scores of others. After the establishment of the State of Israel, murderous acts and waves of destruction continued against the Jews; the government as well harshened its treatment of Jews, such as a prohibition to travel abroad, confiscation of passports and property, freezing bank accounts, forbidding the sale of Jewish houses and limitations on traveling inside Syria. (There were, however, short periods in which Jews were given exit permits in exchange for brutal guarantees.) Yet, it should be noted that in 1949, Syrian ruler Husni al-Za'im proposed negotiating peace with Israel; and in 1952 discussions were held between representatives of the ruler, Adib Shishakli, and Israeli representatives to sign a treaty of non-belligerence. However, these Syrian initiatives failed and the Syrian–Israeli conflict worsened. After the war of June 1967, in which Syria suffered a major defeat, government actions against Jews became harsher, and in Qamishli (mostly Kurdish) 57 Jews were murdered at the hands of Muslims; the Jews of this city and also of Aleppo and Damascus were placed under house arrest for eight months; and after that – under the watchful eye of the security forces.

However, Hafiz al-Asad, of the Alawi minority group and ruler of Syria (1970–2000), adopted a different policy towards the Jews of his country. He instructed to protect them from attacks and harassments by Syrian extremists and Palestinian refugees; and under American pressure, he allowed Jewish girls to emigrate, in 1977 and 1989; in 1992, Asad allowed most of the 4,000 Jews remaining in Syria to emigrate (but not to Israel), leaving only 300 Jews – most of whom were old – remaining in Syria, especially in Damascus. Lately there were only 15 Jews left in Syria

At the same time, Asad was angry at his ally, the Soviet Union, which had allowed its Jewish citizens to immigrate to Israel from 1989 and on. He repeatedly claimed that he is not anti-Jewish, but anti-Zionist: "We do not hate Judaism as a religion, but we hate Zionism as an invasive and colonialist movement". Other Syrian leaders voiced and published anti-Semitic content, such as "The Protocols of the Elders of Zion", and a book about the Damascus libel in 1840, written by Mustafa Tlas, Minister of Defense in

Asad's government.[8] Asad's son and heir, Bashar (from 2000) voiced as a Muslim anti-Semitic statements in his meeting with Pope John Paul II in May 2001. Nonetheless, these statements did not prevent Hafiz al-Asad from lengthy peace negotiations with Israel in the 1990s, motivated by strategic, security-related, political and economic considerations. These negotiations nearly led to a political settlement in 1999, 2000. During the civil war in Syria (since 2011) Israel mostly worked against the Syrian regime and launched numerous military attacks on Syrian, Iranian and Hizbullah positions.

Lebanon

In comparison to Syria, with its Muslim character, Lebanon was ruled for a long period by Maronite Christians, who saw in the Jewish community, the Jewish *yeshuv* and the State of Israel potential allies vis-à-vis their hostile Muslim surroundings.[9] This factor, along with the small size of the Lebanese Jewish community, its relative wealth and its reservations about Zionism, all contributed to the Lebanese Jews' sense of security and prosperity and their adequate relationship with their Muslim neighbors. There were short periods, however, mainly around the establishment of the State of Israel, in which Jews in Lebanon were attacked.

The Jewish community in Lebanon was relatively new. It originated with the settlement in Mt. Lebanon of Jews expelled from Spain, at the end of the 15th century. In the second half of the 19th century, the community numbered about 2500 people, and in the mid-20th century, it numbered 20,000 and consisted of Jewish immigrants from neighboring countries. It won the support of the French mandate governments and the Lebanese constitution, which in 1926 granted the Jews and other minority groups significant ethnic autonomy.

Despite their sympathy and support of the Jewish *yeshuv* in the Holy Land, the Jews in Lebanon refrained from publicly identifying with Zionism, especially after the ruthless attacks in 1929 in Hebron and Jerusalem (the mufti of Jerusalem was then exiled to Lebanon). These events led to anti-Jewish incitement in Lebanon by Muslim nationalists (and Christians – mainly Greek Orthodox). As Palestinian-Zionist polarization worsened in Palestine/the Holy

Land following World War II, the tension in Lebanon between Muslims and Jews increased, especially in Tripoli; in 1945, 14 Jews were killed by Muslim rioters; and in 1948, Muslims attacked Jews in Beirut; in 1950, the central synagogue of Beirut was set on fire.

In 1975, during the civil war in Lebanon, Jews residing in Wadi Jamil in Beirut took shelter in the neighborhood synagogue, *"Magen Avraham"*. According to one report, they received aid and food and other supplies from the PLO. This synagogue had been bombed by the Israeli air-force during the Lebanese War in 1982, but in 2015 the synagogue underwent complete renovation with the support of Hizbullah (see also Chapter 4).[10] This step was taken to demonstrate that Hizbullah is not against Jews in general, and Lebanese Jews in particular, but rather is extremely hostile to the Zionist Jews and seeks to destroy them. But, in fact, Hizbullah killed Jews in Lebanon too and was most likely involved in the terrorist attack on the Jewish Center in Buenos Ares in 1994, which left 85 dead and hundreds wounded. Most likely out of concern for their safety, the Jews in Lebanon unequivocally oppose Israel and supported the Palestinians. Today there are only 200 Jews residing in Beirut.[11]

Iraq

More so than Syria and Lebanon, the Jewish community in Iraq was more ancient and larger, and enjoyed good status and proper relations with its Muslim neighbors over very long periods, except for harsh times starting from the 1930s.

Indeed, the Jewish community in Iraq (or Babylon, Mesopotamia) held a special place in the chronicles of the Jewish people and Muslim–Jewish relations. It was a very ancient community, which began with the exile from the Holy Land to Babylon (586 BC), and which later boasted major Jewish study centers. It was significantly active economically and culturally at different time periods, including that of the Ottoman Empire. (For example, it produced the Babylonian Talmud and established the Talmudic academies of Sura and Pumbadita.) Jews took part in re-conquering Iraq from the Persians in 1638; and as in other Ottoman regions, Jews generally enjoyed tolerant treatment from the governments and the populace (though there were times of harassment and violence from fanatic rulers and ignorant, incited mobs).

The most important Jewish center in Iraq was in Baghdad. During the first half of the 19th century, the Jewish population of Baghdad numbered around 17,000 (compared to 4,000 Christians and 40,000 Muslims); in the early 20th century, the Jewish population grew to 50,000 (compared to 150,000 Muslims). The Jews of Baghdad played a major role in the fields of finance, banking and trade, which also included regional and international trade (with East Asia). Exemplary in this way were the wealthy Sasoon, Kaduri, Daniel and Salem families. However, the majority of Jews were poor and dealt in simple crafts and work.

(The Jews of Kurdistan lived in ambivalent relations with the Muslims: at times they enjoyed prosperity and tolerance, and at other times they lived in poverty and under oppression.)

From the end of the 19th century, Jews enjoyed representation in municipal and regional councils, in the Ottoman parliament, the judicial system, the press, public institutions, various government ministries and even the army (from 1909). As prominent scholars of Iraq wrote:

"The Jewish people in Iraq, who for many centuries have settled along the rivers of Babylon, were considered up to the first half of this century (the 20th) to be very large and even the most progressive of all the Jewish communities in Asia . . . Since the Middle Ages, the Jews of Iraq have accumulated wealth and economic influence." "In 1914, in terms of numbers, Baghdad was a Jewish city more than an Arab city . . . the diligence of the Jewish community, which spoke Arabic and was law-abiding, is felt in every city throughout the land . . . yet, Jews have always borne the shame of their social inferiority."[12]

As stated, there were periods of persecution of the Jews at the hands of rulers and groups of fanatic Muslims, at the end of the 19th century and mainly in 1908, following the rebellion of the "Young Turks", at which time scores of Jews were injured.[13]

After the British occupation of Iraq (1916–1921), the Jews of Iraq enjoyed significant improvement in their economic, security-related, judicial and political conditions. Some preferred British rule and requested British citizenship, and others irritated the Muslims by insulting them. However, from 1920, Jewish leaders joined their Muslim and Christian colleagues, demanding self-governing Arab rule in Iraq; and continued supporting the integration of Jews into Iraqi Arab nationalism.

Leaders of the Jewish community from then on developed an Iraqi and anti-Zionist orientation out of economic, pragmatic and even historic-cultural considerations. Thus, for example, Yehezkel Sasoon, first Finance Minister of an independent Iraq, said in 1921:

> "I have always been an idealist, the opportunity to contribute to the establishment of a great nation fascinated me. My religious brethren have lived in this land for 2,500 years. Many of them con-tributed to its progress in the fields of science, finances, literature and even politics (there were several Jewish delegates in Parliament and one senator), and I saw no reason that would prevent us, the Jews of this generation, to do as they had done . . . " ("He comported himself like a nationalist Arab").

Other educated Iraqi Jews praised the historic roots of Jews in Iraq, who had come even before the Arabs and Muslims. As, for example, stated Naim Katan (born in 1928 in Iraq), a journalist and writer: "Only the Jews can feel the footsteps of the past . . . there is nothing that links the Arabs to ancient Babylon. When they conquered this land, we were already here. We are the true natives of this land . . . in this land we wrote the Talmud, we became great scholars and philosophers." Nonetheless, since the Jews of Iraq lived for centuries in a Muslim and Arab environment, they developed a deep propensity for the Arab language and Muslim culture. A considerable number contributed to Arabic literature and poetry in Iraq and praised the "tolerant Islam"; and there were those who converted to Islam.

Others from the Jewish community joined the moderate Iraqi political parties, the Communist party and Zionist organizations. However, a considerable number among the Jewish leaders and community members disassociated themselves from the Zionist movement and even expressed their opposition, from the time of the Balfour Declaration and up to the establishment of the State of Israel. This stemmed from their concern that Zionism may harm their economic, political and security status and their relations with the Muslims in their common land. Some identified with the ideo-

141

logical Islamic and Pan-Arab heritage and with the Palestinians, and denunciated Zionism as "a tool in the hands of the Imperialists" and a threat to Arab nationalism. Jewish leaders strongly condemned the Zionist activity that had developed amongst Iraqi Jews in the 1920s and 1930s, as well as the UN Partition Plan in 1947, which proclaimed the establishment of a Jewish state in the Holy Land.[14]

Pro-Arab, anti-Zionist positions were especially characteristic of the political-economic-intellectual elite of Iraqi Jews, and stemmed in part from their fear for their status in Iraq ("The law of the land is the law"), whereas others felt a deep, sincere identification with Arab Iraq. For some, this identification continued even after attacks on Jews in the 1930s, the pogrom in Farhud in 1941, the establishment of the State of Israel in 1948, and the emigration of the majority of the Jews from Iraq from 1950 to 1955.

In contrast, from the 1930s, negative changes developed in the condition of the Jews in Iraq and their relations with their Muslim neighbors. This was due mainly to the Palestinian–Zionist conflict in Palestine/the Holy Land, which had a destructive impact on the attitude of the Iraqi rulers and the general public towards both Zionist and non-Zionist Jews. Other influencing factors were the prominent trends of Arab nationalism, fascist Nazi influences, the envy of young Muslims of the Jews' economic success, and the ambition of the newly educated to gain the jobs held by Jews.

The Balfour Declaration in November 1917 marked the beginning of the deterioration of Jewish–Muslim relations in Iraq, with the gradual blurring in distinguishing between Jew and Zionist among the nationalist-Arab–Iraqi-public and media. This trend, which also found expression via mass demonstrations and prayers, grew stronger during the 1929 riots and the Arab revolt in 1936 in Palestine; the Peel Commission Plan in 1937, for dividing Palestine; the propaganda activities of Palestinian refugees from the 1930s and of the Mufti of Jerusalem; and of course in reaction to the UN Partition Plan in 1947 and the establishment of the State of Israel in 1948.

Concurrent with that, from Hitler's rise to power in Germany in 1933, anti-Semitic propaganda in Iraq expanded via the activities of Germany's delegate in Baghdad, Fritz von Grube. He saw to the publication of Hitler's *Mein Kampf* in Arabic in an Iraqi newspaper (along with earlier translations of the "Protocols of the Elders of Zion"). He also actively promoted anti-Zionist, anti-Jewish (and anti-British) propaganda in schools (through Iraq's Education Ministry), and even among army officers and the pre-military organization, *al-Futuwa*. This propaganda was further supported by nationalist leaders and journalists.

On the other hand, moderate senior Iraqi leaders, such as Prime Minister Nuri Al-Sa'id, tried to curb this wave of anti-Semitism. He suggested granting Zionist Jews in Palestine autonomy within the framework of the "Fertile Crescent" program, led by Iraq, with no connection to the Jews of Iraq. Nonetheless, prominent Iraqi Jewish leaders and intellectuals publicly disclaimed Zionism that (supposedly) was harming the Iraqi Jews and the Palestinian Arabs. However, all this could not prevent hundreds of Jews from losing their jobs in government ministries, and the enforcement of new restrictions on Jews' academic studies. Repeated demonstrations, protests, incitements and severe acts violence continued against Jews and their institutions – with scores of killed and wounded.

The height of violence was the pogrom (*farhud*) in Baghdad in 1941, during the holiday of Shavuot, in which 180 Jews were murdered, hundreds were injured and many homes were set on fire. The attackers were members of the military and the police, joined by regular citizens, whose excuse for the violence was the Jews' expression of joy at the restoration of Iraq's old regime supported by the British army, which defeated the nationalist rule of Rashid Ali al-Kaylani.[15] After a period of time in which the status of Iraq's Jewish community was restored, the situation again took a turn for the worse against the background of the UN's international deliberations in 1947. For example, one of the Shi'ite religious leaders publicized a *fatwa* forbidding the sale of land to Jews in all Arab countries; many young Muslims demonstrated and sounded threats against Jews, while Jews were forced to donate money for the war against Israel in 1948. Many others were arrested on the charge of contact with the Zionists; and Zionism was declared illegal. Nearly 15,000 Jews fled to Iran, and others were executed or murdered by Iraqi *Mujahidin* who went to war with Israel.

Following the 1948 war, around 110,000 Iraqi Jews immigrated to Israel or to England, after a law was passed in March 1950 allowing Jews to leave Iraq with but a small amount of money. Those who remained, around 6,000 Jews, including prominent leaders, once again took up economic, educational and community activities out of their "allegiance to the Arab culture that is nourished from

Islamic heritage . . . devotion and loyalty to the Iraqi homeland; and out of economic and other motives as well."[16] This continued despite the hostility towards them from extremist Muslim and Christian factions.

During the rule of General Abd al-Karim Qasim (1958–1961), the condition of the Jews who had remained in Iraq improved, and prisoners who were accused of Zionism and Communism (and being Israeli spies) were released. However, the regimes that followed persecuted the Jews, especially after the June 1967 war. Scores were arrested and tortured and about a dozen were executed, having been accused of spying for Israel. (During that time, Israel provided military help to the Kurd rebels fighting the Iraqi regime, as the Kurdish Muslims' relations with Jews continued to be good.)

In the early 1970s, under international pressure, persecution of Jews lessened and they were requested to leave Iraq, leaving all their possessions behind. At the time, 2500 Jews still remained in Iraq, and later only 500 were left. Nonetheless, even though the magnificent Jewish community in Iraq was wiped out, a failure of the Jewish elite's Iraqi orientation, till today there are a few Iraqi Jewish intellectuals who identify with the Iraqi homeland and its Arab and Muslim heritage (see also a reference to the Shi'ite position in Iraq towards Jews, Chapter 4). It is an interesting point that Muqdata al-Sadr, a senior Shi'ite leader who came in first in the May 2018 elections, invited the Jews of Iraq throughout the world to return to their land and live in full equality alongside Iraq's other residents.

Egypt

Even prior to the Ottoman occupation of Egypt (1517), it was ruled by sultans and Mamluk dynasties (from 1250). The Mamluks were young boys from the Balkan and Caucasus regions and Central Asia, who had been bought/kidnapped and recruited by earlier Egyptian rulers. They were then trained as soldiers and educated as observant Muslims; and with time, they took the reins of government into their own hands and even conquered the Holy Land and Syria.

As fanatic Muslims, most of the Mamluk rulers reinstituted the "Umar Laws" upon Jews and Christians, regarding special rules of dress, collection of the Jizya tax and other taxes, restrictions on religious practice (and attacks on synagogues). Jews were also dismissed from public office and suffered the harassment of the mobs (though there were no massacres). As a result of these harsh conditions and economic decline, many Jews converted to Islam and others emigrated from Egypt. Yet, the suffering of the Jews was not as great as the distress of the Coptic Christians. Jews were also granted autonomy in areas of jurisdiction, marital issues and cultural activities. And the position of the *Nagid*, the community leader, continued to be filled for many years by the descendants of Maimonides.[17]

In the early 16th century, exiled Jews from Spain began immigrating to Egypt and continued coming during the time of Ottoman rule (which was partly nominal). The Jewish educational system developed with the help of Spanish Jews. Later, Jews arrived in Egypt from Italy and from Eastern European countries and, along with the Egyptian Jews, they enjoyed economic and physical security (especially with the opening of the Suez Canal in 1869 and the British occupation in 1882). However, at times Jews also suffered from blood libels and mass harassments (such as in 1844, 1881, 1901, etc.).[18] Nonetheless, for the greater part of the time, Jews were treated with tolerance and affinity and enjoyed economic prosperity. Some held senior positions in the government's financial administration (including the post of director) and in trade; other government positions were also filled by prominent Jews.

The process of prosperity and increasing security for Egyptian Jews (25,000, including 1,000 Karaites at the end of the 19th century) developed during the rule of Muhammad Ali (1805–1848) and his successors, Abbas Sa'id and Ismail (1863–1874). The latter even encouraged European investors – among them a considerable number of Jews – to settle in Egypt and contribute towards its economic growth. Vital economic branches indeed were developed and managed by Jews, such as agriculture, international trade, banking and the railroad. A few Jews contributed significantly to the cultural and public life in Egypt – most prominent among them was Yaqub Sanua (of Italian origin), who was a writer, poet, publicist and journalist. He was an Egyptian patriot ("Egypt for the Egyptians"), who preached for unity between Muslims and Arabs and equality between all religions in Egypt.[19]

At the time, there were manifestations of dialogue and cooperation between Jews and Muslims, such as the pilgrimage to the burial site of Yaacov Abu-Hatzera from Morocco, who was buried in Damanhur in 1880. During those years, Jews defined themselves as Egyptian nationalists, led by Yaqub Sanna who supported the Urabi Revolt (1879–1882) against the Egyptian *Khediv* (deputy to the King) and the British. Other Jewish intellectuals were active at the time in the "*Misr al-Fatah*" movement ("Young, Nationalist Egypt"); and in 1919, a Jewish lawyer, Leon Castro, joined the "*Wafd*" (delegation) Party that led the struggle for Egyptian independence from Britain. In 1923, Rabbi Haim Nahum was appointed Chief Rabbi of Egypt and later as Senator to the Egyptian Council of Delegates, subsequent to Egypt's nominal independence from Britain. He was also one of the founders of the Egyptian Academy for the Arabic Language and was instrumental in re-establishing the Society for the Historic Research of the Jews of Egypt. In 1924, Egyptian Jews won representation in both houses of parliament, and Yusuf Qatawi was appointed Minister of the Treasury and later, senator. As leader of the Sephardic Jewish community, he supported the establishment of an Egyptian Jewish youth movement, whose motto was: "Egypt is our homeland, Arabic is our language". Qatawi also strongly opposed Zionism. A Zionist activist in Alexandria wrote with criticism: "Not only that people are frightened, but the . . . hostility and antipathy to Zionist aims have sprung up. They (the Egyptian Jews) look upon it as a threat to their own peace that must be discouraged."[20]

At the same time, Zionist activity was growing in Cairo, which also found expression in the newspaper, *Israel*. The Egyptian government began treating Zionists, and Jews in general, with hostility in 1926 (though it did not forbid Zionist activity until 1948). For example, the citizenship law of the year 1926 granted citizenship to Muslims or to speakers of Arabic. (Many Jews in Egypt did not speak Arabic and looked upon the Muslims patronizingly).

What turned more hostile towards Jews and especially Zionists was the "Muslim Brotherhood" movement, established in 1928 and supported the Palestinians. This movement was later joined (in the 1930s and 1940s) by nationalist Muslim organizations that called for a boycott of Jews and Zionists. The Arab–Jewish conflict in Palestine during the 1930s greatly augmented the hatred of Muslims towards Jews in Egypt. For example, they blamed the Jewish *yeshuv* in the Holy Land for destroying mosques in Jerusalem; and

146

promoted incitement and violent actions against Jews, which included many incidents of murder and the burning of synagogues and Jewish institutions, both before and after the 1948 war. Many members of the Muslim Brotherhood took part in this war, while pictures of the Dome of the Rock were posted in the streets and printed on postage stamps. The Muslim Brotherhood and the al-Azhar Institute called for Jihad and liberating the Al-Aqsa Mosque. The Egyptian government as well took severe steps against Jews, which included thwarting citizenship, employment restrictions, confiscation of property and extensive arrests.[21] (Prime Minister al-Nuqrashy said at the time that all Jews are potential Zionists and all Zionists are Communists.)

After the war of 1948, 70 Jews were killed and 200 wounded in explosions in central Cairo; as a result, up to 1950 nearly 40% of the Jews in Egypt (75,000) emigrated; many of them immigrated to Israel. In 1954, a number of Jews were arrested, some were tortured and killed, for their involvement in what was to become known as the Lavon Affair (in Hebrew, *Ha'esek HaBish* – the "bad deal"), orchestrated by Israel's Mossad. The Mossad had organized a group of Egyptian Jews, with no military background, to secretly plant bombs in British and American institutions in Cairo, in order to generate a rift in British and American relations with Egypt under Abdul Nasser's leadership. Perhaps the Mossad's activity, which was approved by then Defense Minister Lavon, typified Israel's exploitive attitude towards Egyptian Jews (and Jews in other Arab countries). Concurrently, the social and economic life of Egyptian Jews was harmed, and anti-Semitic incitement increased via the media, and in Egyptian textbooks as well.[22]

After the Sinai–Suez Campaign in 1956, hundreds of Jews were arrested and thousands more were expelled from Egypt without their possessions. After the war of 1967, again hundreds of Jews were detained, some were tortured, and many others were allowed to emigrate without their possessions; most synagogues and Jewish institutions were closed by the authorities. Following the peace treaty between Egypt and Israel (1979), which has remained a cold agreement, civil rights were returned to the Jews of Egypt (just a few dozen). Egypt's new constitution, under the short rule of Mursi, of the Muslim Brotherhood (2012), granted the Jews equality with Muslims and Christians.[23] However, despite this moderation in the attitude towards Jews and Israel, Egyptian support of the

Palestinians has continued, and of Muslim control of the mosques on the Temple Mount.

Mursi too continued to maintain diplomatic relations with Israel and even served as mediator between Israel and Hamas and reached a ceasefire after the IDF's operation against Hamas in Gaza ("Pillar of Smoke"). Abd al-Fatah al-Sisi, who removed Mursi from office (2013), further strengthened the strategic, security-related and political ties with Israel. According to various publications, al-Sisi himself is from Jewish descent, and is well-liked by Egyptian Jews, even though in 2014 he ordered to cancel the annual celebrations in memory of the Moroccan Jewish kabbalist Abu Hatzera, in Damanhur (Egypt). In May 2018, al-Sisi declared that transferring the American Embassy from Tel Aviv to Jerusalem would lead to instability in the region and impact on the Palestinian issue (Reuters, May 16, 2018).

But in January 2020, al-Sisi refrained from criticizing Trump's "Deal of the Century" (*al-Monitor*, February 14, 2020).

CHAPTER

8

Muslim and Arab Ambivalence after the Establishment of the State of Israel

The 1948 war and the birth of the State of Israel intensified and, for the most part, worsened the reciprocal relations between Muslims and Jews in the Middle East and beyond, with greater emphasis placed on the national, religious, political and territorial aspects of the Arab–Israeli conflict.

On the one hand, the harsh and humiliating defeat suffered by the Palestinians (*nakba*) and five Arab states to the small Jewish-Zionist *Yeshuv*, and the establishment of a Jewish state on Arab Muslim land greatly increased among many Arabs and Muslims their feelings of frustration, hostility, revenge (and also fear). They reacted with violence, terrorism, boycotts and siege against Israel, accompanied by anti-Zionist and anti-Semitic/anti-Jewish state-ments by political and religious leaders in their speeches and sermons, and in the schools' textbooks as well.

Israel strongly retaliated against targets in the West Bank (under Jordanian rule) and the Gaza Strip (under Egyptian rule), placing severe limitations upon the Arab population remaining in Israel that came under military rule. However, Israel's governments and most of its Jewish population did not perceive the Arab conflict in religious terms, but rather in national, political, strategic and security-related terms. Thus, for example, fearing possible Egyptian and Pan-Arab aggression, Israel joined forces with Britain and France in October 1956, who initiated the Sinai/Suez

149

Campaign in the aim of occupying the Sinai Peninsula and Gaza Strip. The campaign failed, however, due to pressure from the United States and the Soviet Union, while Israel was increasingly perceived by Muslims and Arabs as a tool of the old European imperialism.

On the other hand, Israel maintained both open and clandestine contacts with some Arab and Muslim countries, in order to break the militant Arab siege and promote political solutions. For example: non-Arab Muslim countries with secular regimes – Turkey and Iran – recognized the State of Israel after its establishment and maintained with it political, economic and strategic security-related ties. Israel also maintained secret ties during the 1960s with Muslim Arab countries, such as Morocco and Yemen, and with Muslim Kurds in northern Iraq, and most recently also with conservative Muslim Sudan.

Israel even conducted secret talks with secular Muslim Arab countries, such as Syria and Egypt, hoping to reach political agreements. However, these failed due to their demands from Israel to make substantial strategic concessions. In contrast, Hashemite Jordan, of Arab Muslim character, nearly signed a political agreement (non-aggression) with Israel in 1950, and later continued to maintain secret strategic, economic and security-related contacts with her. However, the strengthening of Pan-Arab nationalist trends in Egypt (led by Abdul Nasser in 1952) and in Syria (led by the Ba'th regime from 1963) on the one hand, and the unbending reactions of Israeli leaders such as Dayan, Rabin, Alon and Peres on the other hand – led to the eruption of the June 1967 war and an additional defeat for the Arabs (*naksa*). Israel's victory led also to a more critical stage in the relationship between Muslims and Jews, Arabs and Zionists, in the region and outside it .

Israel's conquest of Sinai, the Golan Heights, the West Bank and the Gaza Strip increased anti-Israeli nationalist antagonism among Arab and Muslim countries. However, the occupation of East Jerusalem and the Temple Mount (al-Haram al Sharif) by Israeli Jews, for the first time in history, critically augmented the anti-Jewish (anti-Semitic) Islamic trends in these countries, and especially among the Palestinians.

Egypt, under the leadership of Nasser and Sadat (from 1970) continued its anti-Israel political and military campaign, which was tainted with anti-Semitic Islamic characteristics. Following the War of Attrition in the Suez Canal (1968–1970) Egypt along with Syria initiated the Ramadan War (Yom Kippur War) in October 1973, in order to repossess the Sinai and set in motion a political process vis-à-vis Israel. Yet, despite initial territorial gains, Egypt's military defeat in this war strengthened Sadat's orientation towards finding a political solution to the conflict with Israel. In so doing, he sought to promote the strategic-political and economic interests of his country, which took priority over the anti-Israeli and anti-Jewish ideological aspirations. Probably under Sadat's influence, Egypt's Grand Mufti, Jad al-Haqq, published a *fatwa* in 1979 that sanctioned making peace with the Jews, on condition that Jerusalem be a Muslim city and that the Palestinian problem be resolved.

In the peace talks with Israel, Sadat demanded a solution to the Palestinian problem and Islamic control on East Jerusalem. However, he was forced to accept Israel's dictates on these issues – which continued to prevent full normalization in Egyptian–Israeli relations for many years. In contrast, Syria continued its aggressive stand against Israel after 1973, marked by anti-Semitic tones. Yet under United States influence, it held ongoing political talks with Israel through the 1990s, which nearly led to a peace treaty in 1999–2000.

For the PLO as well, pragmatic considerations became more prominent, overshadowing ideological motivations; in 1988, and especially in 1993, the PLO recognized Israel for the first time and signed political agreements with Israel (the Oslo Accords, 1993, 1995). The 1993 Oslo Accords facilitated Arab Muslim Jordan to translate its de facto peace relations with Israel into an official peace treaty (1994). The Oslo Accords even motivated Muslim Arab and non-Arab countries to establish both official and unofficial relations with the Jewish state. Most prominent amongst them were Morocco, with its strong affinity to Muhammad and Jerusalem; Indonesia, with the largest Muslim population in the world (around 250 million); and other Muslim countries in central Asia, the Balkans and Africa, along with Arab Muslim countries in the Persian Gulf.

In 2002, the Arab League (22 countries) adopted the Saudi peace initiative, which was supported in 2005 by the Islamic states (57 in number, including Arab countries) and, for the first time, made an offer to Israel: Peace, security and normal relations, on condition that Israel agrees to the establishment of a Palestinian state based on the pre-1967 lines, with East Jerusalem its capital (and with full control of Muslim religious sites). Israel's governments, apart from Prime Minister Olmert in 2008, rejected this peace initiative, which periodically was re-ratified by Arab and Muslim countries. In May 2017, in expectation of U.S. President Trump's visit to Israel, it was reported that Palestinian President Abbas was about to propose Olmert's initiative as the outline for peace, after having avoided it in 2008. When Trump visited Saudi Arabia on May 20–21, 2017, Arab and Muslim leaders once again presented the Arab peace initiative of 2002 as the outline for peace between Israel and the Arab nations, and the Palestinians. However, then too, Israel refrained from accepting this initiative, most probably out of concern that it would need to relinquish its control of East Jerusalem and the Temple Mount. Trump's "Deal of the Century" in January 2020 to recognize United Jerusalem as the capital of Israel further increased the polarization between many Muslims and Jews.

It should be noted that Shi'ite Iran under the leadership of Muhammad Khatami, its pragmatic president, refrained from voting on the Arab peace initiative, at a time when the most prominent religious leaders of the Islamic uprising in 1979 led an anti-Jewish and anti-Israeli ideological Muslim line, both in word and deed (terrorism) (see Chapter 4). Others who towed this line were Shi'ite leaders and organizations such as Nasrallah and Hizbullah in Lebanon, and Muqtada al-Sadr in Iraq. Additionally, extremist Sunni organizations, such as Hamas and the Islamic Jihad, which won the support of Shi'ite Iran, continued preaching hatred and violence against Jews and Israelis. More extreme Sunni organizations – al-Qaida and ISIS, anti-Semitic as well – tried to implement terrorism against Jews mainly in Europe, yet hardly carried out any attacks in Israel.

At the same time, amongst Jews both in Israel and abroad, antagonistic attitudes towards Arabs and Muslims developed, mostly influenced by or in response to Arab and Muslim aggression. Up to 1967, most Jews in Israel and abroad perceived the Arabs as a military-political-nationalist threat that seeks to destroy the Jewish state, but those Jews did not strive to occupy East Jerusalem and the West Bank. There were marginal nationalist and religious Jewish groups with ambitions to take control of the Temple Mount (then under Jordanian rule) and restore the third Holy Temple upon the ruins of the Al-Aqsa Mosque and the Dome of the Rock.

However, following the military victory in 1967 and the occupation/liberation of East Jerusalem and the territories in the West Bank/Judea and Samaria, along with the *Likud* party coming into power in 1977, there was a resurgence of nationalist, religious and messianic trends among Jews in Israel and abroad that were Islamophobic in nature. For example, acts of incitement against Islam and Muslims, led by political and religious leaders; attacks on mosques and on Muslims by Jewish extremists; and attempts to harm the mosques on the Temple Mount/al-Haram al-Sharif. True, political and religious leaders, both Jewish and Muslim, continue working towards peaceful coexistence between the two populations, via dialogue and public expression of opinion. However, the absence of an agreed-upon political resolution serves to weaken these trends and reinforce the extremist positions on both sides.

It may be concluded that Islamic Judeophobia and Jewish Islamophobia, which feed upon each other, may lead in the worst-case scenario to a Muslim–Jewish Armageddon, if the pragmatic circles of both Jews and Muslims fail to halt these murky waves and reach political agreement in regard to East Jerusalem/al-Quds and the Temple Mount/al-Haram al-Sharif.

Arab and Muslim Positions

The conflict between Arab-Palestinian and Jewish-Zionist communities during the time of the British mandate grew deeper after the establishment of the State of Israel and expanded into a conflict between Arab countries and Israel, with the Palestinian problem constituting a principal factor. Arab leaders, mostly secular, with a large public following, perceived Jewish Zionist Israel as an aggressive imperialistic entity, an offshoot of European countries that seeks expansion in the region, from the Nile River to the Euphrates, harming Pan-Arab nationalism.

As mentioned earlier, identifying Jews as Zionists among many Arabs and Muslims in the region began earlier, before the establishment of Israel. and was manifested through violence against Jews in Palestine and in different Arab countries. The establishment of Israel as a Jewish state in 1948 (as per the Partition Plan of 1947, and the declaration of Israel's leaders) set in motion the all-Arab military attack upon Israel and increased the severe attacks on Jews and their expulsion from Arab countries. In addition, Arab and Muslim leaders, both secular and religious, denied the Jews' right to national-political determination (certainly those in Muslim Arab Palestine), because they were perceived as a supposedly religious sect and not as a nation. For example, the Palestinian national charter of 1964 (clause 18) states: "Judaism as a divine religion is not national and does not possess an independent reality, hence the Jews are not one nation with an independent persona" (Clause 20 in the revised 1968 charter).[1] In line with this view, Arab leaders prided themselves on the fact that Jews had lived in Muslim and Arab countries for centuries in prosperity and tranquility, until Zionism appeared and destroyed the harmonic coexistence between Jews and Muslims.

Hence, the Arabs' supreme objective was the destruction of "cancerous" Israel and the Zionists-Jews, the "new Crusaders", while at the same time supporting the Palestinians' rights and returning their refugees. All this would be attained through Jihad (Muslim holy war). Indeed, though the Arab discourse was in most part secular anti-Zionist, it was influenced by and included Islamic anti-Semitic/anti-Zionist elements, drawn from Muslim intellectuals who believed their doctrines, and from secular leaders who utilized Muslim religious beliefs held by the general public.[2]

The Muslim anti-Jewish (Judeophobic) trend developed into a central movement in Arab and Muslim countries following the war of June 1967 with Israel's conquest of the Sinai Desert, the Golan Heights, the Gaza Strip and the West Bank – and most notably, East Jerusalem and its Islamic holy sites at the Temple Mount/al-Haram al-Sharif, and the supposed intention of rebuilding the Holy Temple upon the ruins of the mosques.

Even prior to that, a substantial number of Muslim intellectuals presented Jews in an extremely negative light, supposedly leaning on the Qur'an and the Hadith, naming them "traitors, complainers, stubborn, haters, contemptible, primitive, corrupt, fanatic, greedy, arrogant", etc.[3] In addition, these intellectuals praised the war of the prophet Muhammad against the Jews in the Arab Peninsula because the Jews hated him greatly and supposedly plotted to kill him. Muhammad's war against the Jews of Khaybar in 629 CE, for example, is presented via statements proclaimed by Hamas: *"Khaybar, Khaybar, ya Yahud, jaysh Muhammad sa-ya'ud"* (Khaybar, Khaybar, O Jews, Muhammad's army will yet return to fight you). After the war of June 1967 and Israel's occupation of East Jerusalem and the Temple Mount, denunciations against Jews and Zionists (and violent attacks on them) greatly increased, from both Muslim religious clerics and secular political leaders in Arab and Muslim countries.

At a large convention presenting hundreds of Muslim religious leaders at the al-Azhar Institute in Cairo, 1968, harsh defamatory and hateful assertions were spoken against Jews and Zionists, "based upon verses from the Qur'an and the Hadith", such as: "The descriptions in the Qur'an of the people of Israel is not a description of a phenomenon that occurred during the days of prophecy, but rather that of an ancient illness that penetrated the Jews for generations . . . Jews are hostile to all human values . . . They have forever been a curse that has spread amongst the nations that has led to the destruction of Civilization's discoveries . . ."

Other Muslim religious clerics, in both earlier and later periods, described the Jews as "criminals, traitors, arrogant, breaking agreements, conspirators, falsifiers of sacred writings . . . the most cursed of all living creatures on Earth and by nature the most wicked, heretical and abominable . . . ".[4] The elements that continued and still continue to promote their anti-Semitic doctrines, drawn upon the Qur'an and the Hadith, are especially Hamas, the Muslim Brotherhood, Hizbullah, and Muslim newspapers in Egypt, Jordan, Saudi Arabia, Iraq, etc.[5]

In this regard, it is noteworthy that the anti-Semitic/anti-Jewish expressions spouted by Muslim leaders and the Muslim media – both religious and secular – are drawn not just from Muslim sacred texts, but also from classic Christian anti-Semitism, especially in accusing the Jews of killing Jesus, using the blood of children to bake the Passover matzos; "The Protocols of the Elders of Zion" – in other words, a Jewish conspiracy to take over the world; and the Jews' avarice (as in the play, *The Merchant of Venice*).

For example, in 1962, Egypt's Ministry of Education re-published the book, *Talmudic Human Sacrifices*, which notes in the preface that "The Jewish people allow the shedding of blood as a religious requirement, as set out in the Talmud". These accusations, and especially the Damascus Libel affair (1840), were highlighted in the Imams' sermons, in a play by an Egyptian diplomat in 1973, and in several books, including that of Mustafa Tlas, Syrian Defense Minister (*The Matzo of Zion*, 1983); and in statements made by

Saudi King Faisal in 1973. Syrian president Bashar al-Asad (in July 2001) told Pope John Paul II that the Jews aim to destroy the principles of all religions, with the same mentality used in their betrayal of Jesus and their attempt to kill the prophet Muhammad.[6] Similarly, secular Arab leaders such as Nasser, Sadat, Faisal and Arif (in Iraq), at times used anti-Jewish concepts drawn from the Qur'an in their speeches and when meeting with non-Muslim leaders.

For example, in a speech delivered by Muhammad Anwar Sadat, then a minister in the Egyptian government in 1955, he declared: "Our war against the Jews is an old struggle that began with Muhammad . . . it is our duty to fight the Jews in the name of Allah and in the name of our religion and it is our duty to bring to an end the war begun by Muhammad." In another speech given in April 1972, he claimed that "the Jews are a nation of liars, traitors and conspirators". Saudi King Faisal claimed in 1972 that "the Jews are cursed by God . . . They deviated from the teachings of Moses and tried to kill Jesus . . . ".[7] Other leaders such as Hafiz al-Asad and Saddam Hussein, both secular, exploited the Islamic concepts of Jihad and Shahadah (sacrificing one's life) in the wars against Israel, on the issue of the Al-Aqsa Mosque, and in anti-Jewish and anti-Zionist speeches.[8] Muhammad Mursi, one of the leaders of the Muslim Brotherhood in Egypt, prior to being voted in as president, defined the Jews as "the descendants of monkeys and pigs" (as per the Qur'an).

Such Islamic expressions were widely used by Shi'ite revolutionary Iran and Hizbullah; and by the Sunni Hamas, the Muslim Jihad, al-Qaida and ISIS, in the last decades of the 20th century and on. For example, the Hamas charter of 1988 contains harsh anti-Jewish expressions based on the Qur'an and the Hadith and calls for Jihad against Israel and the Jews. However, in early May 2017, a new document of principles of the Hamas was published without annulling its charter. The new document emphasizes the national Palestinian dimension as having priority over the Islamic tenets; it distinguishes between Jews and Judaism as a religion and the "Zionist occupation", against whom the struggle is not religious, but national; Hamas is prepared to recognize a Palestinian state within the 1967 lines with Jerusalem its capital, but does not recognize Israel.[9]

Anti-Semitic/Judeophobic expressions appeared in the Arab media (including in Egypt and Jordan), by religious and secular

Muslim notables, also after the peace treaties between Egypt and Israel (1979) and Jordan and Israel (1994); especially around events in which Palestinians were killed, such as the Intifadas in 1987, 2000 and 2015; and in retaliations by Israel in Gaza in 2008/9, 2012 and 2014. Muslim organizations and leaders especially attacked actions by Israel and Jews against the Al-Aqsa Mosque. For example, in 2016, a conference of the Organization for Muslim Cooperation, which includes 57 countries (of which 22 are Arab countries), severely condemned Israel for "the dangerous attacks of Israeli occupation forces and radical settlers . . . on the holy Al-Aqsa Mosque and hurt the historic status of the mosque and the feelings of Muslims." At a conference held in 2017, initiated by Turkish president Erdoğan, the organization harshly rejected the decision of U.S. President Trump to recognize Jerusalem as the capital of Israel.

The Saudi ambassador, at a convention of this organization "to save Jerusalem from Israeli occupation" (1996), declared that "a billion Muslims will assail upon Israel . . . that supports the desecration of al-Haram al-Sharif". Jordanian King Abdallah II also stated: "We shall continue fighting every attempt to harm the status quo at the Al-Aqsa Mosque . . . with the penetration of extremist Israeli elements into the area of the mosque." The Palestinian president declared (in 2014) the readiness of all Muslims to sacrifice themselves in protection of the Al-Aqsa Mosque . . . Israel is providing protection to the aggressors against al-Aqsa". In mid-July 2017, he harshly condemned Israel for having closed the Temple Mount to Muslim worshippers following the murder of two Israeli policemen at the hands of extremist Israeli Muslims. The king of Jordan did the same, as did the Turkish president who in 2018 voiced anti-Semitic remarks on the issue of Jerusalem.

The Palestinian Authority, which sees in al-Aqsa and East Jerusalem pivotal national symbols, passed a proposal at UNESCO's Board of Directors (in October 2016 and May and July 2017) condemning Israel on various issues related to Jerusalem and especially to the holy sites – the Al-Aqsa Mosque and al-Haram al-Sharif. This proposal was promoted with the cooperation of Egypt, Morocco, Algeria, Lebanon, Oman, Qatar and Sudan, and won support from countries friendly with Israel, such as Azerbaijan, Kazakhstan and Russia, and many other countries. This proposal totally ignores the Jews' historic connection to the Temple Mount and the Western Wall (although in a decision taken in May 2017, UNESCO recognized the affinity of the three monotheistic religions to the Old City of Jerusalem).[10]

If such extreme positions were adopted from time to time by moderate Muslim Arab countries, it is not surprising that extremist Muslim countries and organizations were consistent in noting via symbols and names the violent struggle to free al-Quds and al-Aqsa. Thus, for example, Iran and Hizbullah every year celebrate "Yawm al-Quds" Jerusalem Day and established the "al-Quds Force" to liberate the city. The (secular) al-Fatah organization, after the al-Aqsa Intifada (2000), established the terrorist group "Shuhada al-Quds" (self-sacrifice); the offices of the Palestinian Authority and the Hamas flags bear the images of al-Aqsa as a symbol of their main aspiration. The Hamas organization maintains a television station and a university bearing that name; many violent actions of these organizations and of individual Palestinians are linked to these issues: From the al-Aqsa Intifada in 2000 and the al-Quds Intifada in 2015, the killing of two Israeli policemen at the Temple Mount, the murder of the Salomon family in the Neve Tsuf/Halamish settlement by Muslim extremists in July 2017, and up to the riots and demonstrations by Palestinians following Trump's recognition of Jerusalem as the capital of Israel in December 2017[11] (and in January 2020).

Textbooks in the Schools and Colleges

It should not be surprising that calls against Jews and Israel of Jihad and Shahada (sacrifice), along with anti-Semitic and anti-Zionist statements made by Arab and Muslim leaders, have appeared as well in the textbooks of many Arab and Muslim countries for many years. These countries are in most part totalitarian and use anti-Jewish/anti-Israeli indoctrination in order to satisfy/neutralize extremist Muslim circles or such that are under their influence. Another motive for this hostile policy is the widespread viewpoint among Muslim and Arab governments and populaces that so long as Israel controls the mosques on the Temple Mount, East Jerusalem and the Palestinian territories, there will be no conciliation with Israel and the Jews. This approach is widespread as well in Egypt and Jordan, both of whom signed peace treaties with Israel, in 1979 and 1994 respectively.

The same applies to the Palestinian Authority that signed the Oslo Accords with Israel in 1993 and 1995. Yet, following these accords, hostile ideological expressions against Jews and Israel have lessened or softened (though not by fanatic Muslims). Positive, pragmatic approaches have also surfaced among politicians and intellectuals, and in textbooks, although the core of the indoctrination has remained anti-Israel/anti-Jewish. Exceptions to this phenomenon were Arab Tunisia in North Africa and, to some extent, also Turkey and Pakistan (the large Muslim country with 190 million people, in southern Asia).

As mentioned, the major issues discussed in the textbooks used in Arab and Muslim countries for many years also reflected the positions held by governments and the populace, which were mainly influenced by verses from the Qur'an and the Hadith. For example, Egyptian textbooks, published prior to the 1967 war, described negative characteristics of Jews thus: "Human monsters, a barbaric nation void of any good traits common to all humanity", "They are cursed by God through the prophets and have deviated from the teachings of Moses". Similarly, in Palestinian textbooks from 2002, after the Oslo Accords, Jews are presented as deceitful, avaricious and barbaric, who do not honor agreements; are fanatic and racist, Tartars, oppressors and exploiters, murderers and destroyers . . . Freeing Palestine and al-Aqsa will be done through violence and bloodshed, through Jihad and Shahadah (sacrifice). Similar expressions were written in these textbooks in 2017–2018.[12]

In Egyptian textbooks, after signing of the peace treaty with Israel, Judaism is presented as a monotheistic religion, with humane values shared by Christianity and Islam as well. However, certain aspects of Judaism (and Christianity) are described in a very negative light, such as: "Non-believers, forgers of the Bible, did not obey God's commandments, opposed Muhammad and Islam, they are stubborn, greedy, hypocritical, conspiring and full of hatred towards Islam and Muslims; traitors, they do not honor agreements with Muslims (in modern times). The Zionist movement is spreading, and with terrorist leanings, aspiring to control the entire region, from the Nile to the Euphrates . . . Israel gained control over a country that is not hers (Palestine), expelled its residents and destroyed their homes; the capital of Palestine, Jerusalem, is Arab and Muslim and is holy to the three monotheistic religions. It must be returned to the Arabs, if not peacefully then by military jihad."

With that, Egyptian textbooks do mention the Jews' ties to the Western Wall (without mention of the Temple Mount), and the Egyptian–Israeli peace process; though Israel's intentions are doubtful, as it still occupies the Golan Heights, the West Bank and Arab Jerusalem, including the Al-Aqsa Mosque.[13]

Like Egypt, Jordan too signed a peace treaty with Israel, in 1994 and, prior to that, maintained important strategic relations with the Jewish state. However, Jordanian textbooks from just a decade ago describe Jews as perverts, deviants, swindlers, obstinate and cowardly . . . the way to fight them is through jihad. The murder of King Abdallah on the Temple Mount (1951) motivates the Arabs and Muslims to free the Holy Land from the Zionists; and King Hussein – to sacrifice his life in order to return Palestine to the Palestinians.[14]

In these textbooks, Israel is portrayed as being illegitimate, colonialist, imperialist, aggressive, stealing Arab lands, killing children and destroying homes. Yet at the same time, even after the 1967 war and especially after the Oslo Accords, Israel was cited in Palestinian and Jordanian textbooks as a fait accompli that must be accepted or fought against (via jihad), and its peaceful intentions are not to be trusted. Judaism is mentioned as a monotheistic religion, though without any affinity to the holy sites in Jerusalem (the Jewish Quarter in Jerusalem is mentioned); the Jews in Israel are conquerors and oppressors. Yet parallel to that, Palestinian, Jordanian, Egyptian and Syrian intellectuals showed increasing interest in Israel and its population, to "know thine enemy"; some even publicly supported peace with Israel yet refused to visit Israel as long as the Palestinian problem remains unresolved.[15]

In the textbooks of Saudi Arabia, the standard-bearer of Islam, Islam is presented as the only true and supreme religion, whereas all other religions are false and lead their believers to Hell. Jews and Christians are heretics and the enemies of Islam. Muslims are forbidden to have contact with, to love or befriend non-Muslims. The Jews are an evil nation, characterized by bribery, deceitfulness, dishonesty, treachery, aggression and arrogance; they are the enemies of Allah. They cooperated with the enemies of Muhammad and were punished with expulsion, in one case – took part in killing men and enslaving women and children. Their current occupation of Palestine, Jerusalem and the Islamic holy sites is a danger to the neighboring Muslim countries. They are agents of conspiracy as stated in the Protocols of the Elders of Zion; they are racists, colonialists and aggressors who seek to control the world. It is incumbent upon the Muslims to protect al-Aqsa, the holy sites of Islam and purify them of the conquering Jews through jihad and sacrifice. Amazingly, the Bible too is banned in Saudi Arabia, even though it is spoken of positively in the Qur'an.

It is noteworthy that the Saudi Foreign Minister Saud al-Faisal, in an interview for CBS on September 9, 2002, admitted about his country's textbooks that "ten percent of what we found was questionable; five percent we found abhorrent. So, we have decided to change that, and we have already done so." Faisal's comment referred to the hatred of Americans expressed in the textbooks, but not to the hatred of Jews and Israel, who have remained the object of great loathing. This, despite the Saudi peace initiative (2002) that offered Israel peace and normal relations; and despite the pragmatic approach towards the Jewish *Yeshuv* and the State of Israel by past Saudi monarchs.[16] Only in one Arab Muslim country – in Tunisia – are the textbooks democratic and educate towards tolerance and peace. This stems from a liberal tradition, French influence and neutralizing Islamic influence on the schools' curricula.[17]

Finally, it must be emphasized that the textbooks in Arab Muslim countries usually reflect the ideology, not necessarily the policies of these countries, that is influenced by interests and pragmatic considerations. Additionally, textbooks constitute only one factor in shaping the attitude of students at the different academic levels of schools and colleges. Other factors are the viewpoints held by parents and teachers, by intellectuals and religious clergy. All these factors influence the students, relative to events and developments in the region, and especially the behavior of Israel's government towards Palestinians. Many Muslims and Arabs perceive Israel's behavior as draconian, anti-Muslim and inhuman. They feel a sense of solidarity and identification with the Palestinians who have been suffering under Israeli occupation for fifty two years; they do not define the Palestinians' attacks on Jews as terrorism, but rather see them as freedom-fighters and martyrs (shuhadah).

Summary: The Influence of Extremist Ideology

It may be concluded that the anti-Israel and anti-Semitic extremist ideology held by Arab and Muslim populations has not lessened, but rather has increased in the past decades, in light of continued Israeli occupation and the building of Jewish settlements in the West Bank; and in response to Israeli military actions in the Gaza Strip, the burning of a Palestinian family in the village of Duma (2015) and a Palestinian youth in Jerusalem (2016); as well as the continued activities of extremist Jewish zealots on the Temple Mount. For example, during the Gaza–Israel the IDF attack on the Gaza Strip in July–August 2014, it was reported that 93% of Palestinians and 74% of Arabs and Muslims in the Middle East harbored anti-Semitic feelings.[18] Similar feelings were expressed after the IDF operations in the Gaza Strip in 2008/9 and 2012; the bloody clashes around the Temple Mount in 1996, 2000, 2015 and July 2017; and moving the American Embassy to Jerusalem in May 2018.

Besides the harsh protests by Arab and Muslim (and other) governments, especially since 1967, many hundreds of terrorist actions and violence were implemented against Israeli and non-Israeli Jews in Israel, the occupied territories and throughout the world. This was especially executed by radical Muslim organizations such as Hamas, *Hizb al-tahrir*, the PLO al-Aqsa brigade, Islamic Jihad, Hizbullah, ISIS, and agents of Iran (since the Islamic revolution in 1979).

The most notorious terrorist actions in the past decades included the bombing of the Israeli embassy in 1992 and the Jewish Community Center in 1994, both in Buenos Aires, Argentina, most likely carried out by Hizbullah with Iranian help. Additionally, terrorist attacks were carried out on a synagogue in Djerba, Tunisia in April 2002; on Jewish targets in Casablanca, Morocco in 2003; on synagogues in Istanbul, Turkey in November 2003, all by al-Qaida; also, attacks on the Israeli embassy in Tashkent, Uzbekistan in July 2004, by the Islamic Jihad; attacks on Israelis in Sinai, Egypt, October 2004; hotels in Amman, Jordan ("that host Jews and Crusaders") in November 2005, also by al-Qaida; and terrorist attacks against Jews in Paris, France in November 2015, by ISIS. All this was in addition to hundreds of violent attacks, mostly by Hamas, the Islamic Jihad and other Palestinians in the West Bank and in Israel, which included the cruel lynching of two Israeli reserve soldiers in Ramallah in October 2000, the brutal terrorist attack at the Park Hotel in Netanya in March 2002, the killing of two Israeli soldiers on the Temple Mount and the murder of the Salomon family in Neve Tsuf in July 2017.[19]

On the other hand, along with these anti-Israel and anti-Jewish aggressive statements and violent actions, the past decades have witnessed continued pragmatic and even moderate approaches towards the Jewish state. This has stemmed from strategic, political and economic constraints and interests of Arab and Muslim countries; and dialogues with political leaders and Muslim intellectuals – motivated by cultural, humane and ideological considerations. Before turning our attention to these pragmatic approaches, we should first examine the positions towards Israel and Jews held by two Muslim Arab states, as examples of the ambivalent positions of modern-day Arab Islam: ideological hatred and political pragmatism.

Jordan and Saudi Arabia

These two countries clearly possess a Muslim-Arab character, with strong connection to Islam's holy sites and its cradle of growth. The forefathers of the Jordanian kingdom – the Hashemite family – were related to the prophet Muhammad (the Quraysh family) and to the city of Mecca, and ruled in Mecca and in Hijaz for centuries, until they were expelled by their Saudi opponent in 1924. Even prior to that, Husayn bin-Ali, the Sharif of Mecca, and his son Faisal were the banner-bearers of Muslim Arabism in the revolt they led against Turkish Ottoman rule (1916). And in the war of 1948, Abdallah I, King of Jordan, occupied all the holy sites of Islam in East Jerusalem, but in 1951 he was murdered by a Palestinian extremist at the entrance of the Al-Aqsa Mosque.

His successor, King Hussein, renovated the Dome of the Rock between 1959 and 1962 and saw in the Temple Mount/al-Haram al-Sharif a compensation of sorts for the loss of control over the important mosques of Mecca and Medina. The Hashemite connection with the Temple Mount continued also after Israel's occupation in 1967, in collaboration with Israel; and in the Israeli–Jordanian peace treaty of 1994, Israel committed itself to bestow upon Jordan a privileged status at al-Haram al-Sharif, within the framework of negotiations for a permanent settlement of the Palestinian issue. Even prior to this agreement, over a period of years, secret and significant strategic relationships were developed between Israel and Jordan in areas of security and economics. Yet this did not lessen the anti-Semitic and anti-Israeli indoctrination in the text-books or in the sermons by extremist Islamists. (The same applies to the anti-Western-Christian indoctrination in Jordan, which for the past decades has benefited from strategic, political and economic support from the United States and Britain.)

This dissonance may also be found in Saudi Arabia, protector of the holy sites of Islam and the epicenter for the dissemination of Islamic ideas and publications worldwide. On the one hand, the anti-Jewish (and anti-Western) propaganda has been ongoing for many years; on the other hand, the Saudi kings adopted pragmatic policies towards the Jewish-Zionist *Yeshuv* during the British man-date era; and towards Israel since the 1982 Fez Conference; and up to the Saudi Arabian peace initiative in 2002, and after. It is also worth noting that in the past decade high-ranking Saudis and Jordanians have initiated interfaith dialogues, including with Jews, in their own countries and throughout the world (no Jews live in Jordan and Saudi Arabia, though Jews visited these countries from time to time). Thus, it seems that national strategic interests and considerations of these Arab Muslim countries have at times over-ridden religious ideological motives. The latter reflected the desire of the countries' leaders to win political-religious legitimacy by extremist Muslims, or to weaken their struggle against the govern-ment; at times, the ideological messages were ambivalent.

A blatant and significant example of this is Ibn Saud (Abd al-Aziz Ibn Abd al-Rahman), founder of the Saudi Arabian kingdom in 1902 and its sovereign up to his death in 1953. On the one hand, he voiced anti-Jewish/anti-Semitic opinions, basing them on verses from the Qur'an and the Hadith, such as: "Jews are the enemies of Islam and prophet Muhammad. They are a dangerous and hostile race, sinful, cursed and evil; they are despised because of their exag-gerated love of money; God denied the Jews the right to be a nation forever; they have no historical rights in Palestine; they are endan-gering it as an Arab land; they are worse than the Christians; they must be fought with violence."

On the other hand, at other opportunities, Ibn Saud claimed that the Jews are better than the Christians: "Good friends of the Arabs, and coexistence with them is possible (though not with the Zionists), as a small minority with guaranteed rights"; "Palestine is a land holy to three religions". He opposed declaring jihad on the Jews by a *fatwa*; and condemned Muslim Palestinians that murdered

164

Jews in Hebron in 1929, stating: "Show me the (Muslim) sacred books that authorize you to murder Jews; God will never forgive you for what you have done."[20]

Apparently, the ambivalent positions taken by Ibn Saud were also dictated by political and strategic considerations, most importantly the relations with Britain and later with the United States, the two influential powers in the region. Also, these positions were influenced by the rivalry with the Hashemites that ruled in Iraq and Transjordan and strove to rule over Syria and Palestine within the framework of the Fertile Crescent program. As the Saudis saw it, the Arab–Jewish conflict in Palestine was a potential threat to the region's stability, but they were also concerned that the Peel Program (1937) or the Partition Plan (1947) would enable Transjordan to take control of the Arab section of Palestine. On the other hand, a Jewish-Zionist entity in Palestine, despite its religious-ideological illegitimacy, may bring the Hashemite influence to a halt; and in any case, such an entity is a significant political fact that must be taken into consideration in Saudi strategy.

Zionist and Israeli leaders have failed to understand/appreciate until recently the realpolitik motives of the Saudi Arab rulers and tended to see in them as anti-Semitic and pro-Palestinian fanatical Muslims (who in any event are nothing but "Bedouin sheikhs"). These Israeli concepts stemmed from the Saudis' support of the Palestinian struggle, after 1967, for the liberation of the mosques on the Temple Mount through jihad; and the Saudi oil boycott on Israel in 1973. Israeli leaders did not notice Saudi Arabia's pragmatic orientation, also toward the Egypt–Israel peace treaty in 1979, with the United States' involvement and support.

In August 1981, Amir Fahd, the Saudi crown prince, proposed a solution to the Palestinian–Israeli problem, which for the most was pro-Palestinian, yet with positive references to Israel, such as: a demand to establish a Palestinian state in the West Bank and the Gaza Strip and not throughout all of Palestine; and an assertion that it is the right of all countries in the region to live in peace (Clause 7), including Israel (perhaps based on UN resolution 338 of 1973). This program was presented at the Arab summit conference in Fez, Morocco in November 1981, but was rejected. It was presented again at the Arab summit conference on November 30, 1982, but Clause 7 was altered and stated that the UN security council will provide a guarantee of peace to all countries in the region, including

165

an "independent Palestinian state". The veiled recognition of Israel that had appeared in the original Fahd Plan was removed while the new proposal was approved by the Arab summit.

Saudi Arabia continued supporting Palestinian positions, but also formed contact with the Jewish leadership in the United States; and in September 1993 she supported the Israel–Palestinian Oslo accords, yet strove for a comprehensive Arab–Israeli agreement as a guarantee of its country's and the region's security. In January 1995, the chief mufti of Saudi Arabia, Abd al-Aziz Ibn Baz, published a *fatwa*, a religious ruling, according to which Arabs may sign a peace treaty with Jews in the form of a temporary yet complete truce, and on condition that it is beneficial to Arab-Muslim interests (the chief mufti of Egypt had published a similar *fatwa* in 1979). The mufti, Ibn Baz, even expressed his objection to Muslim suicide bombers and their terrorist actions against Israel. His successor, Abd al-Aziz, published a ruling in 2001 forbidding suicide attacks of Muslims against Jewish targets in Israel. Another Saudi religious leader, Sheikh Ishaq Idris Sakuta, one of the leaders of the Islamic Congress, visited Jerusalem in May 1992, prayed at the Al-Aqsa Mosque, met with Israeli leaders and declared as follows: "I found the Jewish people in Israel longing for peace and good neighborly relations. I saw a beautiful Jerusalem and well-cared-for Muslim sites."[21] Other senior Saudi personages as well visited Jerusalem, leaning on the *fatwa* by the mufti Ibn Baz. Along with that, attempts were made by Israeli business people to implement joint economic projects – including the import of gas from Saudi Arabia to Israel – but with no success.

In February 2002, the Saudi crown prince Abdallah proposed for the first time a peace initiative vis-à-vis Israel (perhaps also influenced by the attack on the Twin Towers in New York in 2001, in which Saudi terrorists had taken part).

In March 2002, this initiative turned pan-Arab and later in 2005 was also supported by Muslim countries. It offered Israel peace, security and normal relations in return for Israel's agreement to retreat to the lines of June 4, 1967, and the establishment of a Palestinian state with East Jerusalem its capital. The Saudi–Arab peace initiative was again ratified at the Arab summit in Riyad, Saudi Arabia in March 2007. The summit also decided "to end the Arab–Israeli conflict and bring about a just and all-encompassing peace that will bring security to all the countries in the region and allow the

Palestinian people to establish its independent state with East Jerusalem its capital." This initiative was repeatedly confirmed by Saudi leaders; and in March 2017 – by the Arab League Summit in Jordan. Even the UN and American governments, including Trump's, adopted this initiative. Prior to that, it was reported that at an international peace conference in Paris, on January 25, 2017, Saudi Foreign Minister Adil Jubair and other Arab ministers, had supported John Kerry's draft (of December 28, 2016). This determined for the first time that Israel is a Jewish state with equality for all its citizens, also based on UN Partition Plan 181 from 1947 that proposed the country's division into two states, Jewish and Arab. Furthermore, Kerry determined that the settlement clusters in the West Bank will be annexed to Israel, the Palestinian state will be fully demilitarized, and the problem of the Palestinian refugees will be resolved in a "realistic" manner that will not change Israel's character.[22]

In newspaper interviews given by Saud al-Faisal, Saudi Foreign Minister in 2006, and Turki al Faisal, Saudi ambassador to Washington in 2009, they said accordingly that "the Middle East can turn into a Garden of Eden in which all the sons of Abraham will be able to live a normal and flourishing life, free of fear and insecurity" . . . "If Israel responds to the Arab peace initiative, will withdraw from all the occupied territories and sign a comprehensive peace agreement, it will enjoy full integration into the Arab world and full normal relationships . . . Israel and the Arab world will enjoy not only diplomatic, economic and political relations, but also cooperation in the fields of education, science and the struggle against violence, shared by all the region's inhabitants." At the same time, King Abdallah initiated interfaith dialogues, some of which were attended by Jewish Israeli delegates, such as Shimon Peres. The king also gave a high reward in the field of medical science to an American Jewish cancer researcher who had also trained at the Weizmann Institute, and attended the ceremony in Saudi Arabia accompanied by his Israeli wife.[23]

A number of Israeli leaders reacted positively to some parts of the initiative, yet not a single Israeli government accepted the initiative as a whole, not even as a basis for negotiations (Prime Minister Ehud Olmert was the only one who presented a similar plan to Mahmud Abbas in 2008, but he did not receive an affirmative response). This Israeli position, that was accompanied by ongoing building of Jewish settlements in the West Bank and the influx of Jewish populations into East Jerusalem, led to deep disappointment and criticism among Saudi leaders; yet did not lead to a rescinding of the Arab initiative. In May 2018 the Saudi king, Salman, condemned the move of the American Embassy to Jerusalem, though his son, crown prince Muhammad, expressed himself more moderately towards Israel.

Hashemite Jordan

More so than Saudi Arabia and most Arab and Muslim countries, Hashemite Jordan with the longest common border with Israel, treated Jews and Israel with respect and at times even with amity, through nearly one hundred years of proximity (and this, despite its anti-Semitic/anti-Jewish ideology). The Sharif of Mecca and patriarch of the Hashemite family, Husayn bin-Ali, who was crowned as King of the Hijaz in 1916, accepted the Balfour Declaration in 1917, under British influence. "Hussein held great respect for the Jews (even though there were no Jews in his country), for he saw in them the 'People of the Book', as written in the Qur'an . . . He did not oppose Jewish settlement in Palestine, and even welcomed it on both humanitarian and religious grounds. However, he clearly opposed the Zionists' gain of control in the region."[24]

His son, Amir Faisal (later, King Faisal) in Syria in 1918–1920, showed his sympathy not just towards Jews, but to the Zionist movement as well; and in January 1919 he signed an historic agreement with Chaim Weizmann, leader of the Zionist movement (under British influence, but with no practical implementation). This agreement noted "the racial closeness and ancient ties that exist between Arabs and the Jewish people . . . all necessary steps will be taken to encourage and motivate the immigration of Jews to Palestine in great numbers, to settle Jewish immigrants on the land". In a letter to Felix Frankfurter, a U.S. judge and Zionist leader, Faisal wrote in March 1919: "We feel that Arabs and Jews are cousins in race . . . and can take the first step towards achieving national ideals together . . . We the Arabs look with deep sympathy upon the Zionist movement . . . we are working together for a restored and renewed Near East, our two national movements complement one another . . . the Jewish movement is nationalist and not imperialist . . ."[25]

Faisal's brother, Abdallah, Emir of Transjordan and King of Jordan (1948–1951), continued to promote the Hashemite tradition of moderation, pragmatism and even a certain sympathy towards the Jews and the Jewish Zionist movement. He too supported the Balfour Declaration and appreciated the political and economic power of the *Yeshuv* and strove towards cooperation with the settlers in order to expand his rule in the region and join forces in his struggle against the Palestinian national movement. He strove to establish a "Semitic Kingdom" under his leadership that would include Palestine and Transjordan and consist of Arabs and Jews living together as equals. Later, he also promoted his idea of a "Greater Syria" under his leadership, in which Jews would be granted full autonomy or equality in the Holy Land/Palestine.[26]

On the eve of the UN Partition Plan in 1947 and immediately after, Abdallah and Golda Meir (of the Jewish Agency) reached a tentative agreement to coordinate military and political activities, with the understanding that Jordan would annex the territory designated for the Palestinian Arabs and would refrain from military action in the territory designated for the Jewish state. However, under pressure from the Arab countries, the (Jordanian) Arab Legion invaded the Holy Land/Palestine on May 15, 1948 and occupied the West Bank and East Jerusalem, annexing them to the Jordanian kingdom. This was done without any intention or the ability to occupy parts of the territory designated for the Jewish state. In 1950, Abdallah's delegates negotiated with Israel on signing a peace treaty or truce agreement, but due to pressure from the Arab League, Abdallah suspended the talks. On July 20, 1951, Abdallah was assassinated by a young Palestinian at the entrance to the Al-Aqsa Mosque in Jerusalem.[27]

Abdallah's successor and grandson, King Hussein, continued for many years to maintain secret dialogue and cooperation with the Jewish state on matters of security, politics and economics, such as the American Eric Johnston Plan (1953–1955) to divide the water resources of the Jordan and Yarmuk rivers between Jordan and Israel. This concurrent to anti-Zionist and anti-Israel incitements and severe incidents along the border of both countries, which led to harsh retaliatory actions by the IDF.[28] These actions, especially in al-Samu village in November 1966, in which tens of Jordanian soldiers were killed or wounded, damaged Hussein's status and the fragile fabric of his relations with Israel.

169

In Israel there was concern that Hussein's rule was endangered by the rise to power of Nasser in Egypt (1952) and pan-Arab nationalism, including the union of Egypt and Syria (1958–1961); the establishment of the "Triangle Federation" between Egypt, Syria and Iraq in 1963, and the decision of the Arab Summit in 1964 to divert the Jordan River's waters and station Arab forces in Jordan. The radical Ba'th regime in Damascus, supported by the Soviet Union, was the major factor leading to the outbreak of the June 1967 war with Israel, and Hussein was forced to join the pan-Arab coalition against Israel, lest he lose his rule.[29] Indeed, he lost the West Bank, but continued his secret talks with Israeli leaders on a peace agreement, alongside severe skirmishes, foremost among them the IDF Karamah attack in Jordan (1968) in which tens of soldiers from both sides were killed. However, in (Black) September 1970, Israel helped Hussein survive vis-à-vis critical military threats from Palestinian organizations and Syrian armored units that infiltrated Jordan from the north.

On September 25, 1973, Hussein warned Golda Meir, Prime Minister of Israel, of a possible Syrian attack; and during the Yom Kippur War Jordan did not open a direct front against Israel, despite Egyptian and Syrian pressure, but only sent an armored brigade to the Golan Heights front, coordinated with Israel. After the war, secret dialogue continued towards a peace agreement between the leaders of both sides including a solution to the issue of the West Bank. However, these talks were stopped after Menahem Begin and the *Likud* party came into power in Israel (1977), and the orientation of Defense Minister Sharon to see in Jordan a Palestinian country. During the time of a national unity government (1984–1990), Shimon Peres as prime minister, and later as foreign minister, took action together with King Hussein to reach a political arrangement; they agreed in April 1987 on the "London Document" as the framework for a comprehensive Arab–Israeli agreement. Prime Minister Shamir strongly objected to this agreement, and Peres withdrew from it. Hussein was bitterly disappointed, and after the outbreak of the first Palestinian Intifada in December 1987, he decided in July 1988 on total disengagement from Jordan's ties to the West Bank and a renewed and clear recognition of the PLO as representative of the Palestinians.

At the Peace Conference in Madrid (October 1991) a Jordanian Palestinian delegation was present, acting both together and

170

separately, in which the Jordanians' talks with Israel were beneficial, and with the Palestinians – they were polarized; all in all, the talks failed. However, after Yitzhak Rabin became prime minister in 1992, the Oslo Accords between Israel and the PLO were signed (1993;1995), which led to improved relations between Israel and Arab and Muslim countries and a contractual peace agreement with Jordan in 1994. Especially relevant to our discussion here is the clause that addresses the issue of Jerusalem, i.e., " Israel respects the unique current role of the Hashemite Kingdom of Jordan in the Muslim holy sites in Jerusalem, when negotiations are held regarding the permanent status, Israel will give high priority to Jordan's historic role in these holy sites." (In 2013, the PLO as well recognized Jordan as the custodian of the holy sites in Jerusalem, and especially al-Haram al-Sharif.)[30]

As mentioned, Hussein had a deep connection to East Jerusalem and al-Aqsa – there he witnessed the assassination of his grand-father, Abdallah, in 1951. As a devout yet liberal Muslim, and the scion of the Hashemite family that ruled in the holy sites of Mecca and Medina, he clung to the sacredness of al-Haram al-Sharif and al-Quds al-Sharif, as an expression of the Muslim legitimacy of his rule. However, unlike many other Muslim leaders, he did not demand Muslim sovereignty over the Temple Mount and the Old City, but did suggest that such sovereignty be placed in the hands of God, wherein these sites be managed by three religions and become a symbol of peace between all the "sons of Abraham". Similarly, Hussein believed that Jerusalem must be united, as a "city of peace", with the western part of the city remaining the capital of Israel and East Jerusalem – the capital of Palestine.[31]

Up to his death (in February 1999), King Hussein did not see the realization of Israel's commitment regarding Jerusalem, nor the realization of a "warm peace" with Israel, in which he believed and promoted. The 'honeymoon' in the relationship between both countries was short-lived, lasting until Rabin's assassination (in November 1995), and did not continue during the period of Netanyahu's first round as prime minister (1996–1999). However, during Netanyahu's government as well, Hussein demonstrated a warm relationship towards the Jews in Israel, when in March 1997 he arrived in Israel to comfort the families of the seven young Jewish girls who had been murdered by a Jordanian soldier at the "island of peace" near Naharayim. Many Israelis deeply valued this gesture, as compared to extremist Jordanians who opposed it. At the same time, Hassan, Hussein's brother and would-be successor, continued to direct the Royal Academy for Interfaith Studies that was established in 1994 and maintained many dialogues with Jews and Israelis. However, these positive points had hardly any impact on the cooling of the "warm peace" between the two countries and their people.

The main factors that led to this cooling of the Jordanian–Israeli peace during Hussein's rule were as follows: (a) Israel's anti-Palestinian actions in East Jerusalem and the West Bank, such as expropriation of Palestinian land and building Jewish settlements; opening the Hasmonean tunnel near the Temple Mount in 1996. (b) The failed attempt of the Mossad to assassinate Hamas leader Khalid Mashal in Jordan's capital city, Amman, in September 1997. (c) The deep disappointment from non-implementation of most of the large economic projects initiated by Israel (especially by Shimon Peres), letting down many Jordanians who had nurtured hopes for a better standard of living. (d) A guarded, cold and arrogant attitude of Israeli leaders (especially Netanyahu and Peres). Thus, for instance, Peres was quoted by his biographer, Michael Bar-Zohar: "I'm not crazy about the Middle Eastern culture . . . Israel's connections with the Middle East are purely geographic, and Israel must try and distance itself from this region and form connections with Europe"; to which, Bar-Zohar added: "Many Arabs claimed that Peres speaks to them patronizingly and with disrespect." Two events that I attended attest to this.

As to Netanyahu, as early as 1993, he claimed that "Jordan is Palestine". Moreover, the prime minister of Jordan said that: "Netanyahu's image is characterized by arrogance and a show of force"; and the journalist Tom Friedman wrote in the *New York Times*: "Bibi, I don't believe you are aware of how you sound to Arab ears; a tone of patronization and scorn has clearly crept into your voice." President Bill Clinton made similar observations and added that "these were traits that especially bothered Arab leaders . . . Netanyahu would sit opposite Hussein with his legs crossed and the soles of his shoes facing the king, even though this is considered a scathing insult in the local culture". Ephraim Halevi, former head of the Mossad, who was involved in the Israeli–Jordanian dialogue, said: "It is sad to see the arrogant attitude of Israeli leaders towards Jordan, and their lack of sensitivity."[32]

All the above led, amongst other things, to the "cold peace" between Israel and Jordan during Hussein's rule; and during the rule of his successor, Abdallah II (from 1999) – it was an "increasingly chilly peace" as defined by the new king. He wrote thus: "This specific prime minister (Netanyahu) has stretched the relationship to the breaking point." To this must be added the words of Shimon Shamir, Israeli ambassador to Jordan (1995–1997): "From statements made by Israeli personages, in which one can discern scorn of the Jordanian Kingdom and even a threat to it . . . the state of the country of Jordan is precarious . . . and Jordan is Palestine."

Nonetheless, Abdallah II stuck to the peace treaty with Israel and at the same time supported the Arab peace initiative of 2002, with emphasis on a solution to the Palestinian problem. He cooperated with Israel in an attempt to ease Muslim–Jewish tensions at the Temple Mount at the end of 2015; and in a condolence letter upon the death of Shimon Peres on September 28, 2016, Abdallah emphasized Peres's support of a two-state solution to the Israeli–Palestinian conflict. However, in July 2017 he strongly objected to Israel's closing the al-Aqsa site to Muslim worshippers, following the killing of two Israeli policemen; and Netanyahu's behavior following an incident at the Israeli embassy in Amman in which an Israeli security guard killed two Jordanians. This led to the recall of the Israeli embassy's staff back to Israel. In December 2017, the Jordanian king denunciated President Trump's decision to recognize Jerusalem as Israel's capital. In May 2018 the Jordanian government condemned the transfer of the American Embassy to Jerusalem, claiming this would have a negative effect on Arab and Muslim public opinion.[33]

At the same time, Abdallah instructed to change the school textbooks, decreasing extremist Muslim implications and presenting a more positive mention of Christians and women, yet with no change regarding Jews and Israel. This attitude, as discussed in the section on textbooks, has remained extremely negative and contains anti-Semitic contents. In comparison, and at the same time, Egyptian President Sisi also instructed to remove from the textbooks extremist Muslim contents and introduce texts supportive of the peace with Israel (to cooperate with Israel out of strategic and pragmatic considerations). Yet, Israel is still presented as an aggressive entity that has crushed Arab Palestine and has taken control over East Jerusalem.[34]

173

Summary: Moderate Positions and Dialogues between Muslims and Jews After 1967

This chapter discussed the ambivalent positions of Muslims towards Jews and Israel: On the one hand, ideological and emotional animosity, manifested through violent words and deeds; on the other hand, the pragmatic and realistic positions taken by Arab and Muslim governments that recognize Israel, some of whom even acknowledge Judaism's bonds to Jerusalem. However, they refrain from any historic-ideological appeasement with Jews and Israel as long as the Palestinian problem has not been resolved, and especially the issue of East Jerusalem and the Temple Mount/al-Haram al-Sharif.

We have reviewed in detail two test cases regarding this issue – Saudi Arabia and Hashemite Jordan and their ambivalent positions towards Jews and Israel. Now is the place to summarize and further note the moderate positions held by other Muslims towards Jews and the ongoing dialogues between them, which stem from personal, cultural and even religious, economic and political motives; this occurs after 1967. Indeed, from 1967 and on, leaders, academicians and journalists continued maintaining positive connections with Israel and with Jews. They also proposed peace initiatives and participated in dialogues with Jews and Israelis, although many Muslims worldwide do not share these positive trends.

The most prominent among such leaders were the kings of Morocco, including Hasan II (1961–1999) who treated the Jews kindly and appointed several of them to ministerial and advisory posts for the crown. In 1985, he said, inter alia: "The crisis in the Middle East divides the sons of Abraham – Jews, Muslims and Christians . . . The future can only exist through dialogue", and at another time he said: "The Arabs are not demanding the full return of all of Jerusalem, as was the situation before 1967, but only the holy sites of Islam. The Arabs are not demanding the Western Wall . . . only what is theirs, such as the Al-Aqsa Mosque, where the prophet Muhammad prayed . . ."

As early as the 1960s, the king was in contact with Israel on security issues; he was involved in the ties between Egypt and Israel in preparation for Sadat's visit to Israel (1977) and instructed to open a Bureau of Interests in Israel following the Oslo Accords (1993). Tunisia as well opened a Bureau of Interests in Israel after the signing of the Oslo Accords; and during the "Arab Spring" (2010–2011), Rashid Ghanushi, leader of the *Nahda* [Resurrection] movement (under the auspices of the "Muslim Brotherhood"), who was elected prime minister, promised to protect the Jews from anti-Semitic attacks.

Tunisian president, Munsif Marzuki, made similar statements during a royal visit (April 2012) to the synagogue in Djerba. Additionally, the leader of the Islamic *Tahrir* (liberation) Party, Ridha Blahaji, said that same year: "No one has an issue with Jews who live here . . . for hundreds of years they have been our neighbors (but not the Zionist Jews in Israel)." Similarly, some of the leaders of the uprising during the "Arab Spring" in Libya made statements supporting the establishment of close relations between Muslims and Jews; and Prime Minister Ali Zaidan announced, in January 2013, that a solution of the Palestinian problem will bring peace with Israel and the integration of the Jews in Libya.[35]

As we have seen above, the Egyptian presidents as well – Sadat, Mubarak and Sisi – maintained peaceful relations with Israel (following Sadat's historic visit to Jerusalem in 1977). The Jordanian kings – Hussein and Abdallah II, did the same, following the signing of the peace treaty in 1994; the kings of Saudi Arabia for years have been developing secret strategic relations with Israel; as did the presidents of Indonesia and Pakistan at different periods (publicly as well). For example, the president of Indonesia, Suharto, welcomed Israel's prime minister, Yitzhak Rabin, to his home in Jakarta in 1993, against a background of secret security and economic cooperation. Abd al-Rahman al-Wahid, leader of the largest Muslim movement in that country, *Nahdatul-Ulama*, and its president (1991–2000), had visited Israel several times prior to that, held discussions with Israeli leaders and took part in Jewish–Muslim dialogue at the Hebrew University.

Pakistan as well, the second largest Muslim country in the world (190 million in number), maintained both secret and open relations with Israel; and after the Oslo Accords (1993) Pakistani and Israeli foreign ministers met publicly. Additionally, President Pervez Musharraf held discussions in New York (2005) with Jewish leaders and promised to officially recognize Israel and maintain normal relations with her after the establishment of a Palestinian state at Israel's side. After the Oslo Accords, and prior to that, not a few Muslim countries in Central Asia and black Africa, in the Caucasus and the

Balkans, formed diplomatic, security-related and economic ties with Israel and treated their Jewish communities fairly. In addition to the Arab peace initiative (2002) supported by the Islamic countries, the Saudi king, Abdallah, initiated interfaith dialogues with the participation of Jewish religious leaders. Similar dialogues were held on other occasions as well,[36] including at the al-Azhar Center in Cairo (2016) and at the initiative of Prince Hasan of Jordan.

Most recently, in March 2017, in an open letter addressed to the Saudi prince, Muhammad bin-Salman (king of Saudi Arabia), Abdul Hamid Hakim, director of the Middle East Center for Strategic Studies in Jedda, wrote, inter alia, as follows, under the title "A Golden Opportunity for Dialogue: People of Israel and Jews throughout the world . . . the holy Qur'an confirms that you are an integral part of the region. Your civilization and the history of your forefathers were and still are a part of the history of our region . . . rest assured that peace can be achieved, your historic role in our region is guaranteed within the framework of the Saudi peace initiative." In May 2018, Muhammad bin-Salman said that Israel has the right to its own land, yet he is concerned in regard to the Al-Aqsa Mosque and Palestinian rights. Another Saudi, Dr. Ali Sa'd al-Musa, had written previously in the Saudi newspaper, *Al Watan*, that Israel has no connection to the bloody struggles in the Arab countries; and a Sudanese religious cleric stated at an interfaith dialogue in Khartum that there is no religious ruling that prevents Sudan from maintaining ties with Israel.

At a Muslim–Jewish meeting held in March 2016, at the Islamic Theological Center, al-Azhar, Cairo, a discussion was held on the connection between the Holy Scriptures of Jews and Muslims; and on the book by Dr. Ali al-Sam'an, president of the International Union for Interfaith Dialogue and Education Towards Peace. The title of the book, which has recently been translated into Hebrew, is *Three Windows in Heaven: Accepting the Other, Dialogue and Peace in the Holy Scriptures of the Three Religions of Abraham*. Recently, Arab publicists condemned the Arab Muslim terrorist attack on the Temple Mount on July 14, 2017, calling it religious madness that is leading the Muslim nation to devastation (many others praised this attack).[37]

At a Muslim–Jewish convention held in Marrakech, Morocco in April 2016, in the presence of King Muhammad VI, a high-ranking Muslim stated that "anti-Semitism and Islamophobia are a threat to our communities, we must work together to prevent prejudice and fanaticism". In this regard, it is noteworthy that moderate Muslims will indicate from time to time those verses in the Qur'an that are supportive of Jews and their place in the Holy Land: "We settled the children of Israel in a respectful place and provided them with the best of all things"; "Moses said to his people . . . My people, enter the Holy Land that God has instructed you" (though there are far more anti-Jewish verses in the Qur'an).[38]

Not a few Muslims recognize Judaism's ties to Jerusalem, but only few of them acknowledge the ancient and historic existence of the Holy Temple built by King Solomon on the Temple Mount compound. Most Muslims worldwide deny this fact and strongly oppose building the Holy Temple on the Temple Mount and under full Jewish sovereignty. However, some Muslim leaders are willing to concede that the Temple Mount shall be under God's sovereignty, wherein Muslims will pray at al-Haram al-Sharif and Jews will pray at the Western Wall, which will be under Israel's sovereignty.[39]

On the other hand, only a small number of Jews agree to this solution, whereas the great majority, including most Israeli governments, demand Jewish sovereignty over the Temple Mount and all of Jerusalem, and not a few fanatic Jews are striving to build the Holy Temple upon the ruins of the mosques. The following chapter will address these positions and the ambivalent attitudes of Jews.

9

Jews, Jerusalem and the Temple Mount
Mitzvah or Anti-Islamism?

Israel, the Jewish state that was established in 1948, mostly related to its neighboring countries and to the minority living in its midst as Arabs and not as Muslims, even though most of the region's population was Muslim. A large portion of this population clung to the religion and culture of Islam, making hardly any distinction between Islam and Arabism. Most Arab regimes in the region were secular-nationalist, yet their laws reflected and emphasized their Muslim character and utilized religious Islamic terms in their wars against the Jewish state.

For her part, Israel formulated her relationship with the countries in the region based upon strategic, security-related and political considerations, and not religious-cultural ones, yet regarded Arab Islam as a strategic and existential threat. In order to weaken or neutralize this threat, Israel has been active since the 1950s in forming ties and treaties with moderate Muslim and non-Muslim countries and groups. For example, Ben-Gurion's unwritten doctrine in the late 1950s – "The Periphery Theory", in which potential, or actual, allies of Israel were the non-Arab Muslim countries such as Turkey and Iran, as well as Muslim countries in Africa. Ben-Gurion stated: "We must break the blockade which the hostile Arab countries have forced upon us and build bridges to the liberated countries of black Africa."[1] This strategy also included non-Arab Muslim minorities, such as the Kurds in Iraq; Christian groups such as the Maronites in Lebanon and the southern Sudanese; also Christian Ethiopia; as well as moderate Arab Muslim countries in the region's periphery – Morocco, Oman, Sudan and Yemen (at various time periods). However, with the passing of time, and especially after 1967, the geopolitical circumstances in the region and beyond underwent changes. In response, Israel developed various approaches to the challenges she faced from Muslim countries and groups. As stated in the previous chapter, the June 1967 war and the occupation of Sinai, the Golan Heights, the Gaza Strip, and especially the annexation of East Jerusalem and its Islamic holy sites – all these empowered Arab-Muslim opposition to the Jewish state, along with religious Islamic motives intertwined with nationalist sentiments.

However, the governments of Israel, of both the *Maarach* (Labor) and *Likud* parties, with the exception perhaps of the governments under Ehud Barak in 2000 and Ehud Olmert in 2008, ignored the protests, threats and proposals from Muslim countries and groups on Israel's continued rule over East Jerusalem (annexed to Israel in 1967 by the government and in 1980 by the Knesset). The same applied to the Judaization of the city and the establishment of settlements upon Arab lands conquered in 1967. These positions were addressed in many decisions of the UN, the Middle East Quartet (United States, Russia, the UN and the European Union), the Pan-Muslim Organization for Cooperation (the OIC, founded in 1969), and that of various Arab and Muslim countries. Especially noteworthy among the suggested political solutions to the question of East Jerusalem and the occupied territories, are the plan proposed by President Clinton in 2000 and the Saudi-Arab peace initiative in 2002, which was supported in 2005 by all the Islamic countries (57 in number, including 22 Arab countries). Yet, despite protests from many Muslim countries against Israel's continued control of East Jerusalem and the territories, Israel has continued to develop since 1967 strategic, security, political and economic ties with numerous Muslim and Arab countries in the Middle East, North Africa and black Africa, southeastern and central Asia and the Balkans.

Thus, for example, after the Oslo Accords (1993), Israel established diplomatic and political relations with seven Arab countries, at different levels: Egypt, Jordan, Morocco, Tunisia, Mauritania, Oman and Qatar; with Muslim (secular) countries in Asia – Turkey, Uzbekistan, Kazakhstan, Turkmenistan, Kyrgystan and Azerbaijan; and with Muslim countries in Africa and black Africa, such as Senegal, Zaire, Gambia, Mali, Guinea, Niger and Nigeria.[2]

179

However, some of these countries limited or severed their diplomatic and other relations with Israel, following Israeli actions taken against Palestinians in the Gaza Strip and the West Bank, and especially in East Jerusalem. It appears that Israel was ready to relinquish its diplomatic and fully normal ties with Arab and Muslim countries, just not to withdraw from its sovereignty over East Jerusalem and its control of the West Bank. For example, Israel rejected proposals by leaders from Indonesia and Pakistan – the largest Muslim countries in Asia – and from leaders in Morocco in northern Africa, to establish full diplomatic relations in return for an agreed-upon solution to the Palestinian problem and East Jerusalem. Similarly, Israel chose to forego full reconciliation with Turkey, Egypt and Jordan with whom it has maintained diplomatic relations for many years, and who repeatedly requested a full resolution of these problems. In December 2017, all the Arab and Muslim countries at the UN General Assembly voted against President Trump's decision to recognize Jerusalem as Israel's capital.

On the other hand, the majority of the Jewish population in Israel, and many Jews abroad who were deeply moved by the "liberation" of Jerusalem and the Temple Mount in 1967, have continued to support till today a united Jerusalem under eternal Israeli sovereignty. Additionally, nationalist secular Jewish and religious Zionist circles (around 30%), continue striving to rebuild the third Holy Temple on the Temple Mount, upon the ruins of the Al-Aqsa Mosque and the Dome of the Rock. Yet, like many Muslims who deny the historic existence of the ancient Holy Temple on the Temple Mount, there are not a few Jews who ignore the importance of East Jerusalem (al-Quds al-Sharif) and the Temple Mount (al-Haram al-Sharif) for Islam and the Muslims. They claim that Jerusalem is not mentioned in the Qur'an (nor is Jerusalem mentioned in the Holy Scriptures, only in the Book of Prophets); and that the Al-Aqsa Mosque is only of marginal importance to Islam ("not mentioned in the Qur'an", yet it is mentioned in Sura 17, verse 1); they ignore the fact that two billion Muslims believe that the mosque located in Jerusalem is the one that in the Qur'an is called *Bait al-Maqdas*.[3] Recently, Jewish Israeli leaders from nearly all political parties (except Meretz) have declared that a united Jerusalem under Israel's sovereignty is more important than peace with the Arabs.

The symmetry in the positions held by both fanatic Jews and Muslims in this sum-zero struggle over East Jerusalem and the fate of the West Bank, have bolstered anti-Semitism and Judeophobia amongst many Muslims, and strengthened Islamophobia amongst Jews, also as reaction to Muslim Judeophobia. The reciprocal hatred nurtures each side, that chooses to define its struggle against the enemy as a war between good and evil.

Continuity and Change in the Positions Held by Governments, Leaders and Groups in Israel

As stated earlier, all Israeli governments from 1967 and on (except for prime ministers Ehud Olmert in 2008 and Ehud Barak partially in 2000), and many religious and political leaders as well, have supported a united Jerusalem under Israeli sovereignty. Especially prominent were Shimon Peres, the architect of the Oslo Accords and Israel's ninth president; and before him, Israel's second president, Yitzhak Ben-Zvi, who said already at a Hanukkah candle-lighting ceremony (1960): "Next year we will be able to light the first candle on the Temple Mount". Only *Meretz*, the United Arab List and liberal Jewish circles continue to advocate East Jerusalem as the capital of Palestine.[4] This has marked a crucial change in Israel's history.

The *Yeshuv*'s main attitude towards Muslims and Arabs during the British Mandate continued after the establishment of Israel, though in different guises and dosages. Viewpoints such as "peaceful coexistence" as applied to a two-nation Jewish-Arab state in the Holy Land, characterized the *Hashomer Hatzair* movement (that established kibbutzim on Arab land after 1948), which was part of the United Workers Party (*Mapam*). The latter discarded this idea after a few years (when it broke off from the nationalist *Achdut Haavoda* party). In the years 1969–1984, *Mapam* joined the *Haavoda* (Labor) party and together established the *Maarach*-Labor and in 1992 it joined the *Ratz-Shinui* party – which later became *Meretz* – with a joint platform to divide the country into two states, Jewish and Arab, with East Jerusalem the capital of Palestine.

This viewpoint was adopted as early as the British mandate era by the Communist Party and continued after 1948 and 1967 in

Maki (Israel's Communist party), *Rakakh* (the new Communist party) and *Hadash* (the Democratic Front for Peace and Equality) – joined by both Jews and Arabs. Most of the independent Arab parties that were started after 1967 sided with this viewpoint as well. At the same time, small Sephardic and ultra-Orthodox circles from the old *Yeshuv* continued their dialogue with Muslim Arabs in Israel, in the hope of reaching coexistence and cultural and religious cooperation.

The Labor Party – Haavoda; *and* Kadima *– The Movement*

The central stream of the Zionist Jewish *Yeshuv* in the Holy Land during the British mandate (led by Ben-Gurion) was ambivalent in its attitude towards its Arab and Muslim neighbors. On the one hand, it maintained dialogues with moderate Palestinian leaders and was even prepared for a short period to agree to a bi-national Jewish–Arab state in the Holy Land with economic and political cooperation. On the other hand, it fought energetically, politically and militarily, against the Palestinian nationalist movement headed by the mufti Amin al-Husseini, while striving to establish a Jewish state on part of the Holy Land, even without Jerusalem. For example, it accepted the Peel Commission's proposal in 1937 and the UN Partition Plan in 1947. (Nor was Jerusalem mentioned in Israel's Declaration of Independence in 1948.)

By accepting these outlines, the leaders of the Zionist *Yeshuv* were in effect relinquishing parts of the Holy Land, including Jerusalem as a part of Israel; and they did so while agreeing to the internationalization of Jerusalem, which suited their secular viewpoint and their indifference to the religious-historic importance of the Temple Mount (though they did see in the Western Wall a historic-cultural symbol). With the establishment of the State of Israel and subsequent to that, Ben-Gurion and other *Mapai* leaders continued in this path and did not make an effort to occupy East Jerusalem in 1948, and for a short time were even hesitant to do so in June 1967, for fear of instigating a religious war with Islam. However, concurrently, up to 1966, the *Mapai* governments enforced military rule on the Arab minority in Israel, which included land expropriation, discrimination, limitations on passage between regions under military rule and political activity –

182

especially of Arab Muslims who were perceived as "fifth column" adherents.

These governments proclaimed their readiness for peace with the neighboring Arab countries, yet were answered with hostility, siege and terrorism from those countries (except Jordan) and from violent Palestinian organizations, such as Fatah and the PLO. However, as mentioned above, the Labor-*Maarach* governments succeeded in building diplomatic, economic and security-related bridges with both Arab and non-Arab Muslim countries, and especially after the Oslo Accords with the PLO (1993, 1995), which were supported by Prime Minister Yitzhak Rabin and Foreign Minister Shimon Peres. These accords seemed to symbolize Israel's reconciliation, led by the Labor Party, with the Palestinian National movement and its orientation towards returning territories occupied in 1967, in exchange for Israeli–Palestinian peace. However, de facto, the *Labor* governments established Jewish settlements in the West Bank, especially in the Jordan Valley – under Israeli military rule. (Other factions of the party, after 1967, joined the Movement for Greater Israel.) Over the years, *Labor* agreed to the establishment of a demilitarized Palestinian state with limited sovereignty in the occupied territories, but without clusters of Jewish settlements in the West Bank, and without East Jerusalem. For example, Shimon Peres, as prime minister, said in 1986 that "Israel's sovereignty over the Temple Mount is incontestable". Additionally, a new chairman, Avi Gabai (in 2017), supported a united Jerusalem under Israeli sovereignty, preferring that to peace with the Arabs.

Indeed, *Labor* and the governments it had formed repeatedly emphasized that a united Jerusalem is the capital of Israel and will remain under Israeli sovereignty. Thus, the party (as part of a national unity government) supported the unification of Jerusalem after the 1967 war, and in 1980 supported the Jerusalem Law (in the Knesset under the *Likud* government). *Labor* platform (1997) reconfirmed this position and has continued it till the present, except for its relinquishment of Palestinian neighborhoods and villages annexed after the 1967 war. Nonetheless, Yossi Beilin and other prominent members of *Labor* held discussions with Palestinians (in 1995 and 2000) in regard to Jerusalem as an undivided open city with two capitals and free access to all religions.[5] Ehud Barak, then prime minister, proposed, in the year 2000 at Camp David, Palestinian custodianship of the Temple Mount, but without sovereignty; administration, without sovereignty, in the Muslim and Christian Quarters of the Old City; and free passage between the holy sites of Islam and Christianity to North Jerusalem as part of the Palestinian State; establishing the city of "al-Quds" (except for the Jewish Quarter and the Western Wall), that will include the villages annexed to Jerusalem in 1967. However, PLO leader, Arafat, rejected this offer and demanded sovereignty over all of East Jerusalem and the Temple Mount. Barak, as Defense Minister in Netanyahu's government, proposed during a press interview that Jerusalem be divided between Jews and Arabs, with a special ruling body in the Old City.

Prime Minister Ehud Olmert, who left the *Likud* and joined the *Kadima* party led by Ariel Sharon, placed before Mahmud Abbas, president of the Palestinian Authority, for the first time, in 2008, a ground-breaking proposal regarding the future of Jerusalem and the Temple Mount, as follows: Establishing a Palestinian capital in East Jerusalem, wherein the Old City and the Holy Basin will come under international supervision with representatives from Saudi Arabia, Jordan, Israel, Palestine and the United States. Abbas delayed his response to this proposal, claiming that Olmert had refused to show him the proposed map and that there still remained major disagreements between them; and that at the time Olmert was under investigation for corruption and did not continue the negotiations. It is noteworthy that Olmert's proposal was not backed by the government and contradicted his promise to the ultra-Orthodox *Shas* party that Jerusalem would not be a topic of discussion with the Palestinians (in parallel talks held by Foreign Minister Tzipi Livni with Ahmed Qurai (Abu Alaa), the issue of Jerusalem was not raised). In June 2009, Olmert claimed that peace will not be achieved unless part of Jerusalem becomes the capital of the "Palestinian" state.[6]

Olmert, who in the past had held extreme views as a *Likud* member, totally changed his opinion on the Palestinian-Muslim issue and especially the question of East Jerusalem. On the other hand, Tzipi Livni (daughter of the chief operations officer for the historic *Irgun* militia,) and leader of *Hatnuah* (the Movement Party), who had fully identified with the *Likud* for many years, has supported in the last few decades the two-state solution, but without dividing Jerusalem. Additionally, Yair Lapid, leader of the *Yesh Atid* Party (later, the Blue and White party and its leader Benny Gantz), prefer a united Jerusalem over peace with the Palestinians and Arabs.[7]

The National-Secular Likud *Party and* Habayit Hayehudi *[Jewish Home] Party*

In the *Likud* there remains not a large group that continues to express liberal positions towards Muslim Arabs in Israel – continuing the line taken by Menahem Begin who, in 1966, initiated the termination of military rule. As to the question of the Palestinian territories, this stream supports, like its party – the *Likud*, annexation (applying Israeli sovereignty) of Judea and Samaria, yet also granting equal rights (gradually or conditionally) to the Palestinian inhabitants and improving their economic conditions ("economic peace").[8] However, those who hold these views also remain faithful to the long-standing position of *Herut* and the *Likud* for generations: United Jerusalem includes East Jerusalem and the Temple Mount "under eternal Israeli sovereignty". Extremist factions in the *Likud* and *Habayit Hayehudi* are even aspiring to rebuild the Holy Temple on the Temple Mount upon the ruins of the Al-Aqsa Mosque and the Dome of the Rock. They are thus preserving and promoting the trend set by members of *Beitar, Etzel and Lehi* and others from the British Mandate era, and that of right-wing intellectuals such as Uri Zvi Greenberg (see above).

To this stream belongs Gershon Solomon, head of the "Temple Mount Faithful" after 1967, who was a member of *Beitar* and the *Likud*, and joined Prof. Yuval Ne'eman, founder and head of the *Tehiya* Party (1981–1992). Both demanded to implement Israeli sovereignty over the Temple Mount. Solomon was consistently proactive for going up to the Mount, annually and offering sacrifices for the Holy Temple. In 1990, his actions led to riots by Palestinian Muslims and to the killing of 17 of them by Israel's Border Police. (Israel's Police Force has tried from time to time to prevent this ceremony and has lately won the backing of the High Court of Justice.)[9] The principal leaders of *Herut* and *Likud* since 1948, and especially after 1967, continued to embrace the policy of applying Israeli sovereignty over East Jerusalem and the Temple Mount, despite extensive Muslim (and international) opposition; and have taken additional anti-Muslim steps towards that purpose.

Menahem Begin, the leader of *Herut*, stated in 1949: "We could have gone up to the most holy of holies, Jerusalem, and redeemed the Temple Mount . . . there is no redemption of Jerusalem without the redemption of the Old City . . . we want all of Jerusalem." After 1967, Begin sided with the destruction of Arab houses in proximity to the Western Wall. At the Camp David talks (1978) with Sadat, Prime Minister Begin (since 1977) opposed the division of Jerusalem and claimed that "Jerusalem is a united city that is not to be divided and it is the capital of Israel for all eternity". He held this line as well in discussions with Egypt regarding Palestinian autonomy (yet in his talks with President Carter, Begin introduced the idea of three national committees – Muslim, Jewish and Christian – to administer Jerusalem).

In 1980, Begin passed the Unification of Jerusalem Law with a significant majority in the Knesset. Yitzhak Shamir, who followed Begin as prime minister (1983–1984, 1986–1992) as the *Likud* Party's candidate, had served as the leader of *Lehi* (the Stern Gang) prior to the establishment of the State of Israel, which formulated plans to destroy the mosques on the Temple Mount and rebuild the Holy Temple in their place. He also abstained from voting for the Camp David accords (1978) and the Peace Treaty with Egypt (1979), in contradiction to his party's position.[10] In 1996, Binyamin Netanyahu, prime minister from the *Likud* (1996–1999), instructed to open the Hasmonean tunnels, next to the Temple Mount, thus causing Palestinian riots and the death of tens of young Palestinians and Israeli soldiers. Even more deadly was Ariel Sharon's ascent to the Temple Mount in September 2000, escorted by one thousand policemen (he was then the head of *Likud*). This led to the al-Aqsa Intifada (2000–2002) and the death of hundreds of Muslims and Jews, as well as very harsh reactions from most Arab and Muslim countries. Sharon angered Muslims also when he supported a change in the status quo of the Temple Mount that would allow Jews to pray there; and when he purchased a house in the Muslim Quarter. He was proactive in establishing Jewish settlements in the West Bank, to neutralize any chance of a Palestinian state in that area and a Palestinian capital in East Jerusalem.[11]

Finally, Prime Minister Netanyahu, who perceives himself as the leader of the Jewish people, also adhered to a united Jerusalem under Israeli sovereignty. As the celebrations marking fifty years of a united Jerusalem approached, in May 2017, he declared: "Fifty years ago, we did not occupy, we liberated . . . Jerusalem was and always will be the capital of Israel, the Temple Mount and the Western Wall will always remain under the sovereignty of Israel." Prior to that, on Jerusalem Day, in May 2014, he stated: "Jerusalem was united 47 years ago; she will never again be divided; we shall never divide our heart – the heart of this nation. Jerusalem is also Mt. Zion and Mt. Moriah (Temple Mount) and the Western Wall – for all eternity." As far back as 1995, Netanyahu promised Yehuda Etzion – leader of the *Chai Vekayam* group that in 1984 had tried to blow up the Temple Mount – to resolve the right of Jews to pray on the Temple Mount, once the *Likud* returns to power. In fact, for many years, Netanyahu turned a blind eye to the visits of thousands of Jews on the Temple Mount and their attempts to hold prayers there. In July 2017 he supported the ban on Jews praying there yet allowed the ascent of 1200 Jews to the Temple Mount in August 2017, and an even greater number in July 2018 and August 2019.[12]

Among the ministers who went up to the Temple Mount and voiced insults against Islam were Uri Ariel (from the *Tekuma* faction of the *Habayit Hayehudi* party), Miri Regev, and Deputy Foreign Minister Tzipi Hotovely (both from the *Likud*). Uri Ariel said, for example, in 2005 that he wanted to build a synagogue on the Temple Mount in place of the mosques, with the guidance of prominent rabbis. He then went up to the Temple Mount and prayed there, calling upon Netanyahu to open the gates of the Temple Mount to Jewish worshippers. In February 2018 he stated that the time has come to build the Holy Temple on the Mount. The ministers Ze'ev Elkin and Gilad Erdan (*Likud*) supported allowing Jews to pray on the Temple Mount ("it is our indisputable right"). Nathan Sharansky, Minister of Jerusalem Affairs in the *Likud* government, said in 2003 that "the Temple Mount is more important than peace". Similarly, Education Minister Naftali Bennett, leader of *Habayit Hayehudi*, stated: "A united Jerusalem is preferable to diplomatic agreements" (Yair Lapid and Avi Gabai made statements of the same nature).

Miri Regev, Minister of Culture & Sports, who was active on this issue, also stated that Jews shall go up to the Temple Mount even if it leads to an Intifada. She and Ayelet Shaked, former Minister of Justice, hold extreme anti-Palestinian positions, which are shared with Deputy Foreign Minister Tzipi Hotovely, who stated in October 2015: "I dream of the day when the Israeli flag flies over the Temple Mount . . . It is the center of Israeli sovereignty, the capital of Israel, the holiest site of the Jewish people." In March 2017, the two ministers, Elkin and Regev, proposed establishing a government fund to cultivate the legacy of the Temple Mount. Apparently, several Holy Temple organizations are the recipients of government funds.[13]

It may be assumed that these declarations and the visits of ministers, Knesset members and many Jewish people to the Temple Mount constituted a significant contributing factor to the outbreak of the al-Quds (Jerusalem) Intifada (the "Intifada of Knives") that began in September 2015. Many Palestinian terrorists justified their actions as protectors of the Al-Aqsa Mosque which, as they saw it, was defiled by the forceful entry of policemen into the mosque. In this regard, the killing of two Israeli policemen must be noted, murdered by three Israeli Muslim Arabs on July 14, 2017, at the entrance to the Temple Mount; and the murder of the Salomon family in Neve-Tsuf-Halamish just a few days later, executed "to protect the Al-Aqsa Mosque", as explained by the terrorist.

Prime Minister Netanyahu, who was disturbed by the Palestinians' violence and Arab and Muslim criticism, promised Abdallah II, King of Jordan, at the end of 2015, to prevent the ascent of Knesset members and Israeli politicians to the Temple Mount, and to limit the visits of activists and other Jews at the site. These steps did significantly decrease Palestinians' violence, but did not end it. Nor did it end the efforts of right-wing secular nationalists and religious Zionists "to liberate the Temple Mount" and rebuild the Holy Temple upon it.

In April 2017, Netanyahu stated that he was considering lifting the ban on Knesset members to visit the Temple Mount. Such a step might anger a great number of Muslims. This, in addition to the increasing number of Jews who have visited the Temple Mount since early 2017; the opening of a visitors' center and a "*Mikveh* Route" at the foot of al-Aqsa; and the Muazzin Edict suggested by the Israeli government that is an insult to Muslim feelings. Indeed, in response to these steps taken by Israel, the Muslim Waqf Council published in March 2017, an announcement which also contained the statement: "The city of Jerusalem and the blessed al-Aqsa mosque have, since 1967, come under insane racist Jewish attack . . . the Muazzin Edict is aimed at ethnic cleansing and driving away the Jerusalem's Muslims and building centers for the settlers."

Turkish president, Erdoğan ("guardian of al-Haram al-Sharif")
at a Erdoğan conference on the Waqf in al-Quds in May 2017, also
attacked Israel for its "racist" policies regarding Jerusalem, and
the prayers of the Muazzin, and called upon masses of Muslims to
visit al-Haram al-Sharif and support their brethren (see also
Chapter 5).[14]

It should be noted here that like the extreme secular right-wing
in Israel, the religious Zionists' rabbis and the nationalist ultra-
Orthodox, represented mainly in *Habayit Hayehudi*, later *Yemina*,
have been heading in the past two decades the anti-Muslim Israeli
faction that aspires to rebuild the Holy Temple on the Temple
Mount, contradictory to the positions held by the religious Zionist
leadership up to 1967.

Dual Positions of Religious Zionism, the Haredim (Ultra-Religious) and Shas after 1967

As reviewed above, the positions held by the religious Zionist parties
– *Hamizrachi*, *Hapoel Hamizrachi* and later the *Mafdal* [NRP –
National Religious Party] – remained moderate up to 1967, when
compared to the secular nationalist right-wing groups on the issues
of Muslims and the Temple Mount. Though many of them
harbored dreams of rebuilding the Holy Temple, they did not take
any steps to implement this dream. Religious Zionist leaders even
disagreed to the occupation of the Old City and the Temple Mount
in 1948, and in 1967 as well. This was also the position of many
Haredim, both Zionists and non-Zionists. As to the attitude towards
Muslims and Arabs, a significant number of religious Zionists felt
loathing and scorn towards them, whereas moderate factions and
many *Haredim* sought peaceful and equal coexistence with their
Arab neighbors. But according to new research, during the 1950s
and 1960s, amongst religious Zionists were heard "no less than
Messianic positions that supported the use of force against Amalek
(Arabs), and for the liberation of Jerusalem and the entire land
through revengeful redemption".[15]

Following the occupation of the Palestinian territories, East
Jerusalem and the Temple Mount in June 1967, anti-Muslim-Arab
positions were gradually and increasingly heard among the religious
Zionists and sections of the *Haredi* Jews – *Habad* and *Shas* –
primarily amongst nationalist *Haredim* and *Gush Emunim*. By

contrast, sections of *Shas* and the Ashkenazi *Haredim* (mostly non-Zionists) have continued to oppose the ascent to the Temple Mount and the rebuilding of the Holy Temple in the present era.

In order to discuss in some detail the controversies between the different religious factions, it must be emphasized that the Chief Rabbinate of Israel and most *Haredi* rabbis have continued to prohibit by religious law the ascent of Jews to the Temple Mount till the coming of the Messiah. (Nonetheless, prominent rabbis, such as Rabbi Kook and others, continued to envisage the rebuilding of the Holy Temple and train *priests* and *Levites* and other Jews in preparation of this momentous redemption.)[16] This Halachic position (pertaining to religious law) was supported by Rabbi Ovadia Yosef and the rabbis of *Shas*, as well as rabbis from the Ashkenazi *Haredi* sector and religious Zionists. With that, however, since 1967 there has been a progressively growing religious-nationalist Messianic trend that, countering the Chief Rabbinate, preaches and is proactive for ascension to the Temple Mount and the rebuilding of the Holy Temple upon the ruins of the mosques.

Rabbi Shlomo Goren led this trend as Chief Rabbi of the IDF (prior to 1967 and up to 1968), as Chief Ashkenazi Rabbi (1972–1983), with the backing of other rabbis from the Chief Rabbinate's Council. As early as 1955, Rabbi Goren preached the use of force to conquer the Holy Land and rebuild the Holy Temple and noted that the Armageddon is part of the course of redemption. Similarly, Rabbi Mordechai Eliyahu, as Chief Sephardi Rabbi (1983–1993), stated in 2012: "It is the Kingdom (of Israel) that declares unhesitatingly that it desires the Holy Temple . . . even if this means destroying the mosques."[17] Other organizations that followed this direction were *Ne'emanai Har Habayit* [Faithful of the Temple Mount) and *Gush Emunim*, after 1974, and an ever-increasing number of Holy Temple organizations from 1984 and on. (In that year, Yehuda Etzion tried to blow up the Dome of the Rock on the Temple Mount.) Further significant support also came from the Rabbinical Council of Judea & Samaria in 1996 (apart from Rabbi Shlomo Aviner and a few others); all were backed by part of the leadership of the *Habayit Hayehudi* party (especially the minister Uri Ariel from *Tequma*).

The endeavor to build the Holy Temple upon the ruins of the mosques developed along with the hatred of Muslims and Islam

(Islamophobia), although in the more moderate circles of Ashkenazi religious Zionists and amongst Sephardi religious Jews there were manifestations of "support and even sympathy towards the Arabs' condition". This stemmed from their acquaintance with "Arab doctrines and mentality" (allegedly in contrast to the hostility and racism of European Jews or towards those of Eastern origin – Jews and Muslims alike).

For example, Rabbi Ben-Zion Uziel, the Sephardi rabbi of Jerusalem, in the past defined the Arabs as "our dear cousins". Other expressions of moderation towards Muslims and the holy sites of Islam may be found in the *Meimad* movement, headed by Rabbi Malkhior Micha'el and Prof. Aviezer Ravitzky, the religious kibbutz movement, and even amongst settlers in Judea and Samaria. Prof. Shlomo Rosenberg of the Hebrew University, and one of the founders of *Meimad*, held that a resolution on the status of Jerusalem must find expression as part of a general reconciliation between Islam and Judaism. Rabbi Yehuda Amital, head of the Har Zion Yeshiva and one of the leaders of *Meimad*, called upon *Gush Emunim* to settle in the hearts of the Arabs, as Islam is close to Judaism.[18]

Moshe Gafni, from the *Yahadut HaTorah* party (*Haredim*), pointed out that "the Palestinians were here before us" and that the historic right of the Jews "lies within the boundaries of the Green Line". He opposed any change in the status quo of the Temple Mount and argued that "One and a half billion Muslims throughout the world are hearing that Jews are trying to change the status quo and see (Israeli Jewish) public figures going up to the Temple Mount, and this causes escalation". Even Rabbi Thau of the religious Zionists spoke out harshly against the Jewish underground that in the 1980s tried to blow up the mosques on the Temple Mount. He labeled it the "Messianic cult" that wishes to bring redemption using arms and negative ideas . . . to redeem Israel by exploding the mosques on the Temple Mount; "They are causing devastation and destruction". Other prominent figures, including the heads of Israel's General Security Services and the Mossad, warned that Jewish attacks on al-Aqsa may lead to a Muslim Jihad. Similarly, Uri Haitner, spokesman for the Golan Hebron in 1994 by Baruch Goldstein – "It is a terrible crime against humanity . . . this massacre brought disgrace upon the Jewish people . . . and did damage to Judea, Samaria and Gaza and the idea of a Greater Israel."[19]

Similarly, this mindset may be found amongst members of the moderate stream of settlers in Judea and Samaria who oppose violence towards Arabs carried out by individuals, who are not members of the armed forces. They support protecting the properties, honor and rights of the Arab residents ("foreign residents" as per Maimonides) within the process of redemption of the Jewish people throughout the country, and granting equal civil rights to Arabs (or even the establishment of a Palestinian state alongside Israel).

This viewpoint is supported more or less by moderate rabbis in the settlements – such as Rabbi Avi Gisser (who believes that there is no Jewish threat to the al-Aqsa mosque); Rabbi Menahem Fruman (who holds that religious closeness between Islam and Judaism, between Muslims and Jews, can serve as a joint basis for peace between Jews and Palestinians).[20] However, this moderate school of thought is not sufficiently consolidated and is in fact marginal, compared to the increasing hate movements towards Muslims and Arabs among religious Zionists and *Haredim*, and the arguments between them on the issues of ascending the Temple Mount and rebuilding the Holy Temple.

After 1967, many *Haredi* Jews – both Ashkenazi and Sephardi (*Shas*) – continued honoring the Chief Rabbinate's orders to refrain from going up to the Temple Mount until the coming of the Messiah. (However, not a few continued to go to the Temple Mount and display hostility and ridicule towards Muslims and Islam.) For example, the popular *Haredi* weekly, *mishpacha* (Family), published the following in 2015: "We, the *Haredi* population, have no interest in going up to the Temple Mount at this time, we firmly oppose it . . . Jewish religious law sees in this a severe prohibition – punishable by excommunication . . . we are not a party to this conflict . . . we aren't exactly Zionists . . . no *Haredi* will go up to the Temple Mount . . . after all, your rage (of the religious Zionists) is directed at the Temple Mount . . . Going up to the Temple Mount is what instigated the terrorism . . . don't irritate the nations of the world even if we are in control here . . . the command to save lives cancels out the *mitzvahs* . . . . Religious Zionism is a nationalist ideology." The senior *Haredi* rabbis – Elyashiv and Shakh – made similar statements. Also the current Chief Sephardi Rabbi, Yitzhak Yosef, opposes Jews ascending the Temple Mount: "The Holy Temple shall be rebuilt by the Holy One, blessed be He."

However, at a later date, Rabbi Yitzhak Yosef said: "A non-Jew (a Muslim?) cannot live in the Holy Land . . . Whoever does not take upon himself the seven precepts of Noah must be expelled to Saudi Arabia – the non-Jews have to serve the Jews."[21] Even more arrogant and vitriolic was his father. In his weekly sermons, Rabbi Ovadia Yosef, leader of *Shas* and former Chief Sephardi Rabbi, said (even though in 1989 he ruled that land can be returned to the Arabs in exchange for peace): "Islam is an ugly religion . . . and we must pray for the death of the Ishmaelite Palestinians (the Muslims)"; or, put another way: "Muslims are stupid, their religion is as ugly as they are", "These evil ones – the Arabs ('snakes'), it is written in the *Gemara* that God regrets having ever created the sons of Ishmael"; and also: "Non-Jews were created only to serve the Jewish people".[22] Similarly, among the religious Zionists and *Haredi* nationalists extreme views developed after 1967, pertaining not only to the Temple Mount and the occupied territories, but also against Arabs and Muslims; these were manifested in speech and writing, as well as through violent actions.

Extreme Anti-Islamic Positions Held by Religious Zionists, Haredim *and Nationalist* Haredim, *after 1967*

The rabbis and theorists who lead these extremist groups, including *Habad*, define Islam and Muslims (Arabs) in a manner similar to the positions held by extreme Muslims towards Jews and Judaism: "Islam is leading the unfathomable hatred of Israel, and Arab nationalism is linked at its core to the religion of the sword; a lowly nation, lagging behind with arrogance and wildness, cruelty and lies; lacking culture, primitives, thieves and robbers; they are anti-Semites, like Amalek, like the evil Haman, the land does not belong to them, only to us, we must expel them, push them out". "There are a billion Arabs (Muslims) in the world and they are meaningless, and revenge upon non-Jews will be taken by the Messiah, the King, with joy and ecstasy."[23]

These anti-Muslim and anti-Arab statements are no less venomous than the statements made by Rabbi Meir Kahana, an extreme racist who said, inter alia: "Non-Jews, such as the Canaanites and the Ishmaelites (Muslims) . . . have no choice but to run away or to face the edict, 'Not every soul shall live' . . . They must be sent out, expelled." Like Kahana, Rabbi Zvi Thau – one of the prominent students of Rabbi Zvi Yehuda Kook (who opposed the destruction of the mosques), compared the Palestinians to the Philistines and claimed that "they have no right to exist but to bring the Jewish people to spiritual and sovereign realization in their land. As soon as this goal is fulfilled, they will no longer exist." Rabbi Dov Lior, the rabbi of Kiryat Arba and one of the leaders of radical religious Zionism, said that "All the Arabs there (in Judea, Samaria and Gaza), from the age of sixteen to sixty, have to be taken and transferred to another place – to Heaven." He also justified the massacre carried out by Dr. Baruch Goldstein at the mosque of the Cave of the Patriarchs in Hebron, in March 1994. Even Rabbi Eliezer Melamed, head of the yeshiva at Har Bracha, compared the Arabs to Amalek and quoted from the Bible: "Erase the memory of Amalek from under the skies." Prof. Hillel Weiss of Bar Ilan University and a member of the new "*Sanhedrin*", in 2014, called "to destroy the Palestinians as rabble, it is a mitzvah . . . they aren't a nation". At a conference of public activists from the religious Zionist movement, in May 2017, Knesset member Bezalel Smotrich, deputy Knesset chairman, proposed three options to the Palestinians: leave the country; live in *Eretz Yisrael* as "foreign residents" – a bit inferior; or, if they refuse – then kill them (women and children too). "In war, as in war."[24]

Even prior to that, in 1980 Rabbi Lior wrote: "Among the three mitzvahs given to the Israelites as they entered the Holy Land was to build the Holy Temple; building the Temple came after the establishment of the Kingdom of Israel and eradicating Amalek." Rabbi Israel Ariel, head of the Holy Temple Institute, wrote at the same time in the same journal that the commandment, "Thou shalt not kill" does not apply to non-Jews, and that non-Jews must be expelled from the land, and it is forbidden to transfer to them or sell to them land in the Holy Land.

Rabbi Yitzhak Shapira, head of the Od Yosef Hay Yeshiva, in 2009 published *The King's Torah*, in which he claims that Jews can kill non-Jews, including children, if they endanger Jews. These Islamophobic incitements and statements among the leaders of a Messianic religious nationalist public were also manifested in demonstrations and other events, especially in Jerusalem in the last few decades, with groups of youngsters shouting: "We will destroy Amalek, Muhammad is a pig, a son of a bitch; Muhammad is dead;

death to the Arabs; Islam is a virus and Arabs are animals; no Arabs
– no terrorist attacks." Also, "The Holy Temple will be built – the
mosque will burn down." Such voices have also been heard during
the flag-waving parades held by religious Zionists in the Muslim
Quarter of Jerusalem in recent years.[25]

In addition to these exclamations, there were several incidents of
setting fire to mosques (and some churches) and books of the
Qur'an in the West Bank and Israel; and many acts of violence
against Arabs, perpetuated by the *Tag Mehir* movement. Most
blatant in recent years were the kidnapping of the young Palestinian
boy, Muhammad Abu Khadir, who was then murdered and his
body set on fire in the Jerusalem Forest, on July 2, 2014; and the fire
set to the home of the Dawabsha family in the village of Duma, in
the West Bank in July 2015, which claimed the lives of both parents
and an 18-month-old child, and severely injured his four-year-old
brother.[26]

Radio Islam reported on September 11, 2014 (with exaggeration) a long line of "aggressive actions against and desecration of
the Al-Aqsa Mosque since June 1967" by "Messianic Jews". This
also included: Setting fire to the *Mihrab* of the Al-Aqsa Mosque by
an Australian Christian, Dennis Rohan, June 21, 1969; the forced
entry into the *Haram* (sanctuary) by Gershon Solomon and his
gang, on August 14, 1970; Allen Goodman, an Israeli soldier,
burst into the mosque with an M16 rifle and fired at the worshippers, killing and wounding sixty Palestinians, on April 11, 1982;
Israeli soldiers shot at a procession of Muslims at the *Haram*,
killing and wounding nearly one hundred, on May 12, 1988;
Israeli authorities instigated a terrible massacre at the Al-Aqsa
Mosque, killing 22 worshippers and injuring more than 200, on
August 8, 1990.

During the al-Aqsa Intifada nearly five thousand Muslims and
Jews were killed and injured, and in the al-Quds Intifada of October
2015 nearly 200 Palestinians and 33 Israelis were killed.[27] This
horrific blood-shedding did nothing to deter fanatic Jews (and
Muslims) from attaining their goals, and perhaps even served to
encourage some of them to persist in their ways.

For example, Yehuda Etzion wrote in the Gush Emunim journal,
Nequda, in January 1994: "Jerusalem will remain ours, she is our
eternal capital and will remain united and in our hands for eternity
... Bring redemption to the (Temple) Mount, rid it of the Muslims'

hold." Even after his release from prison, Etzion continued preaching and planning the rebuilding of the Holy Temple in place of the mosques. Similarly, Baruch Goldstein became a cultural hero of sorts, a righteous, holy figure amongst extremist Jews who every so often frequented his grave, and even edited a book in memory of "the holy one".[28] In this regard, it is notable that wherein many Jewish Israelis, including nationalist religious Jews, condemned the massacre in Hebron, 80% still support Israeli sovereignty over Jerusalem and the Temple Mount, and 30% support the rebuilding of the Holy Temple upon the ruins of the mosques.[29]

Indeed, a growing number of Jews in Israel and abroad (including many soldiers) continue to express their affinity to the Temple Mount and their longing to rebuild the third Holy Temple, in speech, in writing and via actual visits to the site. Moreover, about nineteen Holy Temple organizations in Jerusalem (including the "Women's Organization for the Holy Temple") are busy planning the rebuilding of the Temple, and some are plotting how to destroy the mosques ("the abomination"), ready to sacrifice themselves towards this goal. For example, a video made by settlers [in the West Bank], shows how a plane bombs the mosques while their leaders urge them on "to obliterate the mosques on the Temple Mount".[30]

The extensive ambivalence and the changes in the positions held by religious Zionists on these critical issues were well described by Avraham Burg, son of one of the leaders of the *Mafdal* party, a religious Zionist thinker who had also served as a Knesset Speaker and as head of the Jewish Agency. He wrote in the *Haaretz* newspaper, on April 19, 2017, inter alia, as follows:

> There is no single religious Zionism, at one time perhaps it was possible to define it monolithically as "Torah with civility", Torah and work . . . national redemption, a religious and clearly anti-Messianic way of life; that is who we were up to 1967 . . . . Then a new generation rose . . . and moved into wild regions. The two Rabbis Kook, both father and son, and the holy spirits – Levinger, Porat and their herd – drew everything to the very edge: redemption, lands, Messianism and fanaticism . . . There are the righteous, such as the *Tag Me'ir* movement, and the hate mongers, such as the Tag Mehir movement . . . There are those who consistently sing from their hearts, "and thou shalt love thy neighbor as thyself", and

those who stand under their wedding canopy while brandishing guns and singing with conviction, "and I shall take revenge upon one of my eyes, revenge upon one of the Palestinians' eyes" . . . There are also proud left-wing Orthodox Jews, and racist nationalists from the same Orthodox stream . . . whoever listens, will also hear terrible, horrible voices. . . . Discussions on Jewish blood being preferable to non-Jewish blood, on the Arabs who are a "nation that resembles a donkey" . . . Visions of building a third Holy Temple have turned into practical plans for Temple activists, and what to many seems as a terrible price to pay (the Armageddon – a worldwide holy war), in their eyes is perceived as worthy.

Muslims worldwide, and especially in the Middle East, in the occupied territories and in Israel, reacted through protests, demonstrations and violence against Jews whom they see as endangering the Al-Aqsa Mosque. The name, *al-Aqsa* (and also *al-Quds* and *Bait al-Maqdas*), was adopted by armed groups, the media and many Muslim associations, and served as an inspiration to hundreds of millions of Muslims in the region and throughout the world, strengthening their anti-Semitism/Judeophobia.

Back in 1969, a PLO document called upon the Arab Muslim Palestinian people and all Muslims on Earth to a Jihad, to liberate the Al-Aqsa Mosque. A PLO conference in 2014 expressed the "readiness of all to sacrifice themselves for the Al-Aqsa Mosque – it is a moral, national and religious right against Israel that sponsors aggression against al-Aqsa in holy Jerusalem and the attempt to desecrate al-Aqsa". These have also been the positions held for many years by the Hamas and the (northern) Islamic Movement in Israel (Umm al-Fahm). Apparently, under its influence, three Israeli Muslim Palestinians from Umm al-Fahm killed two Israeli policemen at the entrance to the Temple Mount on July 14, 2017. Since then, Israel has closed the Temple Mount to Muslim worshippers, which instigated furious reactions from Palestinian, Jordanian and Saudi leaders. The Turkish government spokesman defined this Israeli decision as "a crime against humanity . . . against religious freedom". Sometime before that, Turkish president, Erdoğan, called upon Muslims (in 2016 and 2017) to defend Jerusalem and the Al-Aqsa Mosque.[31]

The abysmal Muslim–Jewish divide on the issue of the Temple Mount/al-Haram al-Sharif was manifested also after the murder of

13-year-old Ariel Hillel Yaffe in her home in Kiryat Arba, by Muhammad Nasir Tariya, a 17-year-old Muslim from Banu Na'im. Ariel's mother called for an ascent to the Temple Mount as an anti-Muslim act, whereas Muhammad's sister claimed al-Aqsa as the symbol of the war against the Jews.[32] Thus, in the past few decades the Temple Mount/al-Haram al-Sharif and the Al-Aqsa Mosque have become the symbol and focus of a sum-zero game between Muslims, Arabs and many Palestinians on the one hand, and nationalist Jews, both secular and religious, on the other hand; each side is willing to sacrifice itself and shed blood to gain control of the Mount and prevent the control from falling into its rival's hands. As previously stated, each side perceives its struggle against the opposing side as a war of good vs evil.

The deep polarization between Muslims and Jews, young and old, on the issue of the Temple Mount/al-Haram al-Sharif, East Jerusalem and the Holy Land/Palestine, stems to a great extent from the educational systems and school textbooks on both sides, but especially the Palestinian side (which was extensively reviewed earlier). Now let us examine these issues as they are reflected in the textbooks and educational systems of the Jewish state.

Muslim and Arab Imageries in Israel's Educational Systems and Textbooks

When compared with the textbooks used in Arab countries that depict Jews and Israel in an extremely negative manner, the textbooks used in Israel since its establishment have been more ambivalent and less extreme and impassioned, meaning: they include both negative and positive expressions regarding Arabs and Muslims at different time periods and in different contexts; and they usually reflect the trends in Israel's Jewish population and critical changes that occurred over time.

The textbooks used in secular schools usually have a positive, matter-of-fact and more balanced approach; as compared to those used in religious and *Haredi* schools, which are laden with negative, anti-Arab/anti-Muslim sentiments. The orientation common to most textbooks throughout Israel's existence, and even prior to that, is: Justification of the right of the Jewish people to the Holy Land and denial of the Arabs' right to it; reinforcing Zionist awareness and aggrandizing Jewish culture and values in contrast to the "inferior" culture and values of Arabs and Muslims.

On the positive side, some schools have included in their curriculum, for example, books written by S. Yizhar, *Hirbet hiz'ah* and *Prisoner-of-War*, that address the moral issues faced by fighters in 1948. Various liberal educators have recommended teaching Isaiah's vision of peace, studying the Muslim–Jewish "Golden Age" in Spain, and introducing greater familiarity with Israel's Arab and Muslim neighbors.[33] After the war of June 1967, prominent professors of history and education spoke out against the negative stereotyping of Arabs and the mounting extreme chauvinism amidst the Jewish public. They proposed presenting a multifaceted picture of the conflict, including an objective examination of Jewish and Arab stands in the educational system. Indeed, when Yigal Alon was in office as Education Minister, from the Labor Party in the early 1970s, this policy was implemented. Even Zvulun Hammer, Education Minister from the *National Religious Party* in the *Likud* government (1977), said in 1979: "The State of Israel has always aspired towards peace. We have never preached hatred between nations. A repeated in-depth examination of our textbooks shows that we did not in any way use antagonistic expressions that might be insulting to the Arabs." Hammer also approved programs to expand the teaching of Arab history and culture, including the Arabic language, in schools. These programs were mainly implemented in the high schools' "Eastern studies elective" sectors (from the early 1960s), that were oriented at training Jewish youth to serve in the IDF intelligence services.

Education Minister Yitzhak Navon (1984–1990), from the *Labor* party, emphasized educating towards democracy and Arab–Jewish coexistence; and Education Minister Amnon Rubinstein (the *Meretz* party, from 1992 to 1996) was known for his liberal and highly balanced approach towards Arabs and Islam, who initiated for the first time a teaching syllabus for the educational system that discusses the peace process: "Israel in the Middle East". In his words, the aim of this program was "to develop a citizen who is tolerant, aware of the values of peace, sensitive, alert, involved and knowledgeable", i.e., possessing knowledge of the Arab world, including the Arabs of Israel; learning the different positions held in Israeli society regarding the peace process; and education towards peace. In 1995, the Education Ministry published a series of

199

booklets for teachers and students during Zvulun Hammer's second term as Education Minister (1996–1998).[34]

On the other hand, emphasis was placed on helping "the student feel an affinity, love, pride and belonging to his country, his people and his culture". This included the Jewish ties to a "united Jerusalem". However, even when Hammer was in office, and at other times as well, some shortcomings remained in the textbooks pertaining to Arabs and Islam, such as: inaccuracies, prejudices, demeaning and patronizing biases, and even anti-Muslim/anti-Arab expressions (that in part are similar to anti-Jewish expressions in Arab textbooks).

For instance, some textbooks stated that the culture of Islam is inferior and unauthentic, and in fact was influenced by other cultures, including Judaism; that the religion of Islam is the "religion of the sword" (especially in textbooks used in religious schools). Arabs are characterized at different periods in the textbooks, especially those used in religious and *Haredi* schools, as disloyal, devious, trouble-makers and intriguers. They are compared to a modern Amalek, to Haman, Hitler and Nazis. In a series of textbooks, "The Land and its People", used in Jewish schools (for civil studies courses) in the past years, the inhabitants of neighboring Arab countries (including Egypt and Jordan that signed peace treaties with Israel) are described as "Jew-haters that unceasingly seek opportunities to harm Israel and its inhabitants; antagonistic (Arab) countries that are plotting conspiracies . . . Israel is among the Arab countries like a lamb among wolves." The maps included in these books hardly acknowledge the Arab settlements on both sides of the Green Line, which does not even appear in most textbooks.

Though Israel's Arab citizens were discussed in various textbooks, as part of the "Living Together" study program in the 1980s and 1990s, they were called "Israeli Arabs" or "Arabs of the Land of Israel", without noting their national Palestinian identity. Other textbooks reflected a trend to integrate Arabs as equal Israeli citizens and the injustices caused them were noted, such as the extensive land expropriation in 1948 and the 1956 massacre in Kafr Qasim. At the same time, however, doubts were raised as to their loyalty to Israel and their desire to become an integral part of it. The new lexicon of the Civil Studies sector defines them as antagonistic to the country.[35]

Education Minister Gidon Sa'ar (2008–2013) initiated a program for Israeli high-school students to visit the Jewish sections of Hebron, including the Cave of the Patriarchs, in order to strengthen their Jewish affinity to the site and emphasize that Hebron is part of Israel. However, this was done without mention of the Muslim link to the Cave and the city of Ibrahim – *Al-Halil* (friend of Allah); and with total disregard to the massacre of Muslim worshippers in the mosque at the Cave of the Patriarchs, in February 1994 by Baruch Goldstein.

Naftali Bennett, leader of the *Habayit Hayehudi* party and Education Minister (2015–2019), was supportive of developing the educational system for the Arab sector in Israel, but in fact a huge gap still exists in the budget allocations for the Arab educational system as compared to the Jewish sector, especially the budget for religious education. Bennett even boasted in a newspaper interview: "I've killed a lot of Arabs in my life, and I have no problem with that." He supported Israeli soldier Elor Azariah who had killed a dying Palestinian terrorist in Hebron in March 2016; and in May 2017, the Education Ministry partnered with the Israeli Police in a presentation before elementary school students in Ramat Hasharon, in which police are shown shooting a Palestinian lying on the ground. Bennett also stated that the majority of Palestinians in Judea and Samaria support Hamas that aims at the destruction of Israel, and that Mahmud Abbas is a "terrorist". In a television interview for al-Jazeera in late February 2017, Bennett claimed that all the land of Israel (including the occupied territories) belongs to the Jews and to Israel, as stated in the Bible – and this has precedence over Israel's Supreme Court's rulings. And in June 2017, at the Peace Conference sponsored by the *Haaretz* newspaper, Bennett stated that he prefers a united Jerusalem to reaching a political agreement with the Palestinians. It has lately been reported that the textbooks during his time in office glorify the building of a third Holy Temple. In illustration, at the end of the school year in 2018, children in some elementary school classes and kindergartens of the secular stream were taught and even practiced how to go up to the Temple Mount and build the Holy Temple (while eradicating the mosques from the photo of the Temple Mount). While briefing high-school students before their trips abroad to disseminate informative propaganda about Israel, Education Minister Bennett said, among other things: "The Arab countries don't want the tiny democratic Jewish state to survive", and that "only in Israel can such a democracy be found".[36]

It can be concluded that in most textbooks, at different times, and in the educational system, the attitude towards the Palestinian Arab Israeli citizens, as well as to Arabs and Islam, was ambivalent. It was also influenced by circumstances and political changes, the public's stand and the personal philosophy held by each of the education ministers. Thus, the education ministers of the *Labor* party, *Yesh Atid*, and mainly *Meretz*, demonstrated liberal positions, as compared to those of the religious Zionists – the *Habayit Hayehudi* and the *Likud*, who were antagonistic. In the past decade, for example, Education Minister Shai Piron, of the *Yesh Atid* party (2013–2014), favored better familiarity with the Arabs in Israel and recognized the religious ties of Islam to Jerusalem.

The Jews' Dual Positions towards Arabs and Muslims in Israel

As with the textbooks, the positions held by Israel's governments and the Jewish population towards Palestinian Arab citizens have been and remain ambivalent: On the one hand, official action has expanded to integrate them into Israeli society, to advance them socially and economically, to improve the educational and health systems and increase their democratic representation in the Knesset, alongside greatly increased dialogues and cooperation. On the other hand, suspicions have remained as to their disloyalty – a "fifth column" of sorts; discrimination de facto in various fields – such as budgets for education, municipal bodies, etc.; unemployment, land expropriation and excessive use of force against suspects; infringement upon the Arabs' equal rights as a national minority, recognizing only their religious affiliation. The recently passed Nationality Bill in July 2018 demonstrates that clearly.

The negative-distrustful attitude is targeted mainly at the Muslim population, which today constitutes 84% of the two million Arab inhabitants, 21% of Israel's population; the remaining 16% are Christians and Druze – most of whom are Arabs. (Each group constitutes about 8% of the Arab population.) The Druze enjoy a more positive attitude from the Israeli establishment and the Jewish public. However, it may be asserted that most Arabs in Israel, with the exception of ultra nationalist circles and extreme Islamists, are loyal citizens of the country and formally enjoy equal rights; yet they do not identify with the country's Jewish-Zionist character, but rather with the Palestinian people and with Islam, and feel like deprived second-class citizens.

This ambivalent situation has existed since the establishment of the State of Israel, with trends towards improvement and integration on the one hand, and discrimination in certain areas along with national and Palestinian nationalist politization, on the other hand. Israel's declaration of independence in May 1948, as a Jewish state, endowed all its citizens with equality regardless of religion, race or gender, and called upon its Arab inhabitants "to do their part in developing the country on the basis of full and equal citizenship" (at the time, they numbered 156,000 out of a population of 800,000).[37] However, most of them (75%) in fact came under martial law and the supervision of the security services and the Advisor on Arab Affairs in the Prime Minister's Office. They lived in several closed areas, mainly the Galilee, the Triangle and the Negev, without freedom of movement between areas and other places, unless by special license.

The formal justification for this policy: Security considerations vis-à-vis the Muslim Arab population with its affinity to Israel's enemies across the borders. However, numerous studies have shown that the contribution of this policy to Israel's security was negligible, whereas the main objectives of military-security supervision actually were: The appropriation of land under Arab ownership (nearly four million dunams) and motivating Arabs to vote for the party in power – *Mapai*.[38]

Furthermore, the killing/massacre of 49 Arab villagers in Kafr Qasim in late October 1956 by border patrol soldiers, greatly shook the Arab public and symbolized the brutal attitude of the security forces and the government towards this populace. Martial law was nullified in 1966, under pressure brought by the parties *Herut* (led by Menahem Begin) and the "General Zionists". Nonetheless, the government continued its policy of "Divide and Rule", thwarting the Israeli Arabs' aspiration to coalesce as a political-cultural national body and establish national parties (except for the Communist party – *Maki*, which recognized Jewish nationalism and the State of Israel from its beginning; this was continued later by the *Rokakh* and *Hadash* parties).

A report put out in 1962 by the GSS (Israel's General Security Services) noted that: "It was the government's policy to split up the Arab population into communities and regions . . . This policy actively prevented the consolidation of the Arab population into a single entity." And in 1966, Abba Hushi, head of the Arab Section in the *Mapai* party, stated: "There is danger in the very existence of an Arab party that is independent of Jewish parties . . . A nationalist party that is not identified with the country may eventually bring devastation upon the Arab populace in Israel."[39] (Referral here was to the emergence of the nationalist-Arab movement, *Al-Ard*, that was declared illegal in 1964.) Following the war of June 1967 (during which the great majority of Israeli Arabs remained loyal to Israel), and a reinforced sense of security in the government and the Jewish populace, the status of Israel's Arabs improved significantly.

The political, economic, social and cultural conditions of Israel's Arabs indeed improved, as was noted by a Palestinian Arab researcher in 1998: "The Arabs in Israel enjoy a relatively high income per capita compared to most Arabs in the Middle East. They enjoy relatively high welfare in the education of men and women, freedom of expression, religion, and social and cultural mobility. They can attack government policies, organize public demonstrations, criticize or sue the ruling bodies without fear of punishment."[40] Amongst other things, with the passage of time, an increasing number of Arab representatives were elected as Knesset members on behalf of both Arab and Jewish parties. Currently, there are seventeen Arab Knesset members, of whom at least seven are Muslim, and the others – Christians, Druze or religiously unaffiliated. Notably, two served as ministers, and at different periods a few served as deputy ministers; judges at different levels, police officers, ambassadors, consuls, mayors and heads of regional councils. There is ongoing dialogue and cooperation between Jews and Arabs in many fields – economic, social and cultural.

Over the years, governments – including the *Likud* – initiated numerous programs to improve the economic and social infrastructure for Israel's Arabs and their integration into national institutions (apart from security institutions) and educational networks at all levels. During the government of Yitzhak Rabin (1992–1995), "affirmative action" policies were introduced in different fields and special budgets were allocated. However, many of these plans were left unimplemented or only partially so, for a variety of causes: Ideological – the Jewish character of the State that pushed aside many Muslim Arabs to a more inferior, deprived status, as they saw it; Security issues – they were defined by the GSS and many Jews as a "strategic threat", or "fifth column", "an extremist dangerous population that exploits its capabilities" (though some GSS directors did recommend to increase the integration of Arabs through civil equality); Bureaucracy – encumbrance and non-implementation of government decisions; Political – excluding Arabs from the political system, with the exception of Rabin's government (1992–1995).[41]

The Or Commission, established as an official investigative committee following the bloody events of October 2000 (in which 12 Israeli Arabs and one Israeli Jew were killed), stated in its summary in 2003, inter alia: "The State and all its governments throughout have failed in that they did not address comprehensively and in depth the difficult problems posed by the existence of a large Arab minority within the 'Jewish' State. Government treatment of the Arab sector was characterized mostly by neglect and privation. The establishment did not demonstrate sufficient sensitivity to the needs of the Arab sector, nor did it take action to allocate government resources to the Arab sector in an equal manner. The State did not do enough and made insufficient effort to bestow equality upon its Arab citizens and remove manifestations of discrimination and privation at once and at the same time (particularly in the fields of poverty, crime, unemployment, a shortage of land and schools); not enough was done to enforce the law in the Arab sector, and illegitimate and undesirable elements took root in this sector . . . Part of the leadership in the Arab sector, some of its most prominent leaders, failed to delineate the demands of the Arab minority to legitimate democratic channels alone. They failed to understand that violent riots, roadblocks and identifying with armed action against the State and its citizens constitute a threat to the State's Jewish citizens and severely damage the delicate fabric of Jewish–Arab relations in the country.

This has given rise to a pattern of threats of violence and harsh violent actions to achieve different goals, displayed in reaction to the destruction of homes and appropriation of land, and in regard to negotiations on the future of Jerusalem and the status of the Temple Mount . . . Ariel Sharon's visit to the Temple Mount led to harsh reactions from the Arab sector's leadership and Palestinian leadership in Judea and Samaria."

The Commission accused, amongst others, Sheikh Raad Salah, head of the northern branch of the Islamic Movement, in instigating violence against Israel, which he claims is illegitimate; he further stated that Israel planned to destroy the mosques on the Temple Mount and is responsible for the massacre on the Temple Mount. He called upon the Muslim public to physically protect al-Aqsa. The Commission further determined that in the Jewish sector as well manifestations of incitement against Arabs were found to some extent, along with incidents of extreme violence against Arabs by the police – and recommended that the police force inculcate an approach that perceives Israel's Arabs as citizens with equal rights.[42]

However, after the Or Commission – and prior to it (for example, on Land Day 1976 in which six Arabs were killed) violent clashes took place between the police and Israeli Arabs, ending in the death of tens of Arabs. Concurrent to that, many of the Or Commission's recommendations were not implemented, despite significant improvements and budget allocations. In fact, up to 2018, the policy of discrimination and racism against the Arab sector continued – such as in airport security checks; the actions of undercover counter-terrorism units (*Mistaarvim*) in Arab villages, the destruction of homes, and police violence. Most recent examples are notably the incident in Umm Hiran in February 2017,[43] in which a Bedouin teacher, Yaqub Abu al Qiyan, who was accused by the police of being an ISIS terrorist, was killed, and only later did it become clear that this accusation was totally unfounded. In addition to the police and other security forces, large portions of the Jewish population in Israel (50%–70%) continued perceiving Arabs as a "fifth column", "the enemy", "traitors", disloyal citizens who are not part of the Jewish "authentic democracy" in Israel. A great many of this Jewish populace, especially members of the *Israel Beiteinu* party, support the transfer of Arabs from Israel to the Palestinian Authority. (In contrast, liberal Israeli Jews have continued to actively work for peace and the equality of Israel's Arabs.)

An outstanding example of these anti-Arab positions among numerous Jews in Israel is found in the recently published book, *The Arab Minority in Israel, Open and Hidden Processes*. It was written by Prof. Rafi Israeli from the Hebrew University and was publicly launched with about four hundred *Likud* members, amongst them the Transportation Minister Israel Katz and coalition head, David Bitan. In his book, Israeli claims, inter alia, that "the national and Islamic element in the Arabs' identity prevents them, the Arab population, from integrating into the country; and that, with the help of the naïve left-wing sector, they are a threat to Israel's existence . . . They constitute a heavy economic, social and security burden on the Jewish State . . . Parasites that suckle from the nation's udders . . . sucking out from the general funds more resources than they bring in or that they deserve . . . This is the behavior of a 'fifth column', not of loyal citizens . . . Despite the fact that the Arabs openly identify with our enemies . . . , not only are they not detained in camps, they are permitted to speak out from every platform". Some of those present at this event called the Arab Knesset members "traitors" and demanded "to throw them out of the Knesset and reinstate martial law on Israel's Arabs." In June 2018, Minister Galant spoke out against "Palestinian-Islamic" expansion in the Hebron region, and in Afula Jews demonstrated against Arabs residing in the city, calling out, "We won't give the neighborhood to Islam".[44]

Undoubtedly, these extreme Jewish positions and the strict and discriminatory policies of Israeli governments have caused reinforcement of the currents of alienation and nationalist politization amongst Israel's Arabs, and especially its young generation ("the upstanding generation"). These streams manifested trends of "Palestinization" and Islamization, especially after the occupation of Palestinian territories in June 1967 and the Israeli Arabs' encounter with their brethren across the border. For many Arabs – mainly those who underwent a process of Israelization – their dilemma, or conflict, has worsened since 1967, torn between their loyalty to the country and their identification with the Palestinian people. The Oslo Accords between Israel and the PLO (in 1993 and 1995) nurtured in many Arab Israelis expectations for a resolution of the conflict between their country, Israel, and their Palestinian Arab people. They also established national institutions such as the "Follow-up Committee"; the General Committee of the heads of Arab local councils, and the Joint List for the Knesset-with various agendas.

The General Committee, for example, published in 2006 a document on a "future vision for Palestinian Arabs in Israel", in the aim to promote their Palestinian civil and national rights within the framework of a state of all its citizens, void of any Jewish distinctiveness. However, the severe negative reactions of many Jews and the worsening relations between Israel and the Palestinian Authority (and Hamas in Gaza), further decreased Palestinians' trust in Israel. Additionally, Israel demanded of the Palestinian Authority to recognize Israel as a Jewish State – a demand that many Arabs see as proof of inequality, discrimination and their exclusion. In that regard, the "Nationality Law", initiated in 2017 by prominent Israeli right-wing leaders and ratified in the Knesset in July 2018, was meant to cast down Israeli Arabs, as they understood it, to second-class citizenship, and their language to an inferior level.[45]

Islamization Among Israel's Arabs and Government's Reaction

The historic-primary identity of most Arab citizens in Israel was and remains – Muslim; it developed before, and alongside, their identifying with Palestinian Arab nationalism. Even radical and secular circles, such as Communists and Christians, recognized the importance of the Muslim faith in Palestinian Arab identity.

The central Islamic movement in the region – the "Muslim Brothers" (established in Egypt in 1928) – began operating in 1946 in Jerusalem and Palestine in 25 branches, and appointed Amin al-Husseini as its honorary president. Only after the war of 1948 did it break up between the Gaza Strip – under the close supervision and hard oppression of Abdul Nasser – and the West Bank under Jordanian rule. They merged with the "Brothers" in Jordan who supported the Hashemite king. In Israel they refrained from anti-Israeli political activity, while the Muslim community concerned itself with establishing institutions of religion, education, justice, Waqf and charity, and its representatives cooperated with the government.[46]

After Israel's occupation of the West Bank and the Gaza Strip in June 1967, Islamic (and Palestinian nationalist) trends developed/intensified among Muslim Arabs in Israel. This stemmed from a renewed encounter with their relatives, as well as with the "Brothers" in the occupied territories and beyond; from the possibility to pray at the Al-Aqsa Mosque in Jerusalem and fulfill a pilgrimage to Mecca and Medina; and the chance to study in religious institutions in the West Bank and in Arab countries. However, despite their anti-Jewish/anti-Israel positions, the "Muslim Brothers" and other groups refrained from an armed struggle against Israel after 1967 (unlike the PLO and Fatah, whose leaders had been tied in the past to the "Brothers"). They preferred to conduct a spiritual-cultural jihad against Jews and Israel. Israel even encouraged these orientations – for instance, by supporting in the late 1970s *al-Mujama al-Islami* – a Muslim center of the "Brothers" led by Sheikh Ahmad Yassin (Head of Hamas from 1988, which since then has turned violent). Israel's actions were targeted at fighting the PLO's influence in the Gaza Strip. [47]

However, in comparison to *Mujama*, other Islamic organizations were violent and active against the Israeli occupation, inspired to a degree also by the Islamic revolution in Iran (1979) and the successful terrorist actions of Hizbullah (which was established in 1982). Among the prominent organizations that began prior to the first Intifada (1987) were the Islamic Jihad movement that for a time was led by Fathi Shiqaqi from Gaza; Usrat al-Jihad (1979) led by Sheikh Abdullah Nimr Darwish from Kafr Qasim in the Triangle. After some years in Israeli prison for activating terrorism (1980–1983), Nimr Darwish founded the Islamic Movement in Israel that refrained from illegal violent actions, focused on educational projects and moderate Islamic instruction, and also worked within the framework of public organizations, municipalities, schools and sports teams.

In 1996 the Islamic Movement split up following disagreements as to taking part in national political activities. Nimr Darwish led the moderate southern faction, whereas Raad Salah led the extremist northern faction (from Umm al-Fahm). [48] Abdullah Nimr Darwish preached for understanding and moderation between Muslims and Jews and made frequent appearances on Israeli media and at inter-faith conferences abroad. Amongst other things, he served as co-chairman (with the author of this book) of a forum sponsored by Israel's president, and attended by hundreds of Jews and Muslims, aimed at learning and understanding the religious, cultural and social life of the two peoples. He supported the two-state solution: Palestine and Israel. (He died in May 2017.)

In 1998, Darwish was replaced by Sheikh Ibrahim Sarsur (from Kafr Qasim), a graduate of Bar-Ilan University and Knesset member from the Joint Arab List (2006–2015). Like his predecessor, he supported the integration of Muslims into an Israeli society that is democratic, guarantees equality and seeks peace. However, he attacked Israel's occupation of Palestinian territories. In contrast, Raad Salah, leader of the extremist northern faction, remained a fierce opponent of Israel and voiced anti-Semitic remarks. He consistently worked to protect the Al-Aqsa Mosque from Israeli occupation and was imprisoned many times for inciting violence and racism.[49]

In November 2015, his movement was officially outlawed by the Israeli government, which closed all its branches and confiscated its land-bound properties. In an announcement released by the Prime Minister's Office, Netanyahu said that "these steps were taken against a movement that supports actions of incitement and racism, under the heading, 'Aqsa is Endangered' and the false accusation that Israel is planning to damage the mosque and digress from the status quo . . . It is a sister movement to the terrorist Hamas organization . . . A separatist racist group that does not recognize Israel's institutions and denies her right to exist, and calls for the establishment of an Islamic Khalifate in her stead . . . The step taken is not targeted against the Arab and Muslim population, the great majority of which upholds the country's laws and renounces incitement and terrorism."[50]

One may argue as to the wisdom of the government's decision to outlaw the northern faction, which is a widespread Islamic social-religious movement, thus spurring its supporters to anti-Israeli underground activity. Yet, there is no doubt that the leaders of this movement have connections with Hamas and hold similar viewpoints in their attitude towards Jews and Israel and the question of the Al-Aqsa Mosque. Both see in Sheikh Izz al-Din al-Qassam – who was active in the 1930s against the Jews and the British – as a role model; and see in Israel and the Jews – enemies of Islam. Devotees of both movements worked together, or parallel to each other, using violence "to save the Al-Aqsa Mosque" against attempts by Jews to attack it. This was expressed in the killing of two Israeli policemen at the entrance of the Temple Mount on July 14, 2017, by three Israeli Muslims from Umm-al-Fahm, the center of the northern faction.

Israel reacted firmly against activists from both these movements and against Hamas that controls Gaza and is expanding its influence to the West Bank as well. A clear example is the severe response to the kidnapping and killing by Hamas activists in June 2014 of three Jewish boys in Gush Etzion – Eyal Yifrah, Gilad Shaer, Naftali Frankel. In the *Shuvu Achim* operation (Brothers – Return), which lasted for eleven days, 5 Palestinians were killed and 350 were arrested in the West Bank, most of them Hamas members and some who had been released in exchange for Israeli soldier Gilad Shalit. This operation and Hamas' response (firing rockets from Gaza) led to the *Tzuk Eitan* operation (Operation Protective Edge) against Hamas in Gaza (from July 8 to August 25, 2014), claiming many victims – 73 Jews killed and hundreds more injured, and about 2,200 Muslims killed, including 284 women and 369 children. Additionally, the Gaza Strip suffered massive destruction, with 17,000 houses demolished and thousands of wounded inhabitants.[51] (In May 2017, Hamas altered its views and now makes a distinction between Zionist Israelis – the enemies of Islam, and Jews that are accepted by Islam; it also agrees to the establishment of a Palestinian state within the 1967 lines, yet without recognition of Israel.)

Since then, a ceasefire has generally been maintained in the Gaza Strip, except for the occasional launching of rockets by more extremist Salafi organizations, including ISIS activists who fired at Israeli territory also from Sinai. According to the GSS, ISIS in the past few years has gained some influence over Arabs in Israel, including the Bedouin (who had remained apolitical for a very long time). This led to the formation of underground cells of the organization in Arab villages and dozens of youngsters joined ISIS, some of whom even took part in the fighting in Syria. And, as stated above, the Bedouin teacher, Yaaqub Abu al Qayan from the Bedouin village of Umm Hiran, was unjustly accused by the police of being a member of ISIS, after he had been shot by policemen who came to destroy illegally constructed houses, in January 2017.

In summary, this case, in addition to many similar incidents, testifies to the fact that the police force, its commanders, and significant parts of the Jewish public still see in Israeli Arab citizens a security threat, potential terrorists – and not citizens with equal rights like the Jews. This position is blatantly displayed by Avigdor Lieberman, leader of the *Israel Beiteinu* party and former Defense Minister. Hence, despite significant improvements in the government's policies and the Arabs' socio-economic conditions, many of them continue to harbor feelings of alienation, exclusion and discrimination, and even fear the intention of not a few Jews to expel them from Israel. The continued conflict between Israel and the Palestinians in the territories further increases among the latter their conflict between civil loyalty to the country and their national identification with the Palestinians. This dilemma may vanish or diminish if a trustworthy peace agreement is reached between Israel and the Palestinians, which will include a mutually acceptable solution to the issues of East Jerusalem and the Temple Mount/al Haram al Sharif. Such an agreement may well neutralize or decrease the anti-Israeli and anti-Semitic positions held by extremist Muslim circles among Palestinians in Israel and in the territories, as well as in Arab and Muslim countries.

For example, it is interesting to read the attitude to some of these issues as expressed by Sheikh Raad Salah, leader of the Islamic Movement and mayor of Umm al-Fahm (2003–2008): "I am a citizen of the State of Israel and also a Palestinian, and I cannot disconnect myself from the country, nor can I disconnect myself from being Palestinian . . . Even in our dreams, we do not harbor the thought that Islam shall rule in Israel . . . The democratic way is today one of the tools accepted by all Islamic movements . . . . The Jihad movements mainly brought harm to Islam . . . . I think it all begins and ends with Israel's conflict with the Palestinians and the Arab people . . . And I see that Israel is assimilating into the Middle East, in the Islamic East . . . There is no other way . . . 'The Jewish State' – what does that mean? That I am out? . . . We want to remain in the State of Israel . . . I don't want to be in Palestine, because I am a citizen of Israel . . ." With that, however, Salah also stated: "Whoever dares to lift a hand against the Al-Aqsa Mosque, we will chop his hand off . . . I will be the first *shahid* at the mosque's gates . . . If they try to kill me while defending the Al-Aqsa Mosque, I will not be alone buried under the ground."[52]

It appears that since then, Sheikh Salah has turned more radical in his views of Israel and Jews and has become anti-Semitic/Judeophobic, while still representing a substantial number of Palestinians in Israel and the territories. In contrast, many Palestinians still support a Muslim–Jewish dialogue and a two-state solution – Israel and Palestine (with East Jerusalem the capital of Palestine). These dual positions may be parallel to some extent to the trends found among Jewish Israelis. As we have seen above, a substantial number of Jews, including former prominent figures in the security system, the IDF and the religious Zionist movement, support a political solution of the conflict, whereas an Islamophobic stream, that is nationalist-messianic, and "determined and influential", is relentlessly striving to gain control over the entire land, neutralize its Palestinian Muslim inhabitants and rebuild the Holy Temple on the ruins of the mosques.

These extreme positions, on the Muslim side as well, may lead in the worst-case scenario to a Jewish–Muslim Armageddon, unless the pragmatic streams on both sides succeed in prevailing over the extremists and reach peace agreements and reconciliation between Muslims and Jews. For example: Establishing a Jerusalem Confederation (as proposed by Gabriel Moked and others) of three independent states – Israel, Palestine and Jordan – with Jerusalem as the capital of the Confederation and remains an open city in which the holy sites are jointly managed.

Concluding Remarks

In Chapter 8 we learned that despite the ongoing trends of hostility towards Jews and Israel, the past few decades have witnessed the majority of Muslim governments, along with some religious, political and social leaders, holding positive or pragmatic positions on these issues (except for the extreme Shi'ite Iranian government). This stemmed from motives, interests and considerations that were strategic, security-related and economic. The most outstanding manifestations of these pragmatic positions were (and still are) the Arab peace initiative of 2002, as well as *fatwa*s by chief muftis in Egypt and Saudi Arabia and the positive stands taken by Imams and Muslim public figures.

Compared to these positions, we have seen in Chapter 9 a symmetry of sorts in the positions held by many Jews and Muslims, and asymmetry in the positions held by most governments in the Muslim countries and in Israel, regarding Jerusalem and the Temple Mount. For, apart from Ehud Olmert (2008), Israel's governments have rejected the Arab Muslim peace initiative and other international proposals towards solving the issues of East Jerusalem and the Temple Mount. The majority of the Jewish population in Israel as well (and many Jews abroad) support Israel's sovereignty in these places; and nearly 30% support the rebuilding of the Holy Temple

213

upon the ruins of the mosques. The statements and actions of Jewish extremists against Muslims are closely similar to those of fanatic Muslims' expressions against Jews and include mutual arrogance and violence. As Israeli writer Amos Oz expressed it in his book, *Dear Zealots: Letters from a Divided Land* (2017): "If the messianic zealots succeed in destroying the mosques on the Temple Mount and, in their stead, build the Holy Temple . . . once again we shall bring upon ourselves devastation . . . There are those among us who wish to lead us into a war with all of Islam . . ."

It is also interesting to note the dual positions of *Haredi* Judaism in Israel – Ashkenazi Jews and Jews with origins in Islamic countries. Many of them – even the Chief Rabbinate – oppose the ascension to the Temple Mount and building the Holy Temple, till the coming of the Messiah; whereas a considerable number, especially from the *Shas* party, hold Islamophobic attitudes. True, liberal religious intellectuals and others express positive attitudes towards Islam and Muslims and the question of the Temple Mount. However, they are few in number and lack any real impact, whereas many of the religious Zionists– led by *Habayit Hayehudi* party – fulfill positions of power and influence in Netanyahu's government and promote anti-Muslim positions, while striving to rebuild the Holy Temple, even if upon the ruins of the Temple Mount mosques, and thus may ignite a Muslim–Jewish Armageddon.

It is possible that the new "Unity Government" in Israel (May 2020) will better protect these mosques from Jewish zealots' destructive actions and permit more Muslims to pray at al-Aqsa mosque. This, according to Trump's "Deal of the Century" (January 2020) that most Israeli Jews have accepted. However, Israeli right-wing parties and about 400 radical rabbis have strongly opposed the deal's suggestion to create a demilitarized (mini) state on parts of the West Bank and Gaza strip.

In comparison, most Palestinians, Arabs and Muslims intensely reject Trump's assertion that an undivided Jerusalem should be under Israel's sovereignty and its capital; whereas a Palestinian capital will be situated in some villages adjacent to East Jerusalem.

Both these antagonistic attitudes may in the worst-case scenario ignite an all-out Muslim–Jewish war, overriding and extending beyond the common menace of COVID-19.[53]

Summary
A Critical Historical Change:
Dialogue or Armageddon?

There are two central viewpoints still popularly held by many groups regarding the state of the Jews in Arab and Muslim countries: The first, shared by many Jews – including religious leaders, politicians and some researchers – claims that Jews were persecuted and suffered violence and massacres in the Islamic lands throughout history, because of Islam's historic and perpetual anti-Semitic-Judeophobic attitude. The opposite perception held by many Muslims and Arabs, and a small number of Jews, is that Jews lived in Muslim lands throughout history peacefully and comfortably, up to the emergence of the Zionist movement that severely damaged the delicate fabric of Muslim–Jewish relations, creating a harsh conflict between them.

Though both above viewpoints contain some correct elements, pertaining to certain eras and countries, they are flawed with coarse, imprecise generalizations that ignore the great complexity of Muslim–Jewish relations over long time periods and in different regions, influenced by political-economic-social factors, internal and external, as well as ideological-religious factors.

This book has widely discussed the duality (ambivalence) in the mutual relationships between Muslims and Jews, against a background of great asymmetry between both sides, demographically (2 billion Muslims vs. about 15 million Jews today); geographically (57 Muslim countries today vs. one Jewish country as of 1948); and politically – the rule of Islam for many centuries over minority Jewish communities. However, after the occupation of Arab territories in 1967, a greater clout – political, military, strategic – gradually developed in the positions held by Jews; as the Jewish state rules directly over several million Muslims and indirectly impacts

215

on the feelings of many more millions in Arab and Muslim countries. This has stemmed from Israel's control of the holy sites of Islam on the Temple Mount (al-Haram al-Sharif) and East Jerusalem (al-Quds al Sharif).

We have seen that for long time periods and in different regions, the positions taken by Sunni Muslim rulers (and at times religious leaders), and less so Shi'ite Muslims, towards their Jewish subjects were tolerant and at times even positive, based on specific verses from the Qur'an and pragmatic considerations. These attitudes were usually better than those held towards Christian subjects; and incomparably better than the way Jews were treated for centuries in Christian countries.

Jews integrated in, cooperated and maintained dialogue with Muslims in economic, social and cultural fields (a Jewish–Muslim symbiosis of sorts), especially during the "Golden Era" in Spain and Egypt (10th–13th centuries), the Ottoman Empire (from the end of the 15th century to the early 20th century) and in other Sunni Muslim countries. At times, Jews defined Muslim rule as "a kingdom of benevolence", "an Ishmaelite kingdom of moderation", and even identified with it during difficult periods of war and distress.

On the other hand, Jews also experienced very difficult times in various countries under the Berber dynasties in North Africa in the 11th to 13th centuries; in Shi'ite Iran and Yemen from the 16th century, i.e., persecutions, forced conversion to Islam and violent riots; and in the 19th century, from blood libels (instigated by Christians). These severe phenomena stemmed from or were influenced by adverse Qur'an verses, fanaticism, patronization and religious-fanatic hostility; envy of the Jews' economic achievements; violence by incited Muslim rabbles; and rarely also in response to actions by Jews perceived by Muslims as provocations.

The more critical provocations, from the viewpoint of many Muslims, were the emergence of the Zionist Movement in the Holy Land at the end of the 19th century, the establishment of a Jewish state in 1948 and, above all, the occupation of Arab territories, mainly East Jerusalem and the al-Aqsa compound in 1967. Many Muslims saw these as fatal attacks against an Arab Muslim land and Islam's holy sites, by Jews who had lived for centuries in Muslim countries as inferior protected subjects. In response to that, Jews in Arab and Muslim countries were violently attacked, most of whom

216

were non-Zionists. For a long time, they maintained dialogue with their Muslim neighbors and took steps to integrate into the economy, culture and society in which they lived; some joined the nationalist movements of their countries. But to no avail – ancient Jewish communities were uprooted and expelled, and many immigrated to Israel at different time periods.

Some Arab and Muslim countries, especially the Palestinian National Movement, imposed a military, political and economic war on Israel, while many Muslims were developing anti-Jewish (Judeophobic) attitudes mixed with anti-Zionist feelings. Most pronounced among them were fanatic Muslim factions – both Shi'ites and Sunnis who, since 1967, have been striving to liberate al-Aqsa (East Jerusalem and all of Palestine); and to that end are willing to sacrifice themselves, even if in an all-out war, a Muslim–Jewish Armageddon.

In contrast, in Arab and Muslim countries and amongst the Palestinians there also appeared pragmatic or moderate elements that maintained political, economic and cultural dialogues with the Jewish Zionist *Yeshuv* and with the State of Israel, in order to reach accords and political agreements. These approaches, and especially military constraints (vis-à-vis the IDF's might) along with national security and economic considerations, motivated Egypt, the strongest of the Arab countries, to sign peace treaties with Israel in 1978–1979; and Jordan – that sustained a long strategic dialogue with Israel – reached a formal peace with her in 1994. Moreover, in 2002 all Arab countries, then followed by all Muslim countries (except Iran), proposed peace, security and normal relations with Israel, on condition that it agrees to a Palestinian state alongside it, based on the lines of 1949–1967, with East Jerusalem its capital and Muslim control of al-Haram-al-Sharif.

However, the governments of Israel (apart from Prime Minister Olmert in 2008), which repeatedly stated their desire for peace with the Arab and Muslim world, rejected this draft even at the price of no reconciliation with the Arab and Islamic peoples. These Israeli governments, apparently content with diplomatic, security and economic relations with many Arab and Muslim governments, have not agreed to relinquish control of the Temple Mount and East Jerusalem. These positions significantly reflect ideological outlooks of Israel's governments and of many Jews in Israel and abroad. Some are inconsiderate of and even denigrate Islam and its culture and embrace a European orientation and liaison with Christian Islamophobic Fundamentalists.

There is no doubt that this ideological-political-cultural process, as displayed by religious Zionists and the secular and traditional right, constitutes a critical historical change in contrast to the former viewpoints of the central Zionist movement and the governments of *Mapai* and *Labor-Maarakh*, in regard to Jerusalem and the holy sites of Judaism and Islam. Indeed, the majority of Zionist Jews that immigrated to the Holy Land from Europe were secular; they did not settle in Jerusalem, nor did they sanctify the Temple Mount, though they did consider the Western Wall a national-cultural site. However, with time, and mainly after 1967, nationalist messianic groups, both religious and secular, nurtured aspirations to take control of the Temple Mount and rebuild the Holy Temple, even upon the ruins of the mosques; some are ready to sacrifice themselves towards this goal. Many of these fanatic Jews also express their hatred of Muslims and Islam (Islamophobia) – by speech, publications and actions – such as through acts of violence, and the killing of Muslims; this, in response to the hatred and violence of Muslims towards Jews; and also Jewish religious and cultural contempt towards Muslims.

These extreme Jewish positions are symmetrical or similar to a great degree (but not in their extent) to the positions of the fanatics of Islam who preach the hatred of Jews and Israel, and carry out many acts of violence against them. On the other hand, a positive symmetry may also be found in the positions found in moderate circles on both sides, on issues of peaceful coexistence, religious, political and ideological dialogues; cooperation and historic reconciliation between Muslims and Jews (in Israel and throughout the world). These include religious leaders, educators, academicians and cultural activists.

However, these moderate manifestations are quite limited, lacking any significant influence, and are not always supported by the relevant governments, and are exposed to brutal threats by fanatic groups on both sides. In the worst-case scenario, these streams may lead to a regional, and perhaps worldwide, Muslim–Jewish Armageddon, as estimated by researchers, religious leaders, statesmen and senior Jewish and Muslim security experts. Such a scenario may be set in motion by a severe attack on the mosques of the Temple Mount by fanatic Jews, which will lead to violent reactions from extremist Muslims and include a massive attack of thousands of missiles and rockets from Iran and Shi'ite Hizbullah.

An additional grim scenario is the creation of a Shi'ite-Sunni alliance between Iran and Turkey – that cultivates ambitions to achieve Sunni-Muslim leadership – against the Jewish state that supposedly continues to harm Muslims in the territories and threaten the holy sites of Islam in Jerusalem; and is preventing the establishment of a Palestinian state within the 1967 lines with East Jerusalem as its capital.

It appears that the key to a devastating war, or to historic reconciliation with Islam and the Muslims, is mainly in Israel's hands. If it continues to thwart a resolution of the Palestinian problem and cling to its control of the Temple Mount and East Jerusalem, if it turns a blind eye to the preaching and provocative actions of Jewish zealots – then it may very well lead to severe outcomes: A worsening in its relations with moderate Sunni Muslim countries such as Egypt, Jordan, Saudi Arabia and Indonesia; empowering the extremist elements in the region and beyond – led by Iran and Shi'ite Hizbullah; imposition of diplomatic and economic sanctions against Israel by both Muslim and European countries and UN institutions.

On the other hand, if the State of Israel shows courage and vision and helps to resolve the Palestinian problem and the issue of East Jerusalem and the Temple Mount, in a manner acceptable to the Muslim world and the international community – for example, by following the Clinton Parameters (2000), the Saudi-Arab peace initiative (2002) and Olmert's proposal (2008) – then the outcome will be positive and promising. Palestinian and Muslim terrorism, the hostility from Iran and Hizbullah – may be significantly reduced; dialogues on Israeli–Arab and Jewish–Muslim reconciliations will be reinforced, Israel will gain extensive support from the international community and will also be in a position to formulate a strategic alliance with the Sunni countries against the dangerous Shi'ite-Iranian axis.

Of course, one must not ignore other scenarios in the relationships between Muslims and Jews, Palestinians and Israelis, as well as developments and changes in the region and the world. This includes the positions of the great powers – Russia and the United States.

President Trump's recognition of a united Jerusalem as the capital of Israel – in his "century deal" – January 2020 – has strengthened uncompromising attitudes on both sides. In contrast, it may be possible for a certain time (such as under the common threat of the COVID-19) to maintain the status quo in Jerusalem and in the territories, and the cold peace with Arab and Muslim countries based on their pragmatic considerations. Still, fifty-three years of Israel's occupation of Palestinian territories and East Jerusalem have already contributed to a mutual radicalization of the positions of Jews and Muslims, have damaged contacts with Arab and Muslim countries and marred Israel's status and image throughout the world. Israel and the Jewish people are strong enough militarily, politically and economically to take calculated risks and prevent a far greater danger; and promote historic reconciliation with the Palestinians and the wider Arab and Muslim world.

Notes

Introduction

1 Qur'an, Sura 5, verse 60; Meri, *Muslim–Jewish Relations*, pp. 351–371; Goldberg, *Arab Spring*, November 29, 2011.

2 Almisri (Cairo) in Memri, August 5, 2010; Al-Sharq (Beirut), March 26, 2013; *Maariv*, June 20, 2010. Palestinian television, April 23, 2018.

3 *Haaretz*, March 24, 2011, May 1, 2013; *Yediot Ahronot*, August 10, 2010; *Washington Post*, April 2, 2010, *Al Monitor*, May 21, 2018; Memri, July 9, 2018.

4 *Haaretz*, January 27, 2013, August 6, 2014; April 30, 2018; *Jewish Exponent*, July 15, 2014.

5 *Memri*, April 9, 2013; *Haaretz*, September 9, 2011; *Jerusalem Post*, April 2, 2013; *Al Monitor*, July 10, 2018.

6 *Haaretz*, November 17, 2011; March 30, September 24, 2014.

7 See further on and in my book, *The Meeting of Civilizations*, vii–viii; *Muslim Attitudes*, vii.

8 See chapters 8 and 9.

9 Benny Morris, interview in *Haaretz*, September 7, 2012; Ma'oz, *The Meeting of Civilizations*, *ibid.*; The National Interest, September 2011. *Yediot Ahronot*, July 20, 2018.

10 Mark Cohen, *Myths, Politics*, p. 24.

11 Ma'oz, *Muslim Attitudes*, pp. 11–12.

12 *Haaretz*, November 29, 2011, May 11, 2012; *Time*, October 2, 2012.

13 Reiter, *Fatwa of Mufti of Egypt*, Ma'oz, *Muslim Attitudes*, pp. 93–112; *Haaretz*, November 29, 2011, September 7, 2012, July 8, 2014.

1 Duality and Dialogue: Muhammad, the Qur'an and the Middle Ages

1 Lecker, Muhammad, p. 11 et seq.; Meddeb and Stora, pp. 39–51.

2 Bat Yeor, *The Dhimmi*; Peters, *From Time Immemorial*; Gilbert, *The Tents of Ishmael*, pp. 30–51.

3 Friedman, *Tolerance*; Qur'an, Sura 2 verse 256.

4 Qur'an, Sura 2, verses 62, 136; Armstrong, *The History of God*, p. 170.

5 Qur'an, Sura 109, verse 6; Goitein, *Muhammad, in Lazarus-Yafeh*, p. 58; Stillman, *The Jews of Arab Lands*, p. 87.
6 Qur'an, Sura 2 verse 83; Sura 9, verse 29.
7 Qur'an, Sura 5, verse 82.
8 Qur'an, Sura 9 verse 29; Sura 5 verse 60.
9 Qur'an, Sura 2, verse 256.
10 Hirschberg, *Jews in Islam*, p. 268; Meddeb and Stora, *Jews–Muslims*, p. 650.
11 Ma'oz, *The House of Abbas*, pp. 220–221.
12 Ratzabi, *Borrowed Motifs*, p. 8; Mark Cohen, *Under The Crescent and Cross*, Chapter 6; Gilbert, *Tents of Ishmael*, pp. 53–54, 57–58; Armstrong, *The History of God*, pp. 184–207.
13 Frankel, Miriam, *History (Peamim 92)*, p. 52; Hawary, *Ayyubid Egypt*, p. 68; Gilbert, *Tents of Ishmael*, p. 85.
14 Lewis, *The Jews of Islam*, pp. 44, 54.
15 Bar Asher,"Ancient Shi'a" in *Peamim A*, pp. 11, 29, 34; Yehoshua Raz, *Silken Curtain*, pp. 86–90.
16 Ibn Tibbon, *The Hearts' Obligation;* Gilbert, *Tents of Ishmael*, p. 61; Meddeb and Stora, *Jews–Muslims*, pp. 640–652.
17 Hirschberg, *The Jews in Islam*, pp. 277–278.
18 "What Judaism Owes Islam", *Haaretz*, May 14, 2013; *Haaretz, Sefarim*, July 24, 2013.

2 The Ottoman Empire: Tolerance and Cooperation in the Balkans

1 Levy, *Jews in the Ottoman Empire*, p. 404; Amnon Cohen, *The Temple Mount*, pp. 51–53; Ramon, 'An Entangled City', pp. 41–52.
2 Ben-Naeh, *The Kingdom of Sultans*, pp. 105, 338, 350; Levy, *Jews in the Ottoman Empire*, pp. 19–41.
3 Al-Awra, *Sulayman*, p. 477; Mansur, *Nazareth*, p. 59; Burckhardt, *Travels in Syria and the Holy Land*, p. 180.
4 Cohen, Amnon, *Jews in Court*, pp. 152–162, 442–445; Ben-Naeh, *Sultans*, pp. 95–96; Shaham, *Jews and the Sharia Courts*, p. 112 et seq.
5 David, *Eretz Hazvi*, pp. 53, 76, 87, 147, 175; Ben-Naeh, *Sultans*, p. 340; Benbasa, *Ottoman Jewry*, pp. 14–26.
6 Ma'oz, *Ottoman Reform in Syria and Palestine*, pp. 184–244.
7 Ya'ari, *Masaot*, p. 19.
8 Ma'oz, *Changes in the Status of the Jews*, p. 162; M.A. Ubicini, *Letters on Turkey*, *Part II*, John Murray Pub., No. 856, p. 346.
9 Landau and Ma'oz, *Jews and Non-Jews*, the entire article; Landau, *Blood Libels*, pp. 415–460.

10 Ma'oz, *Ottoman Reform in Syria and Palestine*, p. 206; Frankel, Jonathan, *Damascus Libels*, the entire book.
11 Benbasa, *Ottoman Jewry*, p. 26 et seq.
12 Benbasa and Rodrigue, *The Jews of Spain*, p. 25; Meddeb and Stora, *History of Jewish–Muslim Relations*, pp. 141–196; Gilbert, *The Tents of Ishmael*, pp. 93–96.
13 Ben-Naeh, *Sultans*, pp. 58, 75, 340–342.
14 Benbasa and Rodrigue, *The Jews of Spain*, p. 149.
15 Op. cit., p. 151 et seq.; Kerkkanan, *Yugoslav Jewry*, pp. 27, 29, 39, 45.
16 *Haaretz* supplement, September 23, 2011; *Yediot Ahronot*, Sabbath supplement, May 24, 2013; Algemeiner, October 31, 2013.
17 *The New York Times International*, November 19, 2013; *The Jersey Jewish Standard*, August 21, 2012.
18 Shai, *Terrorism in the Balkans*, pp. 60–61, 70; Memri, June 24, 2012; Associated Press, September 21, 2010.
19 Amikam Nachmani, "The Triangle: Europeans, Muslims, Jews" in Ma'oz, *Muslim Attitudes*, p. 275.
20 Ma'oz, *The Meeting of Civilizations*, XI, *Haaretz*, March 23, 2012; *Haaretz*, February 20, 2015.
21 PEW surveys and AIC; Haltpost; *Haaretz*, August 12, 2014; Nachmani, pp. 279–280; *The Guardian*, October 8, 2014.
22 *Haaretz*, August 12, 2014; *Haaretz* supplement, February 20, 2015; Nachmani, p. 280; *Jewish News*, August 24, 2014; *The Guardian*, October 8, 2014.
23 *Haaretz*, August 12, 2014, January 13, 2015; *Algemeiner*, 7 (January–June 2016); Nachmani, pp. 279–280, July 2017; *News Europe*, December 7, 2016; *The Guardian*, August 7 and October 6, 2014.
24 *Yediot Ahronot*, December 2, 2011; Ynet, December 3, 2011; *Economist*, December 6, 2011.

3 A Dual Relationship in Africa: The Northern and Sub-Saharan Divide

1 Hirschberg, *A History of the Jews*, p. 59 et seq.
2 Ben-Layashi, *Morocco and its Jewish Community*, pp 126–132.
3 Op. cit., p. 132; Gilbert, *The Tents of Ishmael*, pp. 121–122.
4 Gilbert, *The Tents of Ishmael*, pp. 268, 278, 308; Yardena Schwartz, "Jews and Muslims of Morocco", NBC News, July 18, 2017.
5 Hirschberg, *A History of the Jews*, p. 92 et seq.
6 Noah, *Travels in Europe and Africa*, p. 308; *Virtual Jewish World*, Tunisia.
7 Gilbert, *The Tents of Ishmael*, p. 269.

8 *The Guardian,* June 23, 2016; Jewish Virtual Library, Tunisia., Reuters Agency, May 14, 2018.

9 Meddeb and Stora, *History of Jewish–Muslim Relations,* pp. 994–998.

10 Abitbol, *Anti-Semitism in Algeria,* p. 61 et seq. Hoxter, *The Jews of Algiers,* pp. 135–141.

11 Sivan, *The Hatred of Jews,* pp. 92–108.

12 Abitbol, *Anti-Semitism in Algeria,* p. 61 et seq.; Hexter, *The Jews of Algeria,* pp. 135–141.

13 Op. cit., p. 127, 134, 145–148.

14 Op. cit., pp. 180–188; Hirschberg, *A History of the Jews, II,* p. 90.

15 The Virtual Jewish World, Algeria, *Magreb Times,* May 15, 2018.

16 Roumani, *The Jews of Libya,* pp. 1–5.

17 Chalphon, *For Us and For Our Sons,* p. 125.

18 Op. cit, p. 127; Roumani, *The Jews of Libya,* pp. 45–46, 55.

19 Roumani, op. cit., pp. 54–56, 106, 189–199, 218–220.

20 Meddeb and Stora, pp. 1002–1003; The Times of Israel, March 10, 2015.

21 Arye Oded, "African Islam: Its Attitudes towards Israel and Judaism", in Ma'oz, *Muslim Attitudes,* p. 249; Yossi Alpher, *Periphery,* p. 14, et seq.

22 *Jerusalem Post,* July 20, 2016; Ynet, September 12, 2016; New African website, July 7, 2017.

23 *Haaretz,* August 22, 2017. For further reading on Muslim Sudan, see: Mondour El-Mahdi, *A Short History of the Sudan,* Oxford University Press, London 1965; *Haaretz,* September 12, 2017; *Daily Post (Kenya),* May 16, 2018.

4 The Shi'te Positions of Iran, Hizbullah and Yemen

1 Windecker, *Between Karbala, Jabal Amil and Jerusalem,* pp. 103–112.

2 Op. cit., pp. 112–123; Lev Zion, *The Sects in Islam,* p. 291; Hirschberg, *The Jews in Islam,* pp. 299–312.

3 Cohen, Haim, *The Jews in the Middle East,* pp. 56–60; Windecker, *Karbala, Jabal Amil and Jerusalem,* p. 115; Moreen, *The Jews of Iran,* pp. 239–245.

4 Moreen, *ibid.;* Cohen, Haim, *ibid.*

5 Scepihandler, *The Jews of Iran,* pp. 12–14; Netzer, *The Jews of Iran,* pp. 10–16; Orly Rahimiyan, 'Jews of Iran', Jewish Learning Website.

6 Netzer, op. cit., pp. 10–13, 16–29; Elazar, *The Jewish Community in Iran,* pp. 23–29.

7 Netzer, *ibid.*

8 Netzer, op. cit., and also pp. 37–38.

9 Ram, *Not East,* pp. 150, 156, 158; Ram, *Reading Iran,* passim.

10 Aloni, *Revolutionary Messages*, p. 77; Mehran, *Religious Education*, pp. 100, 103, 110.

11 Orly Azulay, *Yediot Ahronot, "Seven Days"*, April 9, 2015; Roger Cohen, "What Iran Jews Say", *New York Times*, February 22, 2009.

12 Menashri, *Iran after Khomeini*, p. 94 et seq.; *Yediot Ahronot*, Friday supplement, August 14, 2015; *Haaretz*, August 19, 2012.

13 For further reading on the meeting between Khatami with Israeli President Moshe Katzav, see also: Ram, *Reading Iran*, p. 182.

14 Ram, op. cit, p. 188; *Washington Post*, October 8, 2004.

15 Windecker, *Between Karbala, Jabal Amil and Jerusalem*, pp. 116, 168, 172, 174, 189; Mutawalis in Lebanon, p. 21.

16 Windecker, op. cit., pp. 194–196, 202–212, 217–218.

17 Windecker, op. cit., p. 330; For further reading on Musa al-Sadar, see: Ajami, *The Hidden Imam*.

18 Windecker, op. cit., p. 330.

19 Shapira, *Hizbullah*, p. 126 et seq.; Petran, *The Struggle for Lebanon*, pp. 267–277; Nakash, *The Shi'ites on the Way to Power*, pp. 140–156.

20 Ynet, March 21, 2017.

21 BBC News, July 18, 2006; Jewish Press, May 20, 2014, al Jazeera, May 14, 2018; *Foreign Policy*, December 12, 2019; *Time Magazine*, November 7, 2019.

22 Tubi, *Jews of Yemen*, pp. 241–257; Tubi, *Yemeni Jews*, p. 88 et seq.

23 Tubi, *Jews of Yemen*, p. 251; Haim Cohen, *The Jews in the Middle East*, pp. 12–14.

24 Gilbert, *The Tents of Ishmael*, pp. 218–220, 262–263, 314–321. *Jerusalem Post*, 26 March 2018; The Times of Israel, December 8, 2019.

25 Kazzaz, *The Jews*, pp. 97, 175–179.

26 Ma'oz, *Muslim Attitudes*, p. 17; *Haaretz*, March 18, 2012; al Jazeera, December 11, 2017; The Times of Israel, December 21, 2019.

27 Ahmadov, *Azerbaijani Perceptions of Jews*, p. 161.

28 Jordan Michael, Jewish Telegraphic Agency, March 17, 2003.

29 Ahmadov, *ibid*.

30 Op. cit., pp. 162–166.

31 *Jerusalem Post*, April 15, 2017; The Times of Israel, April 25, 2017; *Haaretz*, April 29, 2018.

5 Changing Positions of Sunni Turkey and Central Asia

1 Levi, Avner, *Jews in Turkey*, pp. 9–10.

2 Op. cit., p. 52.

3 Lewis, *The Emergence of Modern Turkey*, pp. 66–67.

4 Levi, Avner, *Jews in Turkey*, p. 64, pp. 66–67.

5   Op. cit., pp. 86–91; About the Struma Tragedy: *Haaretz*, February 24, 2012.

6   Levi, Avner, op. cit., pp. 78–80.

7   Landau, *Jews, Arabs, Turks: Selected Essays*, pp. 77–85; Giray, *Turkish Policy*, pp. 174–179; *Haaretz*, March 19, 2008.

8   Louis Fischman, *Haaretz*, September 12, 2016; Yaniv Kopovitch, *Haaretz*, July 5, 2016; *Financial Times*, October 19, 2017; Eldad Pardo, *Impact*, November 2016, January 2017.

9   Giray, *Turkish Policy*, pp. 170–173.

10 *Haaretz*, February 15, 2007; February 2, 2009; September 9, 2011; *New York Times*, May 2, 2005.

11 Soner Cagaptay, Hurriyet, June 6, 2010; *Newsweek*, June 4, 2010.

12 CNN, May 9, 2018, Hurriyet, May 9, 2017; *Times of Israel*, July 22, 2017.

13 Moshe Ma'oz, *Yediot Ahronot*, October 13, 2010; Zvi Barel, *Haaretz*, July 6, September 9, 2011; Amikam Nahmani, *Haaretz*, February 2, 2009. See also papers by both Turkish and Israeli researchers in Bitter Lemons, June 2010.

14 Meddeb and Stora, *History of Jewish–Muslim Relations*, pp. 258, 260–265; Yehoshua Raz, *The Silken Screen*, p. 23 et seq.; Gilbert, *The Tents of Ishmael*, p. 113.

15 Altschuler, *The Jews of Bukhara – by Yaacov Pinchasi*, pp. 11–20; Jewish Telegraphic Agency, 29 December 2006; *The Guardian*, November 2, 2010; Al Jazeera News, May 8, 2015; The Times of Israel, September 15, 2016.

16 Yehoshua Raz, op. cit., pp. 48, 375, 417, 477; *Forward*, November 11, 2015; *The Jerusalem Post*, May 31, 2016.

17 Yehoshua Raz, op. cit., pp. 162, 179.

18 Yehoshua Raz, op. cit., pp. 183, 184, 190; *The Guardian*, February 29, 2012; Radio Free Europe, October 29, 2013; *Times of Israel*, December 7, 2017.

19 Rockower and Cheema, *Israeli–Pakistani Relations*, pp. 188–189; Kumaraswami, *Indian Muslims and Jews*, pp. 216–219.

20 Rockower and Cheema, op. cit., pp. 194–195; Kumaraswami, *Israel and Pakistan*, pp. 123–135.

21 Rockower and Cheema, op. cit., pp. 195–197; Seema Sirohi, *Outlook India Magazine*, August 11, 2009; Moonis Ahmar, *Journal of Asian and Middle Eastern Studies*, No. 2, 2002, pp. 11–12.

22 Rockower and Cheema, op. cit., pp. 203–204; *Haaretz*, September 2, 2005; *New York Times*, September 3, 2005; BBC Service, May 30, 1998.

23 Shafiq, *Teaching Jewish and Christians Interfaith*, pp. 127–143; al-Jazeera, May 14, 2018.

24 Kumaraswami, *Indian Muslims and Jews*, in Ma'oz (ed.), *Muslim Attitudes*, pp. 219–227; *The Times of India*, March 3, 2017; *Jerusalem Post*, 3 July 2017.
25 Ahmad Junaidi, *Jakarta Post*, May 27, 2008.
26 *Haaretz*, December 3, 2010, June 17, 2011; *Jakarta Post*, January 8, 2009, May 6, 2010.
27 *Jakarta Post*, June 11, 2005, May 6, 2012, August 21, 2017; Burdah, "Indonesian Muslims", in Ma'oz (ed.), *Muslim Attitudes*, pp. 230–244.
28 Azra, *Trilogy of the Religions of Abraham*, in Ma'oz (ed.), *The Meeting*, pp. 220–229; *Jakarta Post*, March 27, 2002.
29 *The Economist*, November 13, 2009; *The Diplomat*, March 11, 2015; *Jakarta Post*, June 11, 2005; *Daily Mail*, April 17, 2017.
30 Burdah, op. cit., p. 242; *Jakarta Globe*, February 26, 2018; *Times of Israel*, May 11, 2018.

6 The Muslim–Jewish Relationship in the Holy Land/Palestine

1 Ben Zvi, *Eretz Yisrael*, p. 351 et seq.; Gilbert, *The Tents of Ishmael*, pp. 120, 123–124, 136.
2 Parfitt, *The Jews in Palestine*, p. 38; Gilbar, *Ottoman Palestine*, p. 24.
3 Ubicini, *Letters*, Part 2, pp. 246–247.
4 Harel, *Damascus*, pp. 36–37.
5 Ma'oz, *Ottoman Palestine*, p. 148.
6 Parfitt, op. cit., p. 202; Ma'oz, *Ottoman Palestine*, p. 162; Birjis Baris, Vol. 2, No. 32, 1860.
7 Ro'i, *The Zionist Attitude to the Arabs*, p. 227.
8 Mandel, *The Arabs and Zionism Before World War I*, pp. 47–49, 80–83, 225–228.
9 Rockower and Cheema, *Israeli–Pakistani Relations*, pp. 188–189; Isaiah Friedman, *Multiple Promises*, p. 244, p. 309.
10 Laqueur and Rubin, *The Israel-Arab Reader*, pp. 18–21.
11 Klein, *Connected*, pp. 43, 90–91; Ro'i, op. cit., pp. 227–228.
12 Cohen, Hillel, *The Army of Shadows*, p. 3 et seq., pp. 10–61, 80–85; Frumkin, *The Judge's Way*, pp. 219–221, 281, 370; Klein, op. cit., pp. 37, 58, 69.
13 Cohen, Hillel, op. cit., pp. 21, 32, 67, 93, 124, 164; Mattar, *The Mufti of Jerusalem*, pp. 80–81.
14 Mattar, op. cit., *The Mufti*, pp. 34–37, 40–42.
15 Mattar, op. cit., pp. 30–39; Ma'oz, *Syria–Israel*, p. 20.
16 Mattar, op. cit., p. 36; Cohen, 1929, p. 197 et seq.; Morris, *Victims*, pp. 97, 128 et seq., 190 et seq.
17 Porath, *From Riots to Rebellion*, pp. 103, 105, 232.
18 Ro'i, *The Zionist Attitude to the Arabs*, pp. 203, 218 228, 231.

19 Mandes-Flohr, *A Land of Two Peoples*, p. 88.
20 Cohen, *1929*, pp. 39, 179; Sulayman Masalha, *Haaretz*, April 28, 2016. See also the positive regard of the commander of the Palmach, Yigal Alon, towards Muslims in his youth: Shapira, *Yigal Alon*, p. 63.
21 Ben-Gurion, *Meetings*, pp. 19–20.
22 Eilat, *Hajj al-Husseini*, pp. 58–59.
23 Ben-Gurion, op. cit., p. 34; Porath, *Growth of the Movement*, pp. 214–215.
24 Klein, *Connected*, p. 116; Cohen, *1929*, p. 25; Mattar, *The Mufti of Jerusalem*, pp. 36, 91–92.
25 Cohen, op. cit., p. 92; Klein, op. cit., p. 63.
26 Shlaim, *The Iron Wall*, p. 34; Laqueur, *A History of Zionism*, p. 228; Barak Ravid, *Haaretz*, July 21, 2017; Anshil Pepper, *Haaretz*, April 20, 2018.
27 Cohen, *1929*, p. 137; *Kol Ha'am*, February 16, 1948.
28 Cohen, *1929*, pp. 104, 116, 123; Porath, *From Riots to Rebellion*, p. 282; B. Michael, *Haaretz*, May 2016; Inbari, *Jewish Fundamentalism*, p. 3.
29 Ibn Tibon, *The Duty of the Hearts*. This section is also based on a survey by Yael Kuperman, my research assistant, in September 2016, for which I am grateful to her.
30 Ibn Tibon, op. cit. See also Chapter 1.
31 B.Z. Kedar, *Haaretz*, August 7, 2009; Radio Channel 7, March 6, 2012.
32 Inbari, op. cit., pp. 15–19; Greenblum, *From the Power and Bravery in Religious Zionism*, pp. 38, 41, 100, 229, 390, 397.
33 Lavie, *Religion and Nationality*, pp. 22 et seq.; Cohen, *1929*, p. 151 et seq.
34 Lavie, op. cit., p. 111 and pp. 46–97.
35 Lavie, op. cit., pp. 154–161.

7 Muslim Attitudes towards Jews in Iraq, Egypt, Syria and Lebanon

1 Meri, *Muslim–Jewish Relations*, pp. 42–44.
2 Gilbert, *The Tents of Ishmael*, p. 203.
3 *Haaretz*, November 30, 2016.
4 Harel, *Damascus*, p. 119; Ma'oz, *Israel–Syria*, pp. 14–15.
5 Harel, op. cit., pp. 159–160, also 187, 236, 249.
6 Ma'oz, op. cit., p. 21.
7 Op. cit., pp. 16–26; Cohen, Haim, *Jews in the Middle East*, pp. 49–51.
8 Ma'oz, op. cit., pp. 111, 122–128; Ma'oz, *Muslim Attitudes*, pp. 11–12.

9 Binder, *Politics in Lebanon*, p. 297.
10 Petran, *The Struggle for Lebanon*, p. 17 et seq.; Jewish Press, May 20, 2014.
11 Schultze, *Israel's Covert Diplomacy in Lebanon*; BBC News, July 18, 2006; Jewish Press, *ibid.*
12 Kazzaz, *The Jews in Iraq*, pp. 36–39.
13 Op. cit., pp. 158–182; Ben Yaacov, *Jews of Babylon*, pp. 145–149, 324.
14 Kazzaz, op. cit., pp. 55–71; Meri, *Muslim–Jewish Relations*, pp. 48–50.
15 Kazzaz, op. cit., p. 238 et seq.; Ben Yaacov, op. cit., pp. 150–151.
16 Kazzaz, op. cit., p. 254 et seq.; Cohen, Haim, *Jews in the Middle East*, p. 34 et seq.
17 Gilbert, *The Tents of Ishmael*, pp. 68–74; Stillman, *The Jews of Arab Lands*, pp. 8–90; Winter, *The Jews of Egypt*, p. 5 et seq.
18 Landau, *The Jews in Egypt*, pp. 14–26; Landau and Ma'oz, *Jews and Non-Jews*, p. 6 et seq.
19 Gilbert, op. cit., pp. 118–119; Meddeb and Stora, *History of Jewish–Muslim Relations*, pp. 938–939; Vatikiotis, *Egypt From Muhammad Ali to Sadat*, pp. 107–108, 136, 140.
20 Kramer, *Zionism in Egypt*, p. 352.
21 Gilbert, op. cit., pp. 165–166; Vatikiotis, op. cit., pp. 363–364.
22 Syd Ahmad, *The Jews of Egypt*, a book about the social and economic life of Egyptian Jewry; Ruth Kimche, *Zionism in the Pyramids' Shadow*, Tel Aviv, 2009.
23 Ma'oz, *The Arab Spring*, p. 16.

8 Muslim and Arab Ambivalence after the Establishment of the State of Israel

1 Harkabi, *The Palestinian Covenant*, p. 25.
2 Harkabi, *Positions of the Arabs*, p. 207 et seq.; Ma'oz, *Hatred of Jews*, full article.
3 Harkabi, op. cit., pp. 125–126; Webman, pp. 225–228.
4 Ma'oz, op. cit., pp. 11, 12, 14–15; Webman, *The Image of the Jew in the Arab World*, p. 53.
5 Webman, op. cit., pp. 58–59.
6 Ma'oz, op. cit., pp. 20–23; Ma'oz, *Muslim Positions*, pp. 10–11; al-Sayy'ad (Lebanon) November 29, 1973.
7 Radio Cairo, December 27, 1955; Ma'oz, *Hatred of Jews*, pp. 13, 17. 20–21.
8 Baram, *Saddam Husayn and Islam*, pp. 219–220; Ma'oz, *Assad*, pp. 93, 189.

9 Mish'al and Sela, *Hamas Time*, p. 96 et seq.; Monitor, May 14, 2017.

10 *Maariv*, January 23, 1986; *Haaretz*, March 16, 2016; August 9, 2017; Ynet, July 4, 2017, Kuwait News Agency, August 16, 2016.

11 *Haaretz*, October 14, 2016, August 21, 2017; Luz, *al-Haram al-Sharif*, entire article; Winter, Ofir, *Regimes of Egypt and Jordan*, pp. 96, 207; Palestinian television, April 13, 2018. Memri, June 2, 2018.

12 Groiss, *Palestinian Authority Textbooks* (2002), pp. 3–4; 2001 – p. 4; 2005 – p. 5; Memri, March 18, 2018.

13 Ma'oz, *Hatred of Jews*, pp. 13–15; Groiss, *Egyptian Textbooks*, pp. 6–8, 62–71; Winter, Ofir, op. cit., p. 230.

14 Anderson, *Nationalist Voices in Jordan*, pp. 197–199; Domato, *Teaching Islam*, pp. 84–86.

15 Pasha, *Egypt's Quest for Peace*, p. 65; Groiss, op. cit, 2002, pp. 2–4.

16 Groiss, *Saudi Arabian Schoolbooks*, p. 48; Kahanov, *Saudi Arabia*, p. 212 et seq.; Mustafa Akyo, *International New York Times*, March 17, 2016.

17 Or Kashti, *Haaretz*, January 6, 2011.

18 Jeffrey Goldberg, "Praise Arab Spring, Except For Anti-Semitism", Bloomberg News, November 29, 2011; *al-Shaaq* (Lebanon) March 26, 2013; *Maariv*, June 17 and 20, 2012.

19 Lafree, *Putting Terrorism in Context*; CNN News March 27, 2007; BBC News, October 13, 2000; The Times of Israel, 20 May 2017.

20 Kahanov, op. cit., p. 13 et seq., p. 18 et seq.; Kostiner and Kahanov, *Saudi Arabia and Israel*, p. 113.

21 Kahanov, op. cit., pp. 285–286, 289. About the *fatwa* of the chief mufti of Egypt, see: Reiter, *Islam and the Question of Peace with Israel*, p. 90 et seq.

22 Podeh, *From Fahd to Abdallah*, the entire pamphlet; *Haaretz*, January 20, 30 and March 31, 2017.

23 Kahanov, op. cit., pp. 293–296.

24 Shlaim, *King Hussein*, pp. 27–28.

25 Laqueur & Rubin, *The Israel-Arab Reader*, pp. 19–20.

26 Shlaim, op. cit, pp. 36–37; Y. Porath, "Abdallah's Greater Syria Programme, Middle Eastern Studies", pp. 172–184, 1984.

27 Shlaim, op. cit., pp. 40–49; Shamir, *Peace with Jordan*, pp. 20–25; Sela, *King Abdallah*, pp. 120, 193.

28 Morris, *Border Battles*, Chapters 1–8.

29 Ma'oz, *Syria–Israel*, pp. 74–202; Shamir, op. cit., pp. 27–30; Shlaim, op. cit., p. 321 et seq.

30 Shamir, op. cit., p. 57, and p. 66 et seq.; Shlaim, op. cit., p. 456 et seq.

31 Nusseibeh, *The Future of Jerusalem*, pp. 7–10.

32 Shamir, op. cit., pp. 284–285, 317–318, 545, 594.

33 Op. cit., pp. 555–557; The Jewish Press, October 2015; The Times

of Israel, September 29, 2016; *Haaretz*, July 24, 2017; Reuters, May 18, 2018.

34 Winter, Ophir, *Peace with Israel*, the entire article; Monitor, September 21, 2016.

35 Ben-Layashi, *Morocco and its Jewish Community*, p. 12.

36 *Haaretz*, January 14, 2014; April 14, 2016.

37 Memri, October 6, 2016, January 10, July 19, 2017; Fikra Forum, Washington DC, March 2017; *Mitvim*, May 2018.

38 Qur'an, Sura 10 verse 93; Sura 5 verses 20–21, Sura 7 verse 137; *Haaretz*, April 9, 2016; Monitor, August 15, 2017.

39 Nusseibeh, *The Future of Jerusalem*, pp. 7–10; *Haaretz*, October 14, 2016, July 26, 2018.

9 Jews, Jerusalem and the Temple Mount: Mitzvah or Anti-Islamism?

1 Alpher, *An Isolated State*, p. 14; Oded, *African Islam*, p. 249 et seq.

2 Alpher, op. cit., p. 129; Ma'oz, *Muslim Attitudes to Jews and Israel*, pp. 13, 248, 261.

3 Yoaz Hendel, The Neighborhoods Outside the Walls, in *Yediot Ahronot*, September 16, 2015; Ma'oz, *The Temple Mount*, the entire article; Cohen, Hillel, *The Temple Mount*, pp. 1–19; Channel 7, December 2, 2017.

4 Ramon, *An Entangled City*, pp. 332, 361, 366, 367, 425; *Maariv*, January 15, 1986; *Herut*, December 14, 1960; *Haaretz*, September 18, 2000, February 15, 2017.

5 Document of Israel's Foreign Ministry, June 18, 1994; *Kol Yisrael*, June 9, 1994; Platform of the *Haavoda* party, May 1997; *Haaretz*, September 18, 2000, February 8, 2016; New York Review, October 1, June 13, 2000.

6 Lehrs, *Negotiations Over Jerusalem*, pp. 52–63; Aluf Ben, *Haaretz*, June 26, 2009; The Times of Israel, November 2012.

7 *Haaretz*, December 26, 2017; Ynet, January 14, 2020.

8 Al-Monitor, March 6, 2016; The Times of Israel, April 4, 2017.

9 Sharina Chen, *Holy Temple Devotees*, pp. 263–257; *Maariv*, August 13, 1970; *Davar*, June 12, 1980; *Musaf Haaretz*, April 3, 2017.

10 *Herut*, December 16, 1949, April 9, 1952; Shai Fogelman, *Musaf Haaretz*, November 4, 2011; Ramon, op. cit., p. 356; Ma'oz, *Palestinian Leadership*, pp. 174, 190.

11 Ma'oz, op. cit., p. 199; Reiter, *Sovereignty*, pp. 131, 163, 13, 227; Lehrs, op. cit., pp. 51–52.

12 Reiter, *Sovereignty*, pp. 117, 138; *Haaretz*, April 27, 2016, May 22, 2017. Walla news August 11, 2019.

13 *Haaretz*, May 11, 2015; *Musaf Haaretz*, August 4, 2017; *Haaretz*, February 7, 2018.

14 *Musaf Haaretz*. October 16, 2015; *Haaretz*, April 10, 2016, May 9, July 28, 2017; Al-Monitor, July 19, 2018.

15 Greenblum, *From the bravery of the Spirit*, pp. 38, 40, 116, 149; *Haaretz, Books*, April 7, 2017; CNN News, May 9, 2017.

16 Inbari. *Religious Zionism*, pp. 111–125; Chen, *The Temple Mount*, pp. 647–658.

17 Greenblum, op. cit., p. 165; Lavie, *Religion and Nationalism*, pp. 9–20; Uri Pollak, *The Kippa Site*, May 23, 2012; *Haaretz*, October 9, 2015.

18 Oded Heilbruner, *Haaretz, Culture & Literature*, June 17, 2017; *Nekuda*, September 1994, October 1993.

19 Gadi Gvariyahu, *Haaretz*, August 23, 2013; Avraham Burg, *Haaretz*, April 18, 2017; Carolina Landsman, *Haaretz*, June 24, 2017; *Nekuda*, March 1994.

20 Gottleib, *The Settlers of Religious Zionism*, p. 91 et seq.; *Nekuda*, May 1994; Avi Geiser, *A Different Country*, May–June 2005.

21 Yair Etinger, *Haaretz*, October 30, 2015; *Haaretz*, March 24, March 31, 2016; August 9, 2017.

22 *Maariv*, December 14, 2009; The Times of Israel, October 9, 2013.

23 Aran Gideon, *Haaretz Books*, March 25, 2016; Lavie, op. cit., pp. 11, 26, 30, 32; Rachel Elior, *Haaretz Books*, April 8, 2018.

24 Gottleib, op. cit., pp. 33, 34, 37, 38, 40; Israel Ariel and Dov Lior, *Tzfia*, August 1996; *Haaretz*, October 21, 2014, May 5, 15, 23, 2017.

25 *Haaretz*, April 27, 2015; *Yediot Ahronot*, 18 December 2015;Ynet, June 3, 2019.

26 Or Kashti *Haaretz*, July 7, 2014 and April 27, August 23, 2015, October 27, 2016; *Yediot Ahronot*, December 10, 2015.

27 Radio Islam, September 11, 2014; *al-Hayat al-jadida*, Palestine, August 24, 2000; *The Baltimore Sun*, October 27, 1997; The Times of Israel, June 30, 2016.

28 Ramon, *An Entangled City*, p. 336; Lavie, op. cit., p. 83; *Nekuda*, January 1994; *Haaretz*, February 28, 2010; *The Washington Post*, April 2, 2011; *New York Times*, August 21, 2015.

29 Rabinowitz, *The Western Wall*, p. 403; Reiter, *Sovereignty*, p. 135; *Monitor*, November 29, 2015; *Musaf Haaretz*, June 17, October 10, 2016; *New York Times International*, October 27, 1996.

30 Chen, *The Temple Mount*, pp. 5, 6, 8, 11–15; *Haaretz*, March 22, 2014.

31 PLO, Liberating al-Aqsa; Memri, December 24, 2014, December 14, 2016; *Haaretz*, November 2, 2013, July 26, 2017; *The Gulf Times*, November 16, 2016; CNN News, May 9, 2011.

32 Israel radio, December 10, 2016; The Times of Israel, July 1, 2016.

33 This part is mainly based on compositions by Podeh, *Textbooks*; Adwan, *Parallel Histories of Israel–Palestine.*

34 Podeh, op. cit., pp. 33, 46–47, 51, 57–58; Teff-Seker, *A Palestinian in Israel*, 2016; Update Impact, Jerusalem, 2016.

35 Podeh, op. cit., pp. 47, 59, 75, 118–121; *Haaretz*, July 21, 2017, February 24, September 5, 2014; Peled-Elhanan, *Textbooks*, Chapter Six; Greenblum, *op. cit.*, pp. 225–226, 285.

36 *Yediot Ahronot*, July 24, 2013; February 27, 2017; Nurit Peled-Elhanan, *Haaretz*, September 5, February 24, 2014; David Shipler, *The New Yorker*, November 2, 2015; *Haaretz the Marker*, August 17, 2017; Nasrin Haddad et al., Israel Democracy Institute, December 21, 2018.

37 Studies on Israel's Arabs: Landau, *The Arabs in Israel*; Sabri Jiryis, *The Arabs in Israel*; Ori Stendel, *The Arabs in Israel*; Keren Avraham, *The Arab Society in Israel*; Hatina & Atawna, *Muslims in the Jewish State.* See Bibliograhy.

38 Graitzer, *Mapai and the Arab Minority*, chapters 2–4; Ozacky-Lazar, *Jewish–Arab Relationships*, pp. 40–44; Zureik, *Palestinians in Israel.*

39 Landau, op. cit., p. 93; Firo, *The Druzes in the Jewish State*, pp. 238–239.

40 Manuscript by Tuma given to me by the author.

41 The Abraham Fund, *The Arab Society in Israel*, p. 30 et seq., pp. 61–64; "Coexistence – The Arab–Israeli Crisis", *Musaf Haaretz*, August 2014.

42 The Abraham Fund, op. cit., p. 103 et seq.; official report publication, August 2003, Hatina and Atawna, p. 165.

43 The Abraham Fund, op. cit., p. 61; Haidar Ali, *Or Commission Report; Ziad Abu-Habla*, *Haaretz*, April 25, 2015; Sami Michael, *Yediot Ahronot*, March 18, 2013; *Haaretz the Marker*, May 24, 17 August 17, 2017, May 25, 2018.

44 Smooha, *Autonomy for the Arabs*, pp. 47–67; Smooha, *Ethnic Democracy*, pp. 201–217; Louer, *To Be An Arab in Israel*, pp. 2–4; Rouhana, *The Crisis of Minorities in Ethnic States*, pp. 321–346; *Haaretz*, March 14, June 9, 2017; *Maariv*, February 18, 2017; the Likudnic Site, June 8, 2017; *Haaretz*, July 11, 2018.

45 Ma'oz, *Middle Eastern Minorities*, pp. 38–41; The Abraham Fund, op. cit., p. 21 et seq.; *Haaretz*, May 12, 2017; Adala's reaction, July 15, 2018; *Haaretz*, December 4, 2018; *Maariv*, January 25, 2019.

46 Hatina and Kupferschmidt, *The Muslim Brothers*, pp. 204–205; Mish'al and Sela, *Hamas Time*, pp. 37–39; Stendel, *The Arabs of Israel*, pp. 11–12; Landau, *The Arabs in Israel*, pp. 102, 158.

47 Mish'al and Sela, op. cit., pp. 37–57; Shabi and Shaked, *Hamas*, p. 55 et seq.

48 Hatina and Kupferschmidt, op. cit., pp. 241–242; Stendel, op. cit., pp. 270–273.

49 Yoav Stern, *Haaretz*, February 21, 2006; Ghanem, *The Palestinian Arab Minority in Israel*, pp. 125–129; *Jerusalem Post*, September 26, 2015.

50 Barak Ravid, *Haaretz*, November 12, 2015; Hatina and Atawna, p. 92.

51 *Haaretz*, July 3, 2014, December 30, 2015, March 8, 2017.

52 Ozacky-Lazar and Stern, *Talks with Arabs*, pp. 24–25, 28–29; Ali, *Between Ovadia and Abdallah*, pp. 162,183.

53 Reuters, January 20, 2020; BBC News, January 29, 2020; *Maariv*, January 28, 2020; *Haaretz*, January 29, 2020.

Bibliography

Abitbol, Michael, "The Jewish Community in Algiers" (in Hebrew), *Sefunot*, no. 17, 1983.

——, "Antisemitism in Colonial Algeria 1870–1940" (in Hebrew), Shazar Center, Jerusalem,1993.

Adwan, Sami, et al., *Side By Side: Parallel Histories of Israel – Palestine*, the New Press, New York, 2012.

Ahmadov, Tural, "Azerbaijani Perceptions of Jews", in Ma'oz (ed.), *Muslim Attitudes*, pp. 159–168.

Ajami, Fouad, *The Vanished Imam*, Cornell University Press, Ithaca, 1986.

Al-Awra, Sulayman, *History of the Rule of Sulayman Al-'Adil* (in Arabic), Sudan, 1936.

Ali, Nuhad, *Between Ovadia and Abdullah* (in Hebrew), Resling Publishers, Tel Aviv, 2013.

Al-Misri Newspaper, Cairo.

Aloni, Gil, *Revolutionary Messages in School Textbooks in Iran*, Truman Institute, Jerusalem, 2002.

Al-Monitor (website), The Pulse of the Middle East.

Alpher, Yossi, *Periphery (A Lonely State)* (in Hebrew), Matar Publishers, Tel Aviv, 2015.

Al-Sharq Newspaper, Beirut..

Anderson, Betty, *Nationalist Voices in Jordan*, Texas University Press, Austin, 2005.

Aran, Gideon, "How to Sanctify God" (in Hebrew), *Haaretz, Sfarim*, 25 March 2015.

Armstong, Karen, *The History of God*, Ballantine Books, London, 1994.

Azra, Azyumardi, "Trialogue of Abrahamic Faiths", in Ma'oz (ed.), *The Meeting of Civilizations*, pp. 220–229.

Baram, Amatzia, *Saddam Husayn and Islam (1968–2003)*, Wilson Center, Washington, DC, 2014.

Bar-Asher, Meir, "Jews in Shi'a Literature" (in Hebrew), *Pe'amim*, Ben-Zvi Institute, Jerusalem, 1993–94.

Barnai, Jacob et al. (eds), *Studies in the Jewry of Islamic Countries* (in Hebrew), Haifa University, 1981.

Bat-Ye'or, *The Dhimmi* (in Hebrew), Kaana Publishers, Jerusalem, 1986.

Bibliography

Benbassa, Esther et al., *The Jews of Spain in the Balkan Countries* (in Hebrew), Shazar Center, Jerusalem, 1995.

——, *Ottoman Jews 1906–1920* (in Hebrew), Shazar Center, Jerusalem, 1996.

Bengio, Ofra, *The Turkish–Israeli Relationship*, Palgrave Macmillan, New York, 2004.

Ben-Gurion, David, *Meetings with Arab Leaders* (in Hebrew), Am Oved Publishers, Tel Aviv, 1967.

Ben-Jacob, Abraham, *A History of the Jews in Iraq* (in Hebrew), Ben-Zvi Institute, Jerusalem, 1965.

Ben-Layashi, Samir et al., "Morocco and its Jewish Community", in Ma'oz (ed.), *Muslim Attitudes*, pp. 126–141.

Ben-Naeh, Yaron, *Jews in the Realm of the Sultans* (in Hebrew), Magnes Press, Jerusalem, 2006.

Ben-Sasson, Hayim, "The Image of Eretz-Israel", in Ma'oz (ed.), *Studies on Palestine*, pp. 103–110.

Ben-Zvi, Yitzhak, *Eretz Israel During Ottoman Rule* (in Hebrew), Bialik Institute, Jerusalem, 1954–55.

Binder, Leonard (ed.), *Politics in Lebanon*, John Viley, New York, 1966.

Burckhardt, J. L., *Travels in Syria and the Holy Land*, Elibron Classics, London, 1822.

Burdah, Ibnu, "Indonesian Muslims", in Ma'oz (ed.), *Muslim Attitudes*, pp. 230–246.

Burg, Avraham, "The Dangerous Silence" (in Hebrew), *Haaretz*, April 14, 2017.

Chen, Sarina, "Liminality and Sanctity" (in Hebrew), *Jerusalem Studies in Jewish Folklore*, 24–25 (2007), pp. 245–269.

——, "Visiting the Temple Mount" (in Hebrew), *Jerusalem Studies in Jewish Thought*, 22 (2011), pp. 647–659.

Cohen, Amnon, "The Temple Mount at the Beginning of Ottoman Rule" (in Hebrew), *Cathedra*, no. 33 (1964), pp. 51–53.

——, *Jews in Muslim Courts* (in Hebrew), Yad Ben Zvi, Jerusalem, 2003.

Cohen, Hayyim, *The Jews in the Middle Eastern Countries* (in Hebrew), Hakibbutz Hameuhad Publishers, Tel Aviv, 1972.

Cohen, Hillel, *An Army of Shadows – Palestinian Collaborators in the Service of Zionism* (in Hebrew), Ivrit-Hebrew Publishing House, Jerusalem, 2004.

——, *Year Zero of the Arab–Israeli Conflict, 1929* (in Hebrew), Keter Publishers, Jerusalem, 2013.

——, "The Temple Mount", *Israel Studies Review*, Vol. 32 (2011), pp. 1–19.

Cohen, Mark, *Under Crescent and Cross*, Princeton University Press, Princeton, 1994.

——, "Modern Myths of Islamic Antisemitism" (in Hebrew), *Politika*, 19 (2009), pp. 121–140, Jerusalem.

David, Avraham, *Eretz Hazvi* (in Hebrew), Mass Publishers, Jerusalem, 2013.

Doumato, Eleanor et al. (eds.), *Teaching Islam*, Lynne Rienner Publishers, Boulder, 2007.

Eilat, Eliyahu, *Mufti of Jerusalem* (in Hebrew), Reshafim, Tel Aviv, 1968.

Elazar, Daniel, *The Jewish Community in Iran* (in Hebrew), Jerusalem, 1975.

Fatah, *Liberation of Al-Aqsa* (in Arabic), February 1969.

Firo, Kais, *The Druzes in the Jewish State*, Brill Publishers, Boston, 1999.

Frankel, Jonathan, *The Damascus Affairs 1840*, Cambridge University Press, Cambridge, 1967.

Frankel, Miriam, "History of Jews in Muslim Lands" (in Hebrew), *Pe'amim*, 92, Jerusalem, 2001–2002, pp. 23–61.

Friedman, Isaiah, *Palestine: A Twice-Promised Land* (in Hebrew), Sde Boker, 2004.

Friedman, Yohanan, *Tolerance and Coercion in Islam*, Cambridge University Press, Cambridge, 2003.

Frumkin, Gad, *Path of a Judge in Jerusalem* (in Hebrew), Dvir Publishers, Tel Aviv, 1954.

Ghanem, Asad, *The Palestinian Arab Minority in Israel*, SUNY Press, New York, 2001.

Gilbar, Gad (ed.), *Ottoman Palestine 1800–1914*, Brill, Leiden, 1990.

Giray, Saziya Burcu, "Turkish Policy Towards the Israeli–Palestinian Conflict", in Ma'oz (ed.), *Muslim Attitudes*, pp. 169–185.

Goeitin, S.D., "Muhammad" (in Hebrew), in Lazarus Yafeh, Hava (ed.), *Studies in the History*, pp. 27–61.

——, A *Mediterranean Society*, 5 volumes, 1967–1991, University of California Press, 1999.

Goldberg, Jeffrey, "Praise Arab Spring", Bloomberg News, November 29, 2011.

Gotlieb, Tamara, *The Zionist-Religious Settlers* (in Hebrew), M.A. thesis, Hebrew University, Jerusalem, 2010.

Grayzer, Dina, *Ben-Gurion, Mapai and the Arab Minority* (in Hebrew), Ph.D. Thesis, Hebrew University, Jerusalem, 1995.

Greenblum, Dror, *Power and Bravery in Religious Zionism 1948–1967* (in Hebrew), the Open University, Raanana, 2016.

Groiss, Arnon, *Palestinian Authority Textbooks*, Center for Monitoring the Impact of Peace (CMIP), Jerusalem, 2002.

——, *Saudi Arabian Schoolbooks*, CMIP, Jerusalem, 2003.

——, *Egyptian School Textbooks*, CMIP, Jerusalem, 2004.

Harel, Yaron, *The Beginning of Zionism in Damascus* (in Hebrew), Shazar Center, Jerusalem, 2015.

Harkabi, Yehoshafat, *The Arabs' Position in Their Conflict with Israel* (in Hebrew), Dvir Co. Ltd., Tel Aviv, 1968.

——, *The Palestinian Covenant* (in Hebrew and Arabic), Israel Information Center, Jerusalem, 1974.

Hatina, Meir, et al. (eds.), *The Muslim Brotherhood* (in Hebrew), Hakibbutz Hameuhad Publishers, Tel Aviv, 2012.

——, *Muslims in a Jewish State* (in Hebrew), Hakibbutz Hameuhad, Tel Aviv, 2018.

Hawary, Mohammed, "Muslim–Jewish Relations in Ayyubid Egypt", in Ma'oz (ed.), *The Meetings of Civilizations*, pp. 66–73.

Haydar, Ali, *Or Commission Report* (in Hebrew), Jerusalem, Sikkuy Association, 2005.

Haydar, Aziz (ed.), *The Arab Society in Israel* (in Hebrew), Van Leer, Jerusalem, 2005.

Hirschberg, H.Z., *A History of the Jews in North Africa* (in Hebrew), Bialik Institute, Jerusalem, 1965.

——, "The Jews Under Islam" (in Hebrew), in Lazarus Yafeh (ed.), *Studies in the History*, pp. 262–315.

Hoxter, Miriam, "The Jews in Algiers" (in Hebrew), in S*efunot*, no. 17 (1983), pp. 133–163.

Ibn Tibbon, Judah (translation from Arabic), *The Duties of the Heart* (in Hebrew), Wein Schmichboyer Printing House, 1853.

Inbari, Moti, *Jewish Fundamentalism and the Temple Mount* (in Hebrew), Magnes Press, Jerusalem, 2008.

Ingrams, Harold, *The Yemen*, John Murray, London, 1963.

Jiryis, Sabri (ed.), *The Arabs in Israel* (in Hebrew), Itihad Press, Haifa, 1966.

Kahanov, Michael, *Saudi Arabia and the Conflict in Palestine* (in Hebrew), Israel Publishers, Jerusalem, 2016.

Kahwaji, Habib, *Al-Ard* (in Arabic), Al Arabi Publications, Cairo, 1978.

Kalmer, Ivan and Ramadan, Tariq, "Anti-Semitism and Islamophobia", in Meri (ed.), *Handbook*, pp. 351–372.

Kazzaz, Nissim, *The Jews in Iraq* (in Hebrew), Ben-Zvi Institute, Jerusalem, 1991.

Keren Avraham (Foundation), *The Arab Society in Israel* (in Hebrew), Jerusalem, 2013.

Kerkkanen, Ari, *Yugoslav Jewry*, Finnish Oriental Society, Helsinki, 2001.

Khalfon, Haim, *To Us and to the Children* (on Libyan Jews, in Hebrew), Yad Giborim, Netanya, n.d.

Kimche, Ruth, *Zionism at the Shadow of the Pyramids* (in Hebrew), Am Oved Publishers, Tel Aviv, 2009.

Klein, Menachem, *Lives in Common, Arabs and Jews* (in Hebrew), Hakibbutz Hameuhad Publishers, Tel Aviv, 2015.

Kostiner, Joseph and Kahanov, Michael, "Saudi Arabia and Israel", in Ma'oz (ed.), *Muslim Attitudes*, pp. 113–125.

Kramer, Gurdon, "Zionism in Egypt", in Cohen, Amnon (ed.), *Egypt and Palestine*, Ben-Zvi Institute, Jerusalem, 1969, pp. 348–366.

Kumaraswamy, P. R., "Israel and Pakistan", *Israel Affairs*, Vol. 12, No. 1 (2006), pp. 123–135.

——, "Indian Muslims and Jews", in Ma'oz (ed.), *Muslim Attitudes*, pp. 215–229.

Lafree, Gary, *Putting Terrorism in Context*, Routledge Publishers, London, 2015.

Landau, Jacob M., "Ritual Murder Accusations . . . in Egypt" (in Hebrew), *Sefunot*, 5 (1960–1961), pp. 415–460.

——, "The Jews of Egypt" (in Hebrew), Ben-Zvi Institute, Jerusalem, 1967.

——, "The Arabs in Israel" (in Hebrew), Maarachot Publishers, Tel Aviv, 1971.

—— and Ma'oz, Moshe, "Jews and Non-Jews in Egypt and Syria" (in Hebrew), *Pe'amim*, 9 (1981), pp. 4–13.

——, *Jews, Arabs, Turks*, The Magnes Press, Jerusalem, 1993.

Laqueur, Walter et al. (eds.), *The Israel-Arab Reader*, Penguin Books, London, 1984.

——, *A History of Zionism*, Penguin Books, New York, 2003.

Lavie, Ephraim (ed.), *Religion and the Arab Nationality* (in Hebrew), Carmel Publishers, Jerusalem, 2015.

——, (ed), *Israel and the Arab Peace Initiative* (in Hebrew), Tel Aviv University, 2015.

Lazarus Yafeh, Hava (ed.), *Studies in the History of the Arabs and Islam* (in Hebrew), Reshafim Publishers, Tel Aviv, 1968.

Lecker, Michael, *Muhammad and the Jews* (in Hebrew), Ben-Zvi Institute, Jerusalem, 2014.

Lehrs, Lior, *Negotiations in Jerusalem 1993–2011* (in Hebrew), the Jerusalem Institute, 2013.

Levi, Avner, *The Jews in the Turkish Republic* (in Hebrew), Author's edition, 1992.

Levy, Avigdor (ed.), *The Jews in the Ottoman Empire*, the Darwin Press, Princeton, 1994.

Lev-Zion, Nehemia, "Sects in Islam" (in Hebrew), in Lazarus Yafeh (ed.), *Studies*, pp. 176–198.

Lewis, Bernard, *The Emergence of Modern Turkey*, Oxford University Press, London, 1962.

——, *The Jews of Islam*, Princeton University Press, Princeton, 1984.

Lior, Dov, "Redemption of the Temple Site" (in Hebrew), *Sfiya Journal* (1967–1968).

Louer, Lawrence, *To Be An Arab in Israel*, Hurst and Co., London, 2003.

Luz, Nimrod, *Al-Haram Al-Sharif in the Arab Palestinian Discourse* (in Hebrew), the Floersheimer Institute, Jerusalem, 2004.

Mandel, Neville, *The Arabs and Zionism*, University of California Press, Berkeley, 1976.

Mandes Flohr, Paul, *A Land of Two Peoples*, Oxford University Press, New York, 1988.

Mansur, As'ad, *The History of Nazareth* (in Arabic), Cairo, Egypt, 1924.

Ma'oz, Moshe, "The Abbasids" (in Hebrew), in Lazarus Yafeh (eds.), *Studies*, pp. 199–232.

——, *Ottoman Reform in Syria and Palestine*, the Clarendon Press, Oxford, 1968.

—— (ed.), *Studies on Palestine During the Ottoman Period*, Magnes Press, Jerusalem, 1975.

——, *Hatred of Jews in Arab Media* (in Hebrew), Hebrew University, Jerusalem, 1975.

——, "Changes in the Position of Jews in the Ottoman Empire" (in Hebrew), in Barnai et al. (eds.), 1987, pp. 11–28.

——, "The Damascus Blood Libel" (in Hebrew), *Pe'amim*, no. 20 (1984), pp. 29–36.

——, *Palestinian Leadership in the West Bank*, Frank Cass, London, 1984.

——, *Asad: The Sphinx of Damascus*, Grove Weidenfeld, New York, 1988.

——, *Syria and Israel From War to Peace-Making*, Clarendon Press, Oxford, 1995.

——, *Middle Eastern Minorities*, The Washington Institute, Washington, DC, 1999.

—— (ed.), *The Meeting of Civilizations: Muslim, Christian and Jewish*, Sussex Academic Press, Brighton, 2009.

—— (ed.), *Muslim Attitudes to Jews and Israel*, Sussex Academic Press, Brighton, 2010.

——, "The Arab Spring", *Insight Turkey*, Vol. 14, No. 7 (2012).

——, "The Deterioration of Muslim–Jewish Relations", *Approaching Religion*, Vol. 4, (2014).

—— and Podeh, Elie, "Bashir Versus Bashar" (in Hebrew), in Podeh, Elie et al. (eds.), *The Third Wave: Protest and Revolution in the Middle East*, Carmel Publishers, Jerusalem, 2017.

Mattar, Philip, *The Mufti of Jerusalem*, Columbia University Press, New York, 1988.

Meddeb, Abdel Wahab and Stora, Benjamin (eds.), *A History of Jewish Muslim Relations*, Princeton University Press, Princeton, 2013.

Mehran, Golnar, "Religious Education in Iran", in Doumato (ed.), *Education in the Middle East*, 2007.

MEMRI: The Middle East Media Research Institute, website.

Menashri, David, *Iran After Khomeini* (in Hebrew), Tel Aviv University, Tel Aviv, 1999.

Meri, Josef (ed.), *Muslim–Jewish Relations*, Routledge, New York, 2016.

Mishal, Shaul and Sela, Avraham, *The Hamas Wind – Violence and Coexistence* (in Hebrew), Yediot Ahronot Books, Tel Aviv 1999.

Moreen, Vera Basch, "The Jews in Iran", in Meddeb and Stora, pp. 239–245.

Morris, Benny, *Israel's Border Wars, 1949–1967* (in Hebrew), Am Oved Publishers, Tel Aviv, 1996.

——, *Righteous Victims* (in Hebrew), Am Oved Publishers, Tel Aviv, 2003.

Mutawalis in Lebanon (in Hebrew), the Intelligence Flank, Israel Army, 1956.

Naqqash, Yitzhak, *The Shi'is of Iraq* (in Hebrew), Dvir Publishers, Tel Aviv, 2006.

Nezer, Amnon, *The Jews of Iran* (in Hebrew), Hebrew University, Jerusalem, 1981.

Noah, Mordechai, *Travels in Europe and Africa*, New York, 1819.

Nusseibeh, Sari, "The Future of Jerusalem", in *Jerusalem: Points of Friction and Beyond*, Kluwer Law International, The Hague, 2000.

Ozacky-Lazar, Sarah, *Relations Between Jews and Arabs in Israel* (in Hebrew), Ph.D. thesis, Haifa University, Haifa, 1992.

—— and Stern, Yoav, *Talks with Arab Citizens in Israel* (in Hebrew), Tel Aviv University, Tel Aviv, 2016.

Parfitt, Tudor, *The Jews in Palestine*, Oxford University Press, London, 1984.

Pasha, A.K., *Egypt's Quest for Peace*, National Publishing House, New Delhi, 1994.

Peled-Elhanan, Nurit, *Palestine in Israeli School Books*, I.B. Tauris, London, 2012.

Peters, Joan, *From Time Immemorial*, HarperCollins, New York, 1984.

Petran, Tabitha, *The Struggle for Lebanon*, Monthly Review Press, New York, 1987.

Podeh, Elie, *The Arab–Israeli Conflict in Israei History Textbooks*, Bergin & Garvey, Westport, 2002.

——, *From Fahd to Abdallah*, Truman Institute, Jerusalem, 2005.

—— and Winckler, Onn (eds.), *The Third Wave – Protest and Revolution in the Middle East* (in Hebrew), Carmel Publishers, Jerusalem, 2017.

Polak, Uri, "Rabbi Eliyahu and the Mosques" (in Hebrew), *Kippa* website, May 23, 2012.

Porath, Yehoshua, *The Emergence of the Palestinian-Arab National*

241

Movement, 1918–1929 (in Hebrew), Am Oved Publishers, Tel Aviv, 1976.

——, *From Riots to Rebellion, 1929–1939* (in Hebrew), Am Oved Publishers, Tel Aviv, 1978.

——, "Abdallah's Greater Syria Program", *Middle Eastern Studies*, Vol. 20, no. 2, April 1984.

Rabinovich, Shmuel, *The Western Wall* (in Hebrew), Beit El, 2009.

Rahimian, Orly, "Jews and Iran", *Jewish Learning* website.

Ram, Haggai, "Neither East nor West – The Jews of Iran" (in Hebrew), *Theory and Criticism*, 26 (2005), pp. 67–90.

——, *Reading Iran in Israel* (in Hebrew), Hakibbutz Hameuhad, Tel Aviv, 2006.

——, "Caught In-Between Orientalism and Aryanism", *Hagar*, Vol. 8 (2008).

Rambam (Maimonides), *Letters* (in Hebrew), Shilat Publishers, Ma'aleh Edomim, 1986.

Ramon, Amnon (ed.), *The Jerusalem Lexicon* (in Hebrew), the Jerusalem Institute, Jerusalem, 2003.

Ratzhabi, Yehuda, *Borrowed Motifs in Jewish Literature* (in Hebrew), Bar-Ilan University, Ramat Gan, 2007.

Reiter, Yitzhak (ed.), *Sovereignty of God and Man on the Temple Mount* (in Hebrew), The Jerusalem Institute, Jerusalem, 2001.

——, "Islam and the Question of Peace with Israel", in Ma'oz (ed.), *Muslim Attitudes*, pp. 90–112.

——, *The Eroding Status Quo on the Temple Mount* (in Hebrew), the Jerusalem Institute, Jerusalem, 2016.

Rockower, Paul and Cheema, Aneeq, "Pulling the Veil Off Israeli–Pakistan Relations", in Ma'oz (ed.), *Muslim Attitudes*, pp. 186–214.

Ro'i, Yaacov, "The Zionist Attitude to the Arabs, 1908–1914", *Middle Eastern Studies*, Vol. 4, No. 3, April 1968.

Rouhana, Nadim and Ghanem, Asad, "The Crisis of Minorities – Palestinian Citizens in Israel", *International Journal of Middle Eastern Studies*, No. 30 (1998), pp. 321–346.

Roumani, Maurice, *The Jews of Libya*, Sussex Academic Press, Brighton, 2009.

Schulze, Kirsten, *Israel's Covert Diplomacy in Lebanon*, Macmillan Press, London, 1998.

Sefunot – Studies in Jewish History (in Hebrew), Ben-Zvi Institute, Jerusalem, 1956.

Sela, Avraham, "King Abdullah and the Government of Israel" (in Hebrew), *Cathedra*, No. 57 (1990), pp. 120–162.

Shabi, Aviva and Shaked, Ronni, *Hamas* (in Hebrew), Keter Publications, Jerusalem, 1994.

Shafiq, Muhammed, "Teaching Jewish and Christian Interfaith Initiatives in Muslim Educational Institutions", in Ma'oz (ed.), *The Meeting*, pp. 127–143.

Shaham, Ronni, "Jews and the Sharia Courts in Modern Egypt", *Studia Islamica*, No. 82 (1995), pp. 119–136.

Shamir, Shimon, *Peace with Jordan* (in Hebrew), Hakibbutz Hameuhad Publishers, Tel Aviv, 2012.

Shapira, Anita, *Yigal Alon* (in Hebrew), Hakibbutz Hameuhad Publishers, Tel Aviv, 2004.

Shapira, Shimon, *Hizbullah Between Iran and Lebanon* (in Hebrew), Hakibbutz Hameuhad Publishers, Tel Aviv, 2000.

Shay, Shaul, *Islamic Terrorism and the Balkans* (in Hebrew), IDC, Hertzlia, 2006.

Shlaim, Avi, *The Iron Wall* (in Hebrew), Aliyat Gag Publishers, Tel Aviv, 2005.

——, *King Hussein: A Political Biography* (in Hebrew), Dvir Publications, Tel Aviv, 2007.

Sivan, Emmanuel, "Hatred of Jews in Algeria" (in Hebrew), *Pe'amim*, No. 2 (1979), pp. 92–108.

Smooha, Sammy, "Ethnic Democracy in Israel", *Israel Studies*, Vol. 2 (November 1997), pp. 198–241.

——, *Autonomy for Arabs in Israel* (in Hebrew), Research Center on Arab Society, Ra'anana, 1999.

Spicehandler, Ezra, *Iran's Jews* (in Hebrew), Hebrew University, Jerusalem, 1970.

Stendel, Ori, *The Arabs in Israel* (in Hebrew), Akademon Publishers, Jerusalem, 1992.

Stillman, Norman, *The Jews of Arab Lands*, Jewish Publication Society, Philadelphia, 1979.

Syd Ahmad, Nabil, *The Jews of Egypt, 1917–1956* (in Arabic), Madbuli Publishers, Cairo, 1991.

Teff-Seker, Yael, *Palestinian and Israeli Textbooks*, Impact, Jerusalem, 2016.

Tobi, Yosef, et al. (eds.), *The History of Jews in Muslim Countries* (in Hebrew), Shazar Center, Jerusalem, 1981.

——, "Jews of Yemen", in Meddeb and Stora (eds.), pp. 248–257.

——, *Yemen's Jewry at the Shadow of Islam* (in Hebrew), Misgav Yerushalaim, Jerusalem, 2018.

Tuma, Elias, *The Arabs in Israel* (in Hebrew), author's manuscript, 1998.

Ubicini, M.A., *Letters on Turkey*, two parts, John Murray, London, 1856.

Vatikiotis, P.J., *Egypt From Muhammad Ali to Sadat*, John Hopkins Press, Baltimore, 1980.

Webman, Esther, "The Image of the Jew", in Ma'oz (ed.), *Muslim Attitudes*, pp. 48–66.

Windecker, Gidon, *Between Karbala. Jabal Amil and Jerusalem*, Ph.D. thesis, Hebrew University, Jerusalem, 2009.

Winter, Michael, "Egyptian Jews during the Ottoman Period" (in Hebrew), *Pe'amim*, No. 16 (1983), pp. 4–21.

Winter, Ofir, *Egypt's and Jordan's Peace Treaties with Israel* (in Hebrew), Ph.D. thesis, Tel Aviv University, Tel Aviv, 2015.

——, "Peace with Israel in Egyptian Textbooks", *Strategic Assignments*, Vol. 19, No. 1, April 2016.

Ya'ari, A., *Travels of a Zafed Messenger* (in Hebrew), Tarshish Publishers, Jerusalem, 1942.

Zureik, Elia, *The Palestinians in Israel*, Routledge Publishers, London, 1979.

Index

249

Index

Index

al-Mutawakkil, Khalif, 18

Nadhir tribe, 15, 16
Nadir, Shah, 68
Nadir Shah, King of Afghanistan, 100
Nahda (Resurrection) Movement, 175
Nahdatul Ulama, 11, 109, 175
Nahum, Haim, 146
Nashashibi family, 8, 113, 119, 120
Nashashibi, Raghib, 119
Nasir al-Din, Shah, 68
Nasrallah, Hasan, 77, 152
Nasser, Gamal Abdel, 61, 102, 147, 150, 156, 170, 208
Nassi, Don Yosef, 27
National Liberation Front (Algeria) (FLN), 56
National Religious Party (*Mafdal*), 189, 199
Navon, Yitzhak, 199
Nazi Germany
  Algerian Jews, 55
  influence in Turkey, 89
  Jews of Sarajevo, 38
  links with mufti of Jerusalem, 122
  murder of Greek Jews, 38
  rule in Kosovo, 38–9
  Tunisian Jews, 51
Nebuchadnezzar, 100
Ne'eman, Yuval, 185
Ne'emanai Har Habayit, 190
Nehru, Jawaharlal, 102
Neimark, Ephraim, 100
Nequda journal, 195
Netanyahu, Benjamin
  anti-Muslim/anti-Arab state-ments/actions response, 3–4
  arrogant attitude to Arabs, 172
  East African conference, 63
  Hasmonean tunnels opened, 186
  Indonesian journalists, 110
  Iranian threat, 74
  Islamic Movement outlawed, 210
  Israel front line of Western civilization, 127
  Israeli–Jordanian relations, 171, 172, 173

Jewish visits to Temple Mount, 188
Marmara Affair, 96
relations with Azerbaijan, 85–6
relations with Turkey, 95
state visit to Greece, 97
united Jerusalem policy, 186–7
Neturei Karta sect, 72, 129, 131
Netzer, Amnon, 69–70
New York Times, 172
Niger, 60, 61, 63, 179
Nigeria, 60, 61, 63, 179
Noah, Mordechai Manuel, 50
North Africa
  Almohad Khalifate, 22, 46, 53, 57, 129
  Fatimid Khalifate, 20, 21, 45, 67
  French colonialism, 45, 46
  Italian colonialism, 45
  Jewish conversion to Islam, 7, 49
  Jewish emigration (post-1948), 45, 47–8, 51
  Muslim–Jewish relations, 45, 132, 216
  see also Algeria; Egypt; Libya; Morocco; Sudan; Tunisia
Nunu, Huda, 83
al-Nuqrashy, Mahmud Fahmi, 147

Obama, Barack, 96
Olmert, Ehud
  peace initiative (2008), 113, 152, 167, 179, 181, 184, 213, 217, 219
  secret talks with Syria (2007–2008), 95
Oman, 10, 157, 179
Or Commission, 205–6
Ora Ve-Simcha, 58
Organisation Armée Secrète (OAS), 56
Organization for Islamic Cooperation (OIC), 93, 102, 103, 179
Oslo Accords (1993 & 1995), 10, 113, 159, 171, 179, 183
  Egypt, 174
  India, 106
  Israeli Arabs, 207

261

Index

Index

About the Author

Moshe Ma'oz, Prof. Emeritus, Islamic and Middle Eastern Studies, Hebrew University of Jerusalem, has been a Visiting Fellow at many universities and research centres, including Harvard, Oxford, Columbia, NYU, Beijing, Georgetown, Brookings. He is the author of 20 books and 80 academic articles on the history and politics of Islam, Muslim–Jewish and Arab–Israeli relations. He has served as advisor to Israeli Prime Ministers and Defense Ministers, and to the IDF (Israel Defense Forces) Coordinator in the Territories, at the rank of Full Colonel.